SEXISM AND THE LAW

Sexism and the Law

A STUDY OF MALE BELIEFS
AND LEGAL BIAS
IN BRITAIN AND THE UNITED STATES

Albie Sachs & Joan Hoff Wilson

THE FREE PRESS
A Division of Macmillan Publishing Co., Inc.
NEW YORK

The Free Press
A Division of Macmillan Publishing Co., Inc.
866 Third Avenue, New York, N.Y. 10022

First American Edition 1979

Library of Congress Catalog Card Number: 78-63402

Printed in the United States of America

printing number

  2 3 4 5 6 7 8 9 10

Library of Congress Cataloging in Publication Data

Sachs, Albert Louis
   Sexism and the law.

   (Law in society series)
   Bibliography: p.
   Includes index.
     1. Women--Legal status, laws, etc.--Great Britain.
2. Sex discrimination against women--Law and
legislation--Great Britain. 3. Women--Legal status,
laws, etc.--United States. 4. Sex discrimination again
against women--Law and legislation--United States.
I. Wilson, Joan Hoff   joint author.
II. Title.
K644.S2 1979   342'.41'087   78-63402
ISBN 0-02-927640-3

Contents

Preface

Sexism is all-pervasive in legal life. It surrounds men and women with an intricate network of assumptions and exceptations that are all the more powerful for being largely hidden. By sexism we mean the tendency to think about and behave towards people mainly on the basis of their gender, to generalise about individuals and groups on the grounds of their biology rather than to recognise their actual interests and capacities. This book documents its existence in the legal professions of Britain and the United States. We focus not so much on legal doctrine as on the impact of sexism on the thinking and structure of the legal professions and judiciary themselves. Like many new terms it is inelegant and scientifically inexact; it denotes a reality that is overwhelming to those who claim to experience it, and totally fictional to those who deny its existence. It is clearly more than a description, it is an accusation, that implies a disjunction of perspectives, a clash of world views, a debate about what is right and wrong. As scholars we are happy to use such a term. It sharpens enquiry, forces issues out into the open, and encourages a search for patterns and regularities. We do not expect all our readers to share our standpoint – we believe in full equality between women and men – nor do we expect them to approve of our arguments or agree with our conclusions. But we do hope to persuade them to look at the evidence we have accumulated and to consider the subject seriously.

We believe the issue is of real concern, and not to lawyers only. Inside the profession, gender has a direct bearing on income, status and position; it also dictates opportunities, formulates style and regulates atmosphere. Outside the profession, it affects not only the way in which citizens come into contact with the law, but also the manner in which all of us think about fundamental principles of our society, because in modern society it is the law above all that defines social issues and constructs models of appropriate and inappropriate behaviour. Moreover, the legal profession has been entrusted with a crucial role in the implementation of anti-discrimination measures, a function which lawyers will ill perform if they are tainted with the very practices they are charged with eliminating. We do not feel that the legal profession is any better or worse than any other professional group – on the contrary, the patterns which emerge are all the more relevant for being characteristic rather than extraordinary. Our hope is to see the law functioning as a better instrument for serving the community, and it is to those many women and men struggling inside the profession and judiciary to overcome one of its main areas of backwardness, that we dedicate this book.

A.S.
J.H.W.

PART ONE

THE MALE MONOPOLY CASES

1 *Britain:* Are Women 'Persons'?

INTRODUCTION

The whole city seemed to be in an uproar as the student approached the examination hall. Mud and dirt were thrown, and the crowd began roughly to block the student's progress. The police were not on hand to assist, and only the concerted use of hockey sticks by a group of sympathisers enabled the student to proceed. For months the issue of the student's right to be at the University had provoked clamour and public disturbance. Normally sedate academic gatherings had been interrupted by heckling, and even by the intrusion of a sheep ('Leave it be', one professor had remarked, 'it has more sense than those who put it here'). The great majority of staff and undergraduates objected strongly to the student's presence, and many of the townspeople rallied to their support. As they saw it, a principle was at stake, affecting the honour and dignity both of the University and of the city. They did not claim that the student was unintelligent or insufficiently personable, their objection was simply that the student was a woman.[1]

In writing about the attempt of Sophia Jex-Blake and her colleagues to enter the University of Edinburgh Medical School in the 1860s, it is impossible not to do so in a way that points up the parallel with the disorders that greeted the entry of black students in American universities in the 1960s. Sophia Jex-Blake was the leading personality in a group of seven women who in 1869 had persuaded the Medical School to admit them to instruction. Regulations were passed which authorised females to attend special classes to be conducted by such professors as were willing to teach them, with a view to their qualifying as medical practitioners. At that stage only two women were entitled to practise as doctors in the United Kingdom. The first was Elizabeth Blackwell, who had qualified in the United States and whose registration as a doctor in Britain had prompted the medical profession to seek the aid of Parliament in preventing any other women from following her example. The second was Elizabeth Garrett, who had slipped through a loophole in the legislation which had immediately been stopped up. Sophia Jex-Blake and her companions were willing to submit to the indignity of being taught in segregated classes if this was the only way in which they could pioneer medical degrees for women in Britain. But so fiercely did the majority of professors and students at

Edinburgh object to the idea that somewhere in the city a few sympathetic professors were teaching subjects such as physics and anatomy to females, that the University began to renege on its offers. As one later commentator said of the University's capitulation, there are none so resolute as those who repent of a courageous action.[2] First the University authorities refused to award the Chemistry prize to the woman student who achieved the highest marks in her year. Then they insisted that the women be allowed to sit their final examinations only if they undertook not to ask for a degree if successful. Finally, when the women refused to give such an undertaking, the University terminated the courses altogether. Edinburgh accordingly had the double distinction of being the first University in Britain to admit women to Medical School, and also the first to throw women out.

It was at this stage that the women decided to resort to the courts. The case they brought was one of many initiated during that period by feminists who hoped that they could secure their public rights by recourse to law. The passions that this case aroused penetrated into the courtroom and manifested themselves with unusual vigour. In no other matter was the court so divided, nor did the judges again so openly reveal their attitudes towards women. The judgments in this case accordingly display with unique explicitness the kind of intellectual resistance put up by upper-middle-class men to the attempts by women to breach their monopoly of public occupations.

But this was not the only case in which the judges were called upon to determine how extensive male control of public life was to be. In at least half a dozen other matters, in each of which the litigation was conducted against a background of determined feminist action and stubborn male resistance, the basic issue was whether or not women should by virtue of their sex alone be debarred from public functions. The women contended that, provided they possessed all the necessary qualifications, they could not be excluded from public or professional life unless Parliament in the clearest language imposed disabilities on them. The counter-argument as put forward by male public officials and leaders of the professions was that women were inherently incapacitated on grounds of gender alone from undertaking public functions or participating in professional life, and could be relieved of their legal disabilities only by the most explicit authorisation from Parliament. The judges accordingly had to decide whether, in terms of the common law, women were inherently inferior to men or inherently equal to them. In most cases, the neat technical issue actually was whether women could be included in the word 'persons', this being the gender-free term used in the relevant statutes.

The 'persons' cases, as they came to be called, were launched by feminists in the hope that their arguments needed merely to be stated to be upheld,[3] namely, that an individual's gender was irrelevant to his or her factual or legal capacity, and that females were obviously to be included in the word 'person'. What was self-evident truth to feminists, however, was manifest absurdity to most of the judges. Far from viewing the women as victims of oppressive and capricious behaviour, they treated them with varying degrees of courtesy as misguided attention seekers, much as members of the women's liberation movement would be treated by most men today. Without embarrassment or apology, the judges painted a picture of women being too delicate and refined to undertake public functions, and accordingly classified them legally alongside the insane and the insolvent, and even in one case alongside the inanimate. The decisions show that the judges skirted round historical precedents that favoured the women, introduced a novel legal concept to the effect that rights could be extinguished by custom, and manipulated the meaning of the word 'person' so as to produce results consistent with their picture of womanhood. If this were not enough repeatedly to shatter the perpetually renewed faith of the applicants, the judges insisted that what they were doing was not to impose a disability on women, but to grant them a privilege.

The question that needs to be asked, then, is why did upper-class men, who prided themselves on their education, rationality, fair-mindedness and, above all, their respect for women, behave with such social brutality towards women of their own class who sought in dignified manner to exercise public rights? In recent years, much has been done to document similar examples of habitual and unconscious male arrogance, and to expose the debilitating effect it has had on women's lives, but relatively little has been done to explore its roots. Feminist writers have understandably concentrated on the effects rather than the sources of patriarchal ways, and male writers, also understandably but less commendably, have tended either to give the whole issue a wide berth, or else to treat it as a subject of fun. While there are clearly no barriers of intellect to prevent women from writing about men's consciousness (or men from doing the reverse), there are limitations of experience. Men are therefore in a position to make a special contribution to a debate that involves both sexes, by drawing on their special experience as males living in a male-dominated society.

The British section of this study is in fact being offered more as an exploration of male beliefs than as an exposition of women's rights. The male monopoly cases have been ignored for so long that they deserve to be presented at some length as a reminder of how actual judges actually behaved, in contrast to the sweeping claims for liberalism usually made on their behalf. But these cases may also be used as the basis for far more extensive enquiries. In the sections that follow the exposition of the cases, it will be seen that two separate socio-legal enquiries have been undertaken, each of which explores a different aspect of the general theme of male domination and the law.

The first excursion – entitled 'The Myth of Judicial Neutrality' – uses the cases as a basis for challenging the conventional notion that judges are impartial. This portion of the work might accordingly be of interest to students of law and students of myth formation rather than to persons more specifically concerned with gender relations. The idea of judicial neutrality is central to current legal ideology in Britain, even if it has been severely shaken in the United States. A few British legal academics have delicately pointed out that judicial behaviour in early twentieth-century cases dealing with industrial picketing and workmen's compensation was not always consistent with judicial neutrality. But even these critics have tended to locate such class bias on the fringes rather than at the centre of judicial activity. Whatever inferences can be drawn from the industrial conflict cases, there can be little doubt that the male monopoly cases manifest a gender bias so striking and so explicit as to contradict totally the idea of judicial impartiality. The judges in fact felt far less constraint about making generalised references to women than they did in respect to workers. These judicial utterances about the characteristics and rights of females fairly jump from the law reports, and they strike a note consistently at variance with the current legal claim that the role of the common law and the courts is to vindicate fundamental rights. Yet for all their jurisprudential significance, they have been totally ignored by scholars, and the cases from which they have been drawn do not even rate footnote treatment in discussions of public law. Legal writers may claim that they choose their themes on the basis of intrinsic intellectual merit, but in reality, like all academics working in the field of social studies, they feed parasitically and usually without acknowledgment on the conflicts of their times. Now that the women's movement has renewed its challenges to existing institutions and values, however, the male monopoly cases may be expected once more to claim proper notice.

In law, as in social science, nothing is obvious until attention is directed towards it, so that the self-evident tends to have a curiously retrospective quality. From the time that legal work was first monopolised under the control of a legal profession, half the population was formally excluded from the processes of law formulation and law enforcement, and much of the rest of the population was informally excluded, yet only now is this state of affairs coming to be regarded as startling. Defenders of social hierarchies will always tend to represent them as arrangements that cohere naturally, while critics will depict them as artificially organised forms of privilege. Dr Olive Stone has elegantly pointed out that those who rose to the top in an exclusively male profession were bound to consider that profession to be uniquely well constituted, since it produced such excellent people to lead it.[4] One may add that those denied participation in the benefits of professional life were necessarily less enthusiastic about its virtues. This suggests that, contrary to the common-sense notion that effective criticism can only be made from within, those who participate in a privileged institution almost invariably surrender their critical faculties, and confine their discussion to fringe matters, while those on the outside see the obvious features and are able to discuss the institution's fundamental character. Thus a client may have more of public value to say than a lawyer about the legal system, and a prisoner more than a judge.

The second exploration based on the male monopoly cases – entitled 'The Myth of Male Protectiveness' or what is called in the United States 'Paternalism' – is directed not so much to legal thinking and institutions as to the patterns of thought that lawyers took over from the wider society in which they lived. The particular aim of this exploration is to discover the sources of stereotyped and mythical male beliefs. The crucial assumption underlying this investigation is that the generalised and mythical judicial pronouncements about females masked specific and discoverable material interests that the judges as upper-class males shared generally with members of their class and gender. This attribution of behaviour and beliefs primarily to hidden material interests is not, of course, universally accepted, and the advantages of this approach over those more usually adopted in discussions of gender relations require some defence.

The explicit or implicit assumption in most literature about characteristic actions and beliefs of males is that these are either expressions of innate masculine tendencies to assert and dominate, or else the outcome of socialisation processes. It is suggested, however, that explanations at this level amount at best to description rather than analysis, since a phenomenon cannot be interpreted purely in terms of its manifestations. In addition, there is a moral objection that to regard men as either born to oppress or bred to oppress (dominate, lead, initiate) is to regard them as helpless victims of either biological circumstances or social fate, and not as responsible and tenacious defenders of unfair material advantage. The extent to which the values of masculine supremacy have persisted from generation to generation, surviving feminist onslaughts and general social and political developments, suggests the operation of forces more powerful than the mere cultural inertia suggested by socialisation theory. Yet to locate these forces in innate masculine drives, as much feminist writing implicitly does, is to rely on the very biological determinism that such writing seeks to challenge.

Because the initial classification between males and females is a biological one, it is easy for both supporters and opponents of male ascendancy to assert that behavioural differences between men and women are biologically determined as well. It is particularly convenient for the beneficiaries of social inequality to attribute their advantageous social position to an advantageous biological one. Thus the modern rationale for male supremacy in public life is essentially biological. Simply put, it claims that because women have babies and men do not, there is a necessary division of labour in society between female homemakers and male providers. Those whom God hath put asunder, let no man (or woman) join together. The justification is advanced that men and women are separate and equal, since men are masters of their domains and women mistresses of theirs. The crucial link which binds biological capacity to social necessity is that which purports to equate maternity with domesticity. Since only women can bear children, it is assumed that only women can rear children. The further step is then taken to the effect that looking after children is not merely an important activity for most women, but the only important activity for all women.

Strangely enough, the maternity rationale was rarely put forward in the literature of the nineteenth century, even though there was less control of fertility then than there is now, and childbirth was far more arduous. The argument of disability based on maternity appears in fact to be of relatively recent origin in Britain, and is really the last relic rather than the starting-off point of the biological argument, which used to assert that women were created differently from men in every physical and neurological detail. What the judges said when justifying the legal disabilities on women – and they spoke as the articulators of the views of all right-thinking persons – was that women should be excluded from the harsh world of public affairs because they were possessed of peculiar refinement and delicacy, rather than because they were too busy nursing. This shift in rationalisation suggests that far from biology dictating social patterns, it is the social order that gives significance to biology. Where the biology argument is in fact most demonstrably flawed is in its failure to explain why reproductive capacity should unsuit women only for the more lucrative and prestigious occupations and not for the more poorly paid ones. It is difficult to see why childbirth should prevent women from being surgeons but not from being matrons, and why motherhood should bar the way to women practising law but not to their doing social work or teaching. Furthermore, the maternity rationale is inconsistent with the great changes that have taken place over the centuries in the patterns of female work and employment, and cannot explain why women with a similar physical constitution should be regarded as unfit to sweep streets, sell liquor, pilot planes and preach religion in some countries, and not in others.

In recent years, ethology has been used to present a variant on the biological justification for male ascendancy. In the course of evolution, men are said to have become genetically programmed to seek territory, while women have become constitutionally coded to seek nests, and this has allegedly led to the evolution of a tendency for men to club together, in all senses of the phrase, while women stay at home. Predatoriness and conviviality are said to have combined in the male to produce a bonding to be found in all cultures but which is uniquely manifest in the modern professions. It is interesting to note that the judges did not rely on the precursors of such arguments to justify treating women as unsuitable for studying medicine, practising law, casting a vote or sitting on a council. If anything, the judges attributed to men a superior spirituality rather than a greater physical prowess, as reflected in loftiness of mind, a capacity for reverence, and the ability to indulge in abstract thought. There is nothing in the judicial utterances to indicate that manliness was associated with physical strength or daring or even a special gregariousness; it would seem that it was the two world wars that revived these notions. It would certainly be difficult to explain the distribution of male-exclusive occupations today on the analogy of man as hunter or builder of stockades. Members of the all-male priesthood might obey an injunction to be the fishers of men, but would hardly like to think of themselves as mankind's hunters as well. Similarly, it is rather unconvincing to suggest that it is inheritance of the qualities needed to bash in an antelope's head that explains why only males sit as judges in the House of Lords.

Psychological theories have also been recruited to explain the pervasiveness of male arrogance. One influential view is that bigotry can best be understood in terms of the authoritarian personality and the mechanisms of scapegoating. Yet however useful this approach may be in explaining the more extreme forms of anti-feminism as expressed by particular individuals, it is not very helpful in relation to the ordinary anti-feminism of the psychologically serene man, particularly when his attitudes to females are sanctioned by his culture. As far as the judges were concerned, it will be seen that the same outlook with regard to gender was expressed by men of diverse personality, who, moreover, had little need for finding scapegoats when they could exercise power directly and legitimately. In addition, the way they victimised women was by exalting them rather than defaming them. Similarly, objections can be raised to attempts to use psycho-sexual theories to explain behaviour at the social level. The suppressed eroticism of the Victorian era may have contributed towards the elevation of reverence and spirituality into prime masculine qualities, but could hardly have been the reason why elderly judges more concerned with longevity than virility should have repeatedly turned down women's claims, or why the medical profession should have organised itself so stubbornly against the entry of women into its ranks.

This leaves the possibility that the patterns of behaviour and belief under investigation can best be understood in terms of material or economic interests. In the case of beliefs related to male domination, the argument would be that upper-middle-class men in diverse occupations shared an interest in keeping women as head servants at home and keeping them out of the ranks of competitors at work. In other words, men had and still have a material stake in resisting the emancipation of women.

It is this last approach that has been adopted in this study, since it is the one that appears to throw the most light on the question of why women were so resolutely kept out of the professions. It is consistent with the emphasis that the judges placed on the domestic rather than the reproductive virtues of women, and it also explains why these virtues were expressed through the disguised imagery of delicacy and refinement. If the argument here and in the pages that follow is stated rather baldly, this is done to counterbalance the view that attributes male behaviour to some unexplained genetic essence apparently transmitted from father to son, and female behaviour to an equally mystical inheritance passed on from mother to daughter. The implication of the view adopted in this study is that much of the social, and for that matter sexual, tension that exists between men as a group and women as a group can be explained in terms of clashes of material interests, just as struggles between classes and nations can be explained in those terms. Here again, the emphasis is put rather baldly on the dimension of gender – the sex war as it used to be called – not because gender can ever be separated entirely from such factors as class, or race, or nationality, but because it is usually not separated at all. Even the most vigorous male exponents of conflict theory or male activists in radical movements, are rarely willing to concede that the question of male domination is more than just a matter of nuance or style, to be corrected simply by an improvement of intellectual or political manners. It might be that the issues of class or race are more dramatic than that of sex as sources of social tension in modern society, but that does not mean that the gender struggle should always be submerged in other conflicts, or that it should always be treated as a subsidiary and peripheral matter rather than as an independent and central one.

A third exploration based on the male monopoly cases – 'Towards Equal Opportunity' – moves towards the present day, and probes the extent to which the judiciary and legal profession continue to maintain male domination. The position now is that the principle of male monopoly has given way to the principle of equal opportunity. But has the practice of male domination changed? Formal legal disabilities previously imposed on women have been removed, and there are no longer any technical barriers to women practising law or getting on to the Bench. Women have entered legal terrain in large numbers, and constitute half of all persons concerned with providing legal services, and a third of all persons on the Bench. But closer investigation shows that virtually all the females involved in legal work are secretaries rather than professionals, and all but half a dozen of the female judicial officers are unpaid magistrates.

The question of male domination presents itself most sharply today in terms of who controls entry to and advancement within the profession and the judiciary, but it has dimensions going much deeper. It concerns such diverse matters as the atmosphere in which legal work is conducted, the rigidity of legal manners and style, the principles on which the modern office is organised, the character of the relationship between lawyer and client, and the very institution of professionalism itself. The professions are not merely bodies from which women happened historically to be absent. Women were excluded from the professions as a matter of deliberate policy, and an all-male character helped to elevate the professions above the community at large. The concepts of professional integrity and professional independence became integrated with notions of male loftiness and were used to justify economic monopolies and a special social status for the professions. Traditionally, the wise-women as well as the wise-men in the community had been resorted to for advice just as folk-healers had been approached for medication. They represented a popular, local, community-based and cheap source of aid, as opposed to the elitist, centralised and expensive male professionals. In the hands of the professionals, however, law enforcement became increasingly remote from the community, and developed the pedantry and artificiality so characteristic of the legal process today. The empirically based wisdom of the neighbourhood sages and conciliators was derided in relation to the sophisticated learning of the lawyers, and women formerly regarded as wise oracles were now dismissed as meddlesome gossips. Inasmuch as the professionals controlled litigation, their abstruse knowledge came in reality to be more effective than the practical advice of the locals. The common law ceased to be the property of the common people and became the property of the lawyers. Women of all classes and men of the lower classes were excluded from the professions, and when eventually they did manage to break in, they did so in small numbers and on terms already well-established by upper-middle-class men. Integration into the profession accordingly took place on the basis of newcomers taking over the styles and interests of the existing professionals; it was not asked whether the profession should rather adapt to the ways and experience of the new entrants.

If the law is to be a genuine service to the community rather than just a means of personal self-advancement, then in addition to altering its class base it must find a place for representatives of the female half of the community. And if it does admit larger numbers of women and more persons of working-class background, the gain to the community will be severely restricted if the newcomers are compelled to repudiate their past experiences of the world, abandon their personal ways of seeing and doing things, modify their accents and modes of speech, and generally cultivate the aloofness and pomposity so characteristic of most lawyers today. It would seem that without the large-scale involvement of women, the male-dominated professions can never achieve a more popular, community-oriented character. At the same time, it would seem that women will never be able to enter these professions in large numbers until the professions are radically restructured. Possibly something even more fundamental will be required if the community is to regain control over the processes of law making and law enforcement, and that is the elimination of the monopoly enjoyed by the profession of legal work, and the ending of the divisions whereby those persons possessing legal skills are set apart from the rest of the community rather than integrated into it.

THE CASE OF THE EDINBURGH MEDICAL STUDENTS

Septem contra Edinem – The Edinburgh Seven

In their court action to resist expulsion from Edinburgh Medical School, Sophia Jex-Blake and her associates claimed that in terms of both the general principles of the common law and the express provisions of the University regulations, they were registered medical students and as such entitled to complete their courses and to graduate if they passed their examinations.[5] To this end they asked the court for an order directing that they be entitled to attend mixed classes at the Medical School, that they be given such instruction as would enable them to sit the examinations, that they be permitted to graduate if they passed their examinations, and that the University Senate make such regulations as would be necessary for them to attain these rights.

The University Senate argued that their claim should be rejected on the grounds that the University of Edinburgh had been founded for the education of male students only, as was evidenced by that fact that in hundreds of years the applicants were the only women to apply for admission. Against that background, the University regulations purporting to admit women to the Medical School should be treated as *ultra vires* and of no force and effect, since they exceeded the authority of the governing bodies, whose statutory powers extended only to making regulations for the 'improvement of the internal arrangements' of the University and not to bringing about changes in its basic constitution.

The case at first instance came before Lord Gifford in the Court of Sessions, and he gave judgment substantially in favour of the women. He stated that he could see no reason why women should in principle be debarred from attending University or practising medicine, and that in any event the University regulations clearly gave them the right to receive instruction with a view to qualifying as doctors. He was not, however, prepared to accede to their request to be allowed to attend mixed classes with men.

The Senate appealed from this judgment to the full bench of the Court, which delivered judgment finally in June 1873. The Lord President of the Court declined to participate in the hearing, since he was the Chancellor of the University and as such directly involved in the controversy,[6] but eight other judges sat in the matter, and when they divided four–four, a further four judges were called in. Thus twelve judges in all delivered opinions.

The first was Lord Deas, who said that, independently of the regulations, the women had no right to attend the University. But he could not see how the regulations, which dealt with matters of expediency and propriety rather than law, could be said to be *ultra vires*. The applicants accordingly were entitled to receive instruction in separate classes, and he suggested that to save expense, a partition such as was used at chapel in Pentonville Prison be erected in the classrooms so that the same teacher could instruct both male and female students at the same time.

The second judge, Lord Ardmillan, stated that women were neither inherently entitled to attend the University, nor inherently debarred from doing so. The regulations had been carefully passed, and could not be treated as void. Just as, contrary to previous custom, a Roman Catholic, Jew, Indian or negro had been admitted to the University, so a woman could be admitted, provided she attended separate classes.

The next judge agreed with Lord Deas that the women should be allowed to receive instruction and to graduate, provided they attended separate classes.

Lord Ormidale, on the other hand, held that the University Charters clearly contemplated male students only, as was evidenced by the uninterrupted usage of centuries. The regulations did not give women a right to receive instruction, but merely authorised professors to instruct them if they wished. The court could not require the professors to teach if they chose not to do so, and the women's claim must accordingly fail.

Lord Mure said that the main question was not whether the regulations could be enforced, but whether the University had the power to alter its constitution so as to allow to women the rights and privileges of students. In his view, the University had no such power, and the women's claims must fail.

Lord Gifford, giving the sixth judgment in the full court, indicated that he now relied only on the regulations in support of the women's claims, and wished to make it clear that women had no inherent right to attend the University on the same terms as men.

The following two judgments were given jointly by Lords Mackenzie and Shand, who declared that the regulations permitting professors to hold classes for the women were *ultra vires*, since the University had authority to effect improvements in its internal arrangements but not to alter its constitution. In any event, if the professors chose not to teach, the women could not graduate, so their claims must fail.

The first of the extra judges called in, Lord Cowan, stated that the University had no power itself to change its basic constitution in a matter so essential and inherent, and the regulations accordingly were *ultra vires*.

The next judge, Lord Benholme, agreed that the University had no power to subvert its original constitution by admitting female students.

The eleventh judge, Lord Neaves, conceded that students could not be refused admission on grounds of religion and even less so on grounds of skin colour, but said that nevertheless the law did recognise the difference of sex. The Universities were instituted for the education of males alone, and to purport to admit females was a subversion of the constitution wholly beyond the power of the University.

The last judge, the Lord Justice Clerk, stated that the question of whether women should be admitted to a University was a matter of expediency for the University authorities and not of law for the judges. The University authorities in this case had decided to admit women, and it was not open to the Senate now to challenge the very laws which set out its own duties. The real issue was not whether the professors could be compelled to teach, since other arrangements might be made, but whether if the applicants passed the examinations they were entitled to graduate, and he had no doubt that they were so entitled.

By a majority, then, of seven judgments to five, the claims by Sophia Jex-Blake and her companions were rejected by the court, and their exclusion from medical studies, even in segregated classes, was upheld.

The above summary indicates that the judges were almost evenly divided on the basic legal issue as to whether the University could repudiate its own regulations so as to exclude women in the middle of their studies. All the judges were agreed, however, that the women had no right to attend University on the same terms as men in mixed classes. The most vigorous judgment against the women was that delivered by Lord Neaves, and since it embodies the sentiment which led to the attacks on and eventual expulsion of the women, it will be extensively reproduced.

Lord Neaves Speaks in Scotland[7]

All the judges had agreed, Lord Neaves declared, that the purpose contemplated in founding the Scottish Universities was the education of young men. From the year 1411 to about the year 1860, a period of 450 years, there was no instance produceable of a woman having been educated at any Scottish University. The attempt to answer this was that resort to a University was merely optional, a privilege which could not be lost by non-use, and the case was put of an abstinence from University study by Roman Catholics, Jews, Indians or negroes. It was asked whether the University could not by vote and resolution admit these persons. In his view no such vote and resolution would have been necessary; they could be admitted as a matter of course, since no legal principle existed for excluding them. The general law did not make any distinction of religion in matters of right, and where the national will did so, it operated by imposing a test on admission. As little and perhaps even less could there be any ground for excluding students in respect of the colour of their skin. But the material element was that the law did recognise the difference of sex as an established and well-known element, leading sometimes to the exemption and sometimes to the absolute exclusion of women from a variety of duties, privileges and powers.

Women were long excluded by law from being witnesses, and had always been excluded from judicial office. They were neither compelled nor qualified to sit on juries, except in limited cases of all-female juries. Generally speaking, no political office could be held by any female, 'with one illustrious and solitary exception' (Queen Victoria). With females being undoubtedly excluded in consequence of their sex from functions competent to males, the question arose whether functions connected with University education were designed for men alone or young men and women indiscriminately. The Universities were undoubtedly instituted for the education of male students. Were they equally instituted for females? If so, every female presenting herself as a student at the door of the College was entitled to be admitted to any class on the usual terms. It was impossible to take any middle course in the matter, or to draw a distinction at all between male and female students, except by declaring that while males had a right to a University education, females had none.

Attendance of women in the Medical Faculty could have been merely a matter of waiting upon special arrangements, but a woman bent upon learning Greek and Latin needed no special arrangements for following in the footsteps of the many distinguished women who had successfully applied themselves to those studies. If they had had no right to attend those classes, the exclusion must have rested not upon matters of mere mechanical arrangement, but upon the principle that the University life had not been intended for them, but for the other sex.

> It is a belief, widely entertained, that there is a great difference in the mental constitution of the two sexes, just as there is in their physical conformation. The powers and susceptibilities of women are as noble as those of men; but they are thought to be different, and, in particular, it is considered that they have not the same power of intense labour as men are endowed with. If this be so, it must form a serious objection to uniting them under the same course of academical study. I confess that, to some extent, I share in this view, and should regret to see our young females subjected to the severe and incessant work which my own observation and experience have taught me to consider as indispensable to any high attainment in learning. A disregard of such an inequality would be fatal to any scheme of public instruction, for, as it is certain that the general mass of an army cannot move more rapidly than its weakest and slowest portion, so a general course of study must be toned and tempered down to suit the average of all the classes of students for whom it is intended; and that average will always be lowered by the existence of any considerable numbers who cannot keep pace with the rest.
>
> Add to this the special acquirements and accomplishments at which women must aim, but from which men may easily remain exempt. Much time must, or ought to be, given by women to the acquisition of a knowledge of household affairs and family duties, as well as to those ornamental parts of education which tend so much to social refinement and domestic happiness, and the study necessary for mastering these must always form a serious distraction from severer pursuits, while there is little doubt that, in public estimation, the want of these feminine arts and attractions in a woman would be ill supplied by such branches of knowledge as a University could bestow.

In all this, regard had to be had to the average powers of the female mind and not to the different position of remarkable and gifted women. The true role was to compare the ordinary run of both sexes, and then the rarer examples of superior excellence among men and women – the Agneses, the Lady Jane Greys, the Martineaus and the

Somervilles, with the Galileos, the Bentleys, the Adam Smiths and the Isaac Newtons.

In the first and most elementary schools designed for children, there was no reason why both sexes should not be taught together, and in some of these schools there had been thought to be no incongruity in teaching in union not only both sexes, but all ages, as in the General Assembly's school in the Highlands. When they came to schools of a higher kind, designed for the more advanced education of pupils of riper years, it had been the uniform tendency to make a divergence, and to keep the education of the two sexes distinctly separate. So far as he knew, it had always been the rule in their grammar schools to exclude females, and this had certainly been the case in the distinguished grammar school with which they were all acquainted in the city, and to which many of them owed so much. The same rule had unquestionably been observed in all their Universities, and surely there were very cogent reasons for such a system.

> The period of life attained by the youth who are there educated, say from sixteen to twenty-two, is the most of all susceptible of the more tender feelings of our nature; and, without the slightest suggestion of anything in the least degree culpable, how is it possible to feel secure that, with a number of young men and women assembled together at a University, there shall not occur hasty attachments and premature entanglements, that may exercise a blighting influence on all their future life? What effect it might exercise upon their immediate studies it would be hazardous to conjecture. It might, in some cases, produce a strange emulation; it might in others lead to total idleness among those mixed school-fellows. In any view, he would be a bold man who would collect together at a College, and send out some hundreds of young men and women 'Inter sylvas Academi quaerere verum', with whatever number of chaperons he might try to guard them.

The Universities were corporations, which had a public charter, and as a general rule members of such corporations were exclusively male. It was possible that in some peculiar cases, as in some trading guilds, there may have been a custom of extending, at least partially, the benefits of some corporate privileges to the widows or even to the daughters of guild brethren, but if so the exceptions were created and limited by custom. In the higher corporations no such exception existed. He had never heard it suggested that a woman could be a member of the College of Justice 'though it has been alleged that the elderly part of the sex is not unrepresented in high quarters'. As little could a woman claim to be a member of a University, especially to be made a doctor of any faculty, since the doctorate was not a mere trade, but an office, which involved originally the power and the right to teach, and was not a mere licence to practise but a status implying certain privileges of precedence and otherwise recognised by law.

On all these grounds he was satisfied that the non-attendance of women at the Universities in the past had not been a mere accident or arbitrary abstinence, but had arisen from a consciousness shared by women with the whole community that 'the Universities were not instituted for them, though women would undoubtedly receive indirectly the benefits the Universities were calculated to confer, in making better men of their fathers, their brothers, their husbands, and their sons'. The ladies themselves had not regarded the University regulations as a satisfactory basis for their claims. They complained that the regulations evaded their just legal demands and left their position on a very precarious and slippery foundation. He did not wonder at this feeling, since reliance on the regulations would be a great calamity for all, because the regulations could be modified or repealed from time to time, and privileges could be suddenly withdrawn or curtailed, to the great disappointment and injury of those interested. There could be no fixity of tenure and no class in the community; no individual woman could trust to medicine as an available professional opening. In the meantime the question would remain a subject of keen and bitter contention, and make the University councils a permanent battlefield. How far this would conduce to the interests of science and to the peace and prosperity of their Universities, it was not difficult to conjecture.

But apart from these views, he considered the regulations wholly illegal and palpably beyond the statutory power conferred on the University councils. The proposal to admit women to the study of medicine was not an internal regulation but an external innovation, of the most serious kind. It could not be considered a matter of mere arrangement whether one half of the population had or had not a right of admission to the University. 'To admit those who in consequence of their sex, had no legal claim to University study, and to declare that they now should have such a claim, appears to me to be an essential and fundamental alteration, or rather subversion, of the established consuetudinary constitution of the University, which it is wholly beyond the power of a University to effect.' The University could not make any change that it pleased. If it had enjoyed a system of mixed classes of medical study, he thought that even some of the judges who favoured the women's claim would have held such a regulation as incompatible with the law and constitution of the University. Nor did he suppose that the objection would be removed by the adoption of the Pentonville Prison partition, which had been suggested. Similarly, a regulation requiring professors who refused to have separate classes for the sexes, to devote their single classes to women only, would be disregarded by a Court of Law as utterly null. Furthermore, the regulations as they existed were wholly unenforceable, and it was not the business of the courts to pronounce judgments that led to nothing.

He agreed in thinking that the examples that had been cited of women connected with foreign Universities, had no bearing on the case. 'Those examples after all come to very little, and chiefly amount to this, that, besides some honorary titles conferred on women, it has happened that in one or two instances a wife or daughter was allowed to read her husband's or father's lectures, – an indulgence which might be easily conferred by the autocratic authority of the Pope or Emperor for the time being, to whom the Universities were subject.'

He considered attempts to relate the absence of women from the Universities to the position of women in Scotland and the course of national history generally, to be wholly unsuccessful. Though naturally and willingly keeping aloof from public life, the condition of Scottish women in the fifteenth and sixteenth centuries was anything but slavish or degraded, nor had they been considered as very timid or submissive. Such women could not easily have been stopped from asserting a legal right intended for them, but they were doubtless aware that their proper place was at home, learning to rule their husbands and bring up their children, with those happy domestic results of which Scotland had so much reason to be proud.

In deciding this case, as he was bound to do, upon strict legal grounds, he did not take up the time of the court in saying much as to the personal feelings which it was calculated to excite.

I will say this, however, that I have felt great sympathy with these ladies, both as to the object they had in view and as to the position in which they have been placed. I think that, from very natural motives and with the best intentions, but with unfortunate results, their friends have led them to form expectations which could never be realised in the way contemplated. Again, I think it very natural for those ladies who feel a vocation in that direction to wish to make themselves useful, and to earn an honourable independence, and I have no doubt there are departments of medical or surgical practice in which women may be fitly and successfully employed.... There was an important branch of surgical practice in which their sex was long exclusively engaged, and which continued indeed to be their appanage from the time when Moses was found in the ark of bulrushes down till the beginning of the sixteenth century, for in 1522 a doctor was burnt alive in Hamburg for personating a woman in an obstetric case. That branch of practice in women's hands may now be looked upon with some contempt, but this I think a great mistake, and it might probably with great advantage be associated with other branches of domestic practice for which women would be well adapted. This might surely be done without any material change in the constitution of the Universities. The rules of the London University, with its advanced notions, throw some light on this subject, for they refuse to accord to women the honour of graduation. In fact, any grievance of the pursuers arises out of the Medical Act of 1858. It is for the Legislature to determine the matter; but, if it was thought right, that Act might be amended by opening a somewhat wider door for medical qualification.

The case certainly affords no ground for subverting the constitution of our Universities, or affecting the dignity and weight which belong to the highest honour attending the medical profession. The national object here is, and ought to be, to accomplish and adorn the character of a British physician, not only with all medical and physiological science, but also with the highest philosophy, intellectual and moral, and with all the resources of literature and learning which can aid him in his high functions. Any change that would incur the risk of lowering the standard that now exists, and which we have seen exemplified in so many of our great physicians and professors, is infinitely to be deprecated, and such a danger, I think, would be incurred by the revolution in the medical teaching of our Universities that has here been attempted to be brought about; while at the same time it would otherwise affect, and, in my opinion, deteriorate our Universities in a way unknown to any period of their history.

THE 'PERSONS' CASES

The case of the Edinburgh medical students dealt only indirectly with an issue with which British judges were to wrestle for six decades, namely whether or not a woman could in law be regarded as a 'person'. A series of statutes provided that access to public office, entry to professions and entitlement to vote should be granted to any 'person' who possessed certain qualifications. When women as part of the emancipation movement of the time presented themselves to the authorities duly equipped with the appropriate qualifications, they were confronted with the one major disqualification, namely that they were not in fact 'persons', and this is the story of how Her (and His) Majesty's judges responded.

Women Voters in Manchester

The question of whether or not a woman was in law 'a person' first cropped up at the tail-end of a series of cases brought by women in Manchester against their exclusion from the voters' roll. The background to these cases was the passing of the Second Reform Act in 1867, in terms of which the Parliamentary franchise was extended to all householders. When the legislation was debated in Parliament, John Stuart Mill sought to ensure that the vote was extended to women by substituting the word 'person' for 'man' where it appeared in the key clause. His amendment was rejected by a fairly large majority, but one of his supporters claimed that even the use of the word 'man' would enfranchise women, since it had previously been enacted by Parliament that unless the context indicated otherwise, all references to males included females. When pressed for a ruling on this point, Benjamin Disraeli on behalf of the Government said the question was one for the 'gentlemen of the long robe' (the judges), but that he had little doubt that they would rule against the interpretation contended for.[8]

Supporters of votes for women decided to test the issue, and in several parts of the country women householders sought to have their names placed on the electoral register. In Manchester there was a particularly strong response, and more than 5000 women, representing, it was claimed, over 90 per cent of those canvassed, put their names forward.[9] Dr Richard Pankhurst, whose future wife Emmeline and daughters Christabel and Sylvia were a generation later to play such a prominent part in the suffragette[10] movement, argued the legal points, achieving varying degrees of success in the different areas; most officials rejected the names of women but some placed them on the register. The revising officers, however, eliminated all the names of the successful women, in some cases after objection had been lodged and in other cases without there having been objection. A whole series of court cases were thereupon brought, each slightly different from the other. From a technical point of view, the group of women in the strongest position were those whose names had been placed on the register and then removed by the revising officer without anyone having asked him to do so, since there was clear law to the effect that revising officers had no power to erase names on their own initiative. It was laid down by statute that 'any persons' aggrieved by a decision of a revising officer could appeal to court to have their names restored. This section was relied upon in the case of *Wilson v. Town Clerk of Salford*, but during argument one of the judges suggested that removing the name of a woman from the voters' roll was like removing the name of a dog or a horse,[11] and the Chief Justice eventually held, with the concurrence of his colleagues, that since women were not 'persons' within the meaning of the statute that governed appeals, they had no legal standing to bring their case.

In the law reports this case does not feature prominently, and the judges' ruling on the meaning of the word 'person' appears to have been based on improvised rather than considered thinking. The main issue before the court in the group of cases from Manchester was whether or not women were included in the term 'man', that is, whether the term as used in the Reform Act should be understood generically to refer to both males and females, or restrictively to mean male persons only. This question was decided in the case reported as *Chorlton v. Lings*, in which Dr Pankhurst appeared as junior counsel to Sir John Coleridge on behalf of the women applicants. The law provided that 'every man' of full age 'not subject to legal incapacity' and owning a house should be entitled to vote. The basis of Coleridge's argument was a statute of 1850, which stipulated that in all Acts, words importing the masculine gender should be deemed and taken to include females, unless the contrary was clearly expressed. He suggested that the phrase 'not subject to legal incapacity' referred to people incapacitated by lunacy, imprisonment and bankruptcy, and could not be taken to refer to sex unless the whole female population was deemed to be too imbecilic to exercise the vote. The principle underlying the extension of the franchise was that representation should be co-existent with taxation, and women ratepayers were themselves the best judges of whether they could wisely exercise the vote or not. Historical precedent showed that in earlier times women had in fact voted, and there was no case law to indicate that they were barred from the franchise.

The four judges who heard the matter rejected these arguments without apparent difficulty. The Lord Chief Justice said that the early examples of women voting and even of taking part in legislative deliberations counted for little against the uninterrupted usage of several centuries. The common law rendered women incapable of voting, and if Parliament had intended to change the common law it would not have done so by using the word 'man'. He agreed with the reasoning of the judges in a similar case unsuccessfully brought by feminists in Scotland earlier in the year [*Brown v. Ingram*]. A second judge referred to the eloquence of Coleridge's plea as to the injustice of excluding women from the vote, but said that if Parliament chose in its wisdom to remove this incapacity, it would use explicit language to do so. Another judge said he hoped the case would forever exorcise and lay the ghost of a doubt which ought never to have made its appearance.

Women Councillors in London

One of the results of the women's campaign for the Parliamentary franchise was that they were granted the municipal vote in 1869; Sylvia Pankhurst later contended that the gentlemen in Parliament took little interest themselves in local matters, and accordingly were prepared to let women participate at this level. The question then arose whether women could sit on municipal and county councils as well as vote for them. In 1889 Lady Sandhurst stood as a candidate and was elected to the London County Council by a clear majority over her nearest unsuccessful opponent. The defeated candidate thereupon applied to court for an order declaring her election void and himself elected on the grounds that she did not come within the expression 'fit person of full age', because she was a woman. She countered by saying that there was nothing in the relevant statutes to exclude women from the council – if they were fit to vote they were fit to be voted for, and there was an express provision to the effect that the qualifications for a councillor were the same as those for a voter. The common law could not be used against her since the London County Council had only been in existence for a few years, and was not comparable to Parliament, from which women had been excluded by the usage of centuries.

Judgment was given against her by Sir James Fitzjames Stephen, uncle of Virginia Woolf, and, incidentally, author of a pamphlet that advised women not to be mutinous towards their husbands. He said that he could not accept the argument that if women were not expressly excluded by the statute, the presumption was that they were included. If it had been intended to make an exception to the general rule that women could not hold public office, such an exception would have been made in perfectly plain language.

The case was then taken on appeal before a court of five judges headed by Coleridge, who had by now risen to the position of Chief Justice [*Beresford-Hope v. Lady Sandhurst*]. If Lady Sandhurst had hoped that his earlier eloquence in favour of votes for women would predispose him to decide in her favour, she was to be disappointed. He did not even find it necessary to listen to counsel for her opponent before rejecting her appeal. He based his ex tempore judgment on a provision that stated that 'for all purposes connected with the right to vote at municipal elections, words in the Act imparting the masculine gender included women'. Since this general provision applied only to 'the right to vote', it must by implication exclude the right to be a councillor. Two of the other judges indicated that but for this section they would probably have held that women were entitled to be councillors, while another judge declared that the most that could be said was that there might be a doubt on the question, in which case the law remained unaltered, namely that women had no right to be on a council. The Master of the Rolls, Lord Esher, however, took a firmer stand against Lady Sandhurst, relying on the statements in the Parliamentary Voters' case to the effect that women had been admitted to public office only in the case of somewhat obscure offices exercised often in a remote part of the country where nobody else could have been found to exercise them, or else where they had inherited the office. This being the common law of England, unless a statute expressly gave women the power to exercise public functions, it must be construed so that the powers were confined to men.

The effect of the judgment, then, was that although Lady Sandhurst was clearly of full age and had been elected by the voters, she was disqualified because being a woman she did not fall within the term 'fit person'. On this basis the judges interposed themselves between the electors and the Council, and treated the votes cast for her as having been thrown away, accepting in the words of the law report that it had been a 'matter of notoriety' in the district that Lady Sandhurst was a woman.

Subsequent events indicated that a considerable number of people in London disagreed with the outcome of the case. Shortly after Lady Sandhurst was excluded from the Council, another woman was elected. This time no male opponent came forward to challenge her qualifications, and she allowed a year to elapse before taking her seat, so as to benefit from a provision in the relevant statute to the effect that every election not questioned for a year should be deemed to be good and valid. She was, however, prosecuted and convicted under a section that penalised 'any person' who acted in a corporate office without being qualified. Her argument was that because the twelve-month period had elapsed without objection, she must be regarded as having been duly elected; alternatively, if she was not a 'fit person' to be a councillor, she was by equal reasoning not 'any person' who could act without qualification and so become liable to penalties.

The case came before three judges, who agreed in upholding the penalties against her, though their reasons for doing so differed [*De Souza v. Cobden*]. Coleridge accepted the contention that her election could not be challenged after a year, but said that nevertheless she held the seat contrary to the law of the country, and had acted though disqualified. The Master of the Rolls declared that once more he would take a stronger view than did other members of the court, and reiterated that women were incapable of exercising public functions except where well-recognised exceptions to the contrary had been established as in the case of overseers of the poor. With regard to her liability for penalties, at first sight the section applied only to male persons since the word used was 'he'; but the statute dealing with general rules of interpretation could be applied here, that is, words importing the male gender be applied to females, since there was nothing in the context to indicate otherwise. The third judge, Lord Fry, asked whether the election of a woman was like the election, for instance, of a dead man or of an inanimate thing that could not be elected. He was inclined to think that as the law stood a woman was absolutely disqualified by nature from being elected, and that her election was a mere nullity. The section dealing with penalties was in his view entirely different, since it dealt not with the validity of an election but the disqualification of an individual, and so applied to her.

The judges thus formally accepted a proposition that feminists had previously advanced as a campaigning point to demonstrate absurdity and unfairness, namely, that women were 'persons' for the purposes of legal disabilities but 'non-persons' for the purposes of legal rights.[12]

Women Law Agents in Scotland

The next case to be considered is the application made by a woman in Scotland to be admitted to examinations with a view to qualifying for practice as a Law Agent [*Hall v. Incorp. Society of Law Agents* (1901)]. The Law Agents Act, 1873, used the word 'person', and the applicant claimed that as a 'person' possessed of all the requisite qualifications she had been wrongfully refused the right to sit the examinations by the Society of Law Agents. Her counsel argued that the judges controlled entry to the profession and were not debarred by any law from admitting her. There was ancient precedent for a woman acting as a lawyer in Scotland – Lady Crawford had appeared in the High Court as an advocate in 1563 – and contemporary examples of women practising as lawyers in America and France. The Society contended that inveterate custom in Scotland indicated that the practice of law in all departments had been confined to men. Thus it was doubtful whether women had a legal right to be admitted; none had applied in England and Ireland. Nevertheless, they did not 'consider it to be their interest or duty to maintain that women ought not to be admitted to practise the profession of the law'.

The judges held that their powers to admit applicants to legal practice were governed by the 1873 Act, which referred to the word 'person'. Four judges expressly declared that they regarded this as an ambiguous term, which accordingly had to be interpreted in the light of inveterate usage. 'Person' therefore meant 'male person' and only the Legislature could authorise any change. Five of the judges formulated the matter differently in arriving at the same conclusion – in their view, before the Act was passed women had not been eligible and there was nothing in the Act that made them eligible.

Women Barristers in London

In 1903 Bertha Cave applied to join Gray's Inn as a barrister. The Benchers of the Inn refused to call her to the Bar, and she appealed against their decision to a special tribunal consisting of the Lord Chancellor, the Lord Chief Justice and five other judges. The Benchers contended in a written statement that the regulations of the Inns of Court indicated that males and males alone were to be admitted to practise at the Bar, and that no female had ever been admitted to the Inns of Court. In proceedings which lasted five minutes, Bertha Cave addressed the tribunal herself, and the Lord Chancellor replied that there was no precedent for ladies being called to the English Bar and the tribunal were unwilling to create such a precedent.[13]

Women Graduate Voters in Scotland

The next 'persons' case arose out of the claim by women in Scotland that they be allowed to vote in what were known as the University constituencies. Partly as a result of the furore over the exclusion of Sophia Jex-Blake and her colleagues from Edinburgh Medical School, Parliament in 1889 passed a statute authorising women to graduate at Scottish Universities. One of the automatic rights of a graduate was to vote for Members of Parliament representing respectively the Universities of St Andrews and Edinburgh, and Glasgow and Aberdeen, and eventually in 1906 five women graduates from Edinburgh University sought to exercise this vote. The University authorities refused to issue them with voting papers, and they took the matter to court [*Nairn v. Scottish Universities*]. The key provision stipulated that 'every person' whose name was on the register and who was 'not subject to any legal incapacity', should be entitled to vote. The Scottish judges held that it was a principle of unwritten constitutional law that only men could vote for Parliament, and that the word 'person' accordingly meant 'male person'. Alternatively, women were excluded by the phrase 'not subject to legal disability'.

The case was taken on appeal to the House of Lords in London, which, as the highest judicial body in the country, was not bound to follow the earlier rulings by lower courts on the meaning of the word 'person'. This was a period when agitation by women for the vote and for entry into the professions was reaching large proportions. Chrystal Macmillan, a leading suffragist, argued the matter in person together with her colleague Frances Simson. The essence of their case, which they presented with all the technical trappings of a complex appeal, was that they were 'persons' and therefore entitled to the vote. The word 'person' in its ordinary meaning, they contended, was not ambiguous but included both men and women. Had Parliament intended to exclude women from the term it could have done so by substituting the word 'man' or inserting the word 'male'. The phrase 'persons not subject to legal incapacity' had been interpreted to allow women to vote for school-boards in Scotland and for Members of Parliament in New Zealand. The custom of women not voting could not be regarded as a constitutional principle since women had voted until late in the sixteenth century, and there were cases up to the mid-seventeenth century supporting their right to vote. Moreover, ancient customs could not have a bearing on what was a recently created University franchise. Men graduates voted not as 'men' but as graduates; women graduates with identical qualifications should be entitled to vote in the same way.

The case was heard by the Lord Chancellor and three other judges, who did not even call upon counsel for the Scottish Universities to argue the case against the women.

The Lord Chancellor, Lord Loreburn, noted that the appeal had been argued temperately, on the issue of what the law in fact was and nothing beyond that. He conceded that 'in the vast mass of venerable documents buried in public repositories, some of authority, others of none', there might be found traces of women having taken part in some Parliamentary elections. But no authentic and plain case of a woman giving a vote had been brought before the court. Students of history knew that at various periods members of the House of Commons had been summoned in a very irregular way, and it was quite possible that just as great men in a locality had been required to nominate members, so also women in a like position may have been called upon to do the same; or other anomalies may have been overlooked in a confused time. A few equivocal cases had been referred to. He was surprised how few. And it was the same with regard to judicial precedents. Two passages could be found in which judges were reported as saying that women could vote at Parliamentary elections. These were 'dicta derived from an ancient manuscript of no weight'. Old authorities were almost silent on the subject, except that Lord Coke at one place incidentally alluded to women as being under a disqualification, not dwelling upon it as a thing disputable, but alluding to it for purpose of illustration as a matter certain. 'This disability of women has been taken for granted .... It is incomprehensible to me that any one acquainted with our laws or the methods by which they are ascertained can think, if indeed, any one does think, there is room for argument on such a point.'

The second judge, after referring to the careful arguments advanced by the women, said the case turned mainly on the meaning of the word 'person', which was an ambiguous word. Obscure and unexplained old cases carried little weight against the uninterrupted usage of centuries, and he had no doubt that in its context the word 'person' meant 'male person'. If it had been intended to make a vast constitutional change in favour of women graduates, one would have expected to find plain language and express statement.

The third judge indicated his displeasure at having had to listen to the women by remarking that the court had not had the assistance of counsel but that fortunately the question had not been very difficult. The central fact was that from time immemorial men only had voted in Parliamentary elections. Clear expression of an intent to depart from this distinction had to be found before it was inferred that 'so exceptional a privilege' had been granted in the single case of Scottish Universities. In truth, the case for the appellants rested on a very narrow and slender basis, and that was the word 'person'. It was difficult to say that Parliament had by a roundabout way enabled University authorities to authorise votes by authorising degrees, and at the same time retain conventional respect for Parliament.

The fourth judge concurred in dismissing the appeal.

The House of Lords accordingly rejected the claim to the franchise of the women, the majority of judges expressly holding that women did not fall within the term 'person' as used in the relevant Act.

Women Solicitors in London

Six years later the question of whether women could in law be included in the term 'person' arose once more, this time in relation to entry into the solicitors' branch of the legal profession. After taking a degree at Oxford, the applicant applied to the Law Society to be enrolled as a solicitor's clerk. The Solicitors Act, 1843, provided that any 'person' possessing certain qualifications was entitled to be articled to a solicitor with a view to qualifying for the profession. The Act further stated that 'every word importing the masculine gender only shall extend and be applied to a female as well as a male' unless there was something in the subject or the context repugnant to such construction. The Law Society rejected her request for articles on the grounds that it would be futile to allow her to undertake them if she could never, as a woman, be admitted to practice as a solicitor. She thereupon applied to court for a declaration that she was in fact a 'person' and accordingly could become a solicitor [*Bebb v. Law Society* (1913; 1914)].

The judge who first heard the application gave judgment for the Law Society, mainly on the grounds that in terms of the common law women were debarred from all public offices. The applicant appealed, and the case finally came before the Master of the Rolls and two other judges in the Chancery Division.

Lord Robert Cecil argued the appeal, conceding at the outset that only unmarried women could claim equal rights with men, and that in general no women could hold public office. He contended, however, that unmarried women had *prima facie* the same legal rights as men, and that historically there was nothing to show that women could not act as attorneys. On the contrary, in early years women had so acted, while later statutes did nothing to exclude them, and the Solicitors Act clearly authorised them by using the word 'person'. Women were permitted to practise as solicitors in many of the colonies and in foreign countries, and there was nothing in any Act of Parliament or in the nature of things to prevent women from practising in England, especially as solicitors did not discharge public functions.

The judges went out of their way to compliment Lord Cecil on his arguments, but nevertheless they rejected what he said. The Master of the Rolls declared that all that had to be considered was whether at the date that the Solicitors Act had been passed women were under a disability to become an attorney or solicitor. Three hundred years previously, Lord Coke had stated that women could not be attorneys, and no woman had ever applied to be one.

> We have been asked to hold, what I for one assent to, that in point of intelligence and education and competency women – and in particular the applicant here, who is a distinguished Oxford student – are at least equal to a great many and, probably, far better than many, of the candidates who will come up for examination, but that is really not for us to consider. Our duty is to consider ... what the law is, and I disclaim absolutely any right to legislate in a matter of this kind. In my opinion that is for Parliament and not for this Court.

Both the other judges emphasised that their function as judges was merely to declare the law, and that only Parliament could say what the law should be. The first judge said that anciently in England, parties to a suit had appeared in person, but ever since the profession of attorney had arisen, at least as early as 1402, no instance of a woman attorney seemed to have existed. The inveterate practice of several centuries showed what the law was.

The second judge also stressed that he approached the matter in the light of it being his primary duty to declare the common law. He conceded that in early days when there had been no profession of attorney, and particularly when perhaps the husband might have been following the King's suit at war in another country, a woman had occasionally been appointed the attorney or representative of a litigant, just as a woman might have a power of attorney to perform acts of conveyancing at the present day. But from the time attorneys had become a profession there had been no instance of it having been considered that a woman could be an attorney or solicitor. Originally in the Court of Chancery the only representatives permitted had always been men because they had been at least in minor religious orders.

All the evidence taught them that there was an inveterate usage to the effect that this was a profession that had not hitherto been open to women. The cases as to women holding certain parochial offices had been distinguished on the ground of their being offices which, in the view of the courts, were suitable to women. 'I do not say that this may not be an office suitable to women; what I say is that it has never been, in the view of the Courts, suitable to women.' In all the discussions in those cases and in all the quotations with respect to hereditary offices that a woman might hold or her husband might hold in her right, there had never been a suggestion that the office of attorney was one that was open to women. A further difficulty was that it would be a serious inconvenience if, in the middle of her articles, or in the middle of conducting a piece of litigation, a woman was suddenly to be disqualified from entering into contracts by reason of her getting married.

The Chancery judges therefore were unanimous in rejecting the claim by the applicant that she fell within the term 'person' as used in the Act.

Peeresses in the House of Lords

The peculiar tenacity with which the judges resisted women's claims was manifested by the opposition they organised to the seating of a woman in the House of Lords. In 1918 Parliament eventually acceded to the demand that women be enfranchised and be allowed to stand for election to the House of Commons. In the following year the Sex Disqualification Removal Act provided that no person should be disqualified by sex or marriage from the exercise of any public function. The question soon arose as to whether this general removal of legal disabilities entitled women who inherited a peerage to take their seat in the House of Lords.

In 1922 Viscountess Rhondda, who in earlier years had been active in the suffrage movement, applied for a writ entitling her to take the seat that went with her hereditary title. The matter was considered by a special Committee of the House of Lords, consisting of three members who were judges and four who were not. The Attorney-General on behalf of the Government argued in favour of Lady Rhondda's claim, and the Committee duly reported that in their opinion she was entitled to take her seat. In the ordinary course, the report of such a Committee would have been sufficient to end the matter, but the Lord Chancellor remained obdurate in his opposition. His special position as leader of the House of Lords and head of the judiciary enabled him to have the recommendation of the Committee referred back to a larger committee which was substantially weighted against the admission of women to the House of Lords. It appears that against the strong objection of members of the original committee, he quickly pressed the matter to a vote, with the result that what had originally been an unopposed report in Lady Rhondda's favour was converted into a decision against her by 20 votes to 4, with 5 abstentions. The opinions given by the judges were remarkable for their rancour and sarcasm. Lords Haldane and Wrenbury, who were in the minority supporting Lady Rhondda's claim, said in effect that the Lord Chancellor had steam-rollered the matter through in such an irregular fashion that the decision of the enlarged committee was worthless. The Lord Chancellor (Birkenhead) replied even more robustly by in effect accusing his two 'noble and learned friends' of gross hypocrisy.

The fact remains that for a further forty years the senior section of the Mother of Parliaments refused entry to women.

Sir James Easte Willes Speaks in England

It will be noted from the above recital that in every single case heard by the English and Scottish judges in which a decision had to be given on whether women were debarred merely by sex from exercising public functions or entering a profession, that decision went against the women. It made no difference whether the terms to be interpreted were 'man' or 'person ... not under a legal disability' or merely 'person'; in each case the words were regarded as excluding women. It also made no difference whether the arguments to the courts were addressed by the women themselves or by distinguished male lawyers, whether they were couched in wide constitutional terms or based on close historical research; the judges consistently and unanimously used their interpretation of the common law to cut down the apparently wide words of the statutes and reject the women's claims.

Whether this should be regarded as judicial intransigence or judicial consistency is a question that will be considered later. At this stage it is appropriate to consider the rationale offered by the judges for the exclusion of women from public life. An explanation to which a succession of judges referred with approbation was that offered in the Manchester Voters' case by Sir James Easte Willes ('and a finer judge never lived'):

> What was the cause of [the exclusion of women], it is not necessary to go into: but, admitting that fickleness of judgment and liability to influence have sometimes been suggested as the ground of exclusion, I must protest against its being supposed to arise in this country from any under-rating of the sex either in point of intellect or worth. That would be quite inconsistent with one of the glories of our civilization, — the respect and honour in which women are held. This is not a mere fancy of my own, but will be found in Selden [the legal historian], in the discussion of the origin of the exclusion of women from judicial and like public functions, where the author gives preference to this reason, that the exemption was founded upon motives of decorum, and was a privilege of the sex.

The custom of the ancient Britons was that women took part in deliberation of all public matters whether relating to war or peace, but the Saxons confined their councils to those who bore arms. The only women in Saxon and later times who signed Charters were apparently the Queen or ecclesiastics of rank and wealth; women who inherited land held by military tenure which carried public office with it, exercised their authority through a male deputy, the one exception being Ann Countess of Pembroke, who as 'a person of unusual gifts both of body and mind, had thought fit to discharge the duties in person'. Women could not be judges or sit on juries, and although women had once been able to appoint proxies to sit in the House of Lords, and later to be represented by their husbands, it was clear that such a right had long ceased to exist. The absence of the right of representation in Parliament in both Houses was

> referable to the fact that in this country, in modern times, chiefly out of respect to women, and a sense of decorum, and not from their want of intellect, or their being for any other such reason unfit to take part in the government of the country, they have been excused from taking any share in this department of public affairs.

A Note on Women Lawyers in Canada and South Africa

Reference to judgments in other countries on the question of whether or not women should be refused entry into the legal profession on grounds of sex, should provide some evidence as to whether English[14] judges were particularly insensitive or hostile to women's claims in the public law field, or whether they were merely articulating a conception of the law universally maintained in countries with the common law tradition. In making the comparison, it should be borne in mind that the English legal profession as a whole remained adamantly and overwhelmingly opposed to the admission of women until the end of the First World War, apparently with unanimous support from the judges.

What will be looked for in the non-English judgments, then, is not only the outcome of the cases, but whether the judges were unanimous and whether they expressed any views to indicate that the exclusion of women might be inequitable or prevent women from achieving economic independence.

The position in *Canada* was tested by at least two applications brought by Mabel French. The first was that she be admitted to legal practice in New Brunswick, and was unsuccessful [*Re French* (1905)]. Presumably the law was changed by legislation, because when she later applied to be admitted to the Bar of British Columbia she stated that she was an attorney in New Brunswick. The second case eventually came before the British Columbia Court of Appeal, which unanimously rejected her application. The Chief Justice relied heavily on the common law exclusion of women, and held that this exclusion could only be set aside by clear statutory language. He went on to say, however: 'That there are cogent reasons for a change, based upon changes in the legal status of women, and the enlarged activities of modern life, may be admitted, but this was a matter for the Legislature, not the Court to resolve.' The judges in Quebec, called upon to decide a similar matter, held that women could be admitted neither to the study of law nor to the legal profession in Quebec [*Langstaff v. Bar of Quebec* (1915)].

Second, women in *South Africa* pressed to be admitted to legal practice, and on being opposed by the local Law Societies took the matter to court. In the first case the applicant was unsuccessful. She sought to become an attorney in the Transvaal, but the opposition of the Law Society was upheld by the Transvaal Supreme Court (which, incidentally, had overruled an objection by the Law Society based purely on race to the admission of an African – the word 'person' thus included black men but excluded white women) [*Schlesin v. Incorporated Law Society* (1909); cf. *Mangena v. Law Society* (1910)]. The second case was brought by Madeline Wookey in the Cape Supreme Court in 1912. A firm of country attorneys was willing to enrol her as an articled clerk, but the Cape Law Society refused to register her. She applied to the Cape Supreme Court for an order compelling the Society to register her, and her application was upheld. The judgment (by Judge President Maasdorp) therefore stands out as the first one in which the term 'person' was construed so as to include women. In fact, of all the judgments in the various jurisdictions in which the courts were called upon to open the way for women to enter legal practice, this appears to be the only one in which women were held to be 'persons'. The judge went extensively into Roman, Roman-Dutch, English and Scottish law on the subject, and came to the conclusion that although in Holland and England the practice had been for men only to be in the profession, 'there was no law compelling the Court to follow that practice, nor was there any law preventing the Court from altering it'. The word 'persons' in his view ordinarily included females as well as males, and so included the applicant.

The Cape Law Society appealed to the South African Appeal Court [*Incorporated Law Society v. Wookey* (1912)]. Acting Chief

Justice Rose-Innes, who was friendly with a number of South African feminists, including the writer Olive Schreiner, summarised the issues as follows:

> It is hardly necessary to point out that the question is one of the utmost importance, not only to the applicant herself, and to others who may be desirous of following her example, but to the profession and the public. If it was rightly answered in the Court below, the result will be materially to widen the area of women's economic activities, though that be done by opening to a host of new competitors the doors of an already congested profession. If it was wrongly answered, then the law of the country will be denying to one-half of its citizens, on the mere ground of sex, the right of employing their natural abilities in the pursuit of an honourable calling.

After this introduction, he set out the gist of the views of the Cape Judge President and then declared that it was with real regret that he felt constrained to differ from them. In his opinion the exclusion of women from legal practice in Holland had not been merely a question of practice, but related to the general position of women in the law. 'The law of Holland was astonishingly broad and liberal on this subject ... but it certainly did not place men and women in a position of equality. It went out of its way to protect women, but it protected them as being the weaker vessels, and subject to natural and legal disabilities .... Rightly or wrongly that was the point of view of the ... law.' He felt forced to the conclusion that the word 'persons' in the relevant statute must be taken to have denoted 'male persons' and not 'any persons'. However much he might sympathise with the position of the applicant and others in like position, it was impossible for a court of law to help them achieve equality of opportunity in regard to the practice of the legal profession.

The second judge (Solomon, members of whose family had joined the militant suffragettes in England) said that ordinarily the term 'person' included women as well as men, but was often used to refer to one sex only. Looking at the statute in the context in which it was passed, it seemed inconceivable to him that if the Legislature had intended to introduce so great a change and to throw open the doors of the profession to women, it would not have done so in clear and unambiguous language, instead of leaving it as an inference to be drawn from the use of the word 'person', which might or might not include women as well as men.

The third judge (de Villiers) conceded that the word 'person' was wide enough to embrace women as well as men, but to understand its meaning in the statute it was necessary to look at the history of the subject. The Roman Praetorian Edict showed that boys under seventeen years of age were excluded from the profession of attorneys or advocates, as also were women, the deaf, and the blind. The later Christian Emperors introduced further restrictions, which were also adopted into Dutch practice: pagans, Jews, pronounced heretics, persons, for example, who denied the Trinity.

> Some of these restrictions are undoubtedly obsolete. It would be difficult to maintain that a blind person duly qualified in other respects cannot be admitted as an attorney on the ground that he cannot see and therefore cannot pay the proper respect to the Magistrate. The prohibitions, too, based on race and religion, are notoriously obsolete. Can the same be said of the prohibition based on sex? I am of opinion that the answer must be in the negative. No doubt many of the disabilities under which women have laboured in the past have been abolished. The onward march of civilisation, new needs of society and of women, fresh burdens upon all alike, women as well as men, have called for remedial legislation in various directions. But we cannot ignore the fact that from the time that Carfania vexed the soul of some too nervous praetor with her pleading down to our own day the profession of an attorney has been exercised exclusively by men; and this applied not only in Holland, but also to England.

It may be noted that in its comments on the case the *South African Law Journal* asked why, if Jews, heretics and blind persons were no longer disqualified, women should be excluded. In the *Journal*'s view the word 'persons' would include women in law as in common sense.[15]

WOMEN BECOME 'PERSONS'

It was Parliament rather than the judiciary that was responsible for the removal of legal disabilities on women. In 1918 the vote was granted to women aged thirty years or more and a decade later it was extended to all adult women on like terms with men. In 1919 the Sex Disqualification Removal Act formally revoked all disabilities on women from holding public office or exercising public functions. These statutes did not, however, expressly declare that women were 'persons' in the eyes of the law, and the question still lay with the judges.

Women Senators in Canada

The last of the 'persons' case emanated from Canada, where feminists had sought the right for women to be nominated to the

Senate.[16] The case came by way of appeal from the Canadian Supreme Court to the Judicial Committee of the Privy Council in London, the body that heard appeals on important questions of law from all parts of the British Empire. The British North America Act of 1867 provided that the Governor-General should from time to time summon qualified 'persons' to the Senate. The legal issue was once more whether the term 'persons' could be said to include women, and the Canadian Supreme Court unanimously decided it did not. The Chief Justice and three other judges based their judgments substantially on the common law disability of women and on the various cases in which it had been held that the term 'persons' did not include women. The fifth judge rejected this general approach, but held that there were special indications in the statute which suggested that the word 'persons' applied to men only.

Five judges, presided over by the Lord Chancellor (Sankey) heard the appeal in London, and, as was the custom in the Judicial Committee, expressed their decision in a single judgment, which was delivered by Lord Sankey [*Edwards v. Attorney General, Canada* (1929)].

Their Lordships, he declared, were of the opinion that the word 'persons' *did* include women (his emphasis).

> The exclusion of women from all public offices is a relic of days more barbarous than ours, but it must be remembered that the necessity of the times often forced on man customs which in later years were not necessary. Such exclusion is probably due to the fact that the deliberate assemblies of the early tribes were attended by men under arms, and women did not bear arms.[17]

Yet the tribes did not despise the advice of women, as Tacitus made clear.

> The likelihood of attack rendered such a proceeding unavoidable, and after all what is necessary at any period is a question for the times upon which opinion grounded on experience may move one way or another in different circumstances. This exclusion of women found its way into the opinions of Roman jurists [such as Ulpian]. The barbarian tribes who settled in the Roman Empire, and were exposed to constant dangers, naturally preserved and continued the tradition.

He then set out the legal disabilities which in England had prevented women from holding public office below the level of Queen or Regent, or from entering the legal profession. After dealing with most of the earlier 'persons' cases, and suggesting some reasons why they might not be applicable to the case in hand, he stated that 'the word [persons] is ambiguous and in its original meaning would undoubtedly embrace members of either sex'. The fact that no woman had served or claimed to serve a public office was not of great weight when it was remembered that custom would have prevented the point from being contested. The appeal to history in the particular matter was therefore not conclusive, particularly in regard to a statute that created a constitution for a new country.

The word 'person' may include members of both sexes, and to those who ask why the word should include females, the obvious answer is, why not? In these circumstances the burden is upon those who deny that the word includes women to make out their case.

The Judicial Committee of the Privy Council accordingly held that women were 'persons' in the eyes of the law.

THE MYTH OF JUDICIAL NEUTRALITY

The debut of women into person-hood was acknowledged by the judges as an event deserving of special ceremony. Contrary to the usual practice of stating only the conclusion of a judgment, Lord Sankey read out the court's decision in full to the representatives of various women's organisations who crowded the chamber.[18] This little ritual to mark formal sexual emancipation was greeted with celebratory telegrams across the Atlantic, while newspaper editorials marked the event with that stiffly gracious prose reserved for congratulating women on the progress they were making. Journals, which for years had equivocated on the question of women's rights, which had suppressed, distorted or jeered at the aims of the suffragette window-breakers and hunger-strikers, greeted the judgment as though it represented the culmination of the smooth and automatic unfolding of an idea. The women were praised for their perseverance, the judges for their adherence to principle, and society as a whole for its possession of such women and such judges. Displayed to the full was the special capacity of writers on the English constitution for healing and hiding the wounds of bitter past battles, not by enveloping them with glory as writers in other countries do, but by pretending they never existed.

The Persons case, as the piece of litigation had become known, brought to an end sixty years of rejection by the judiciary and the legal profession of women's claims. The English common law, which had so often been extolled as being the embodiment of human freedom, had in fact provided the main intellectual justification for the avowed and formal subordination of women; English legal scholars, such as A. V. Dicey who had written so influentially on the Rule of Law, had turned their pens to detailed explanations of why women should not have the vote; and English lawyers, who over the centuries had proclaimed their adherence to the principles of justice and had fought against restraints on trade, had consistently refused to allow women into their ranks.

From a technical legal point of view, all that the Canadian Senator's case decided in substance was that it was no longer necessary to assume that participation by women in public life was so startling a concept that only the clearest authorisation by Parliament could permit it. Six decades of precedent stating that women could not be included in the term 'persons' were swept aside by the simple proposition: 'The word "person" may include members of both sexes, and to those who ask why the word should include females, the obvious answer is, why not?' What had suddenly changed to render manifestly correct propositions that had been dismissed as virtually unarguable by earlier judges?

There is nothing in legal logic itself which explains the turn-around of the judges in the Canadian Senator's case. Nor is it likely that in case after case the judges happened by a coincidence of subjective moods arbitrarily to arrive at unanimous decisions against the women, and then by an equally mysterious coincidence happened suddenly to agree that the women were entitled to succeed. The cases thus provide little support for those sceptical realists who emphasise the subjective and erratic character of judicial decision-making. Judicial dyspepsia is not all that rare, and counsel have their own folklore about how judicial behaviour is affected by lunch if not by breakfast, but the chances of all the judges having been afflicted by indigestion at the same time are rather remote, and in any event, the nexus between stomach discomfort and anti-feminism would still have to be established. Sylvia Pankhurst did remark that it was whispered at the Bar that Lord Coleridge's metamorphosis from being counsel for the women in one case to becoming head of the court that rejected their claims in another, was due to his second wife having been more of a Tartar than his first. But the malice that barristers reserve for private discussion is as unreliable a guide to truth as is the concomitant show of solidarity they muster for public display.

In the absence of any other satisfactory explanation, the conclusion becomes inescapable that what had changed was not the meaning of the word 'person', nor the modes of reasoning appropriate to lawyers, but the conception of women and women's position in public life held by the judges.

It should be remembered that political events in Britain had produced changes not only in the climate in which the issues were being decided, but also in the personnel of the judiciary. It could hardly have been coincidence that the first judgment in which women were held in law to be 'persons' was delivered by Lord Sankey, who had been appointed by the Labour Administration as Lord Chancellor in an effort to liberalise the judiciary, and who sat in the Cabinet alongside Margaret Bondfield, the first woman to hold Cabinet office in Britain.[19] Of course, none of these political factors is referred to in the judgment, which is expressed in traditional form with emphasis on questions of linguistics rather than matters of policy. Yet the only inference that can be drawn by a present-day reader from the judgment is that Lord Sankey and a majority, if not all, of his colleagues thought it absurd that women should be debarred from public office solely on grounds of sex, and even more absurd that the word 'person' should be the instrument for achieving this result. Having arrived at that conclusion, or rather, having started off on that premise, it was not difficult for them to write a judgment that paid conventional respect to all the earlier decisions while totally ignoring their effect. In practice, if not in theory, they accepted the view so emphatically denied by their predecessors on the Bench, namely that the law was the instrument of the judges rather than the judges the instrument of the law.

What is so striking is that judicial neutrality was most adamantly asserted precisely during the period of greatest judicial partisanship, when the Bench was being packed to the greatest extent, and manoeuvring by the leading judges was being done in the most flagrant fashion. In the period 1832 to 1906 half of judicial appointments went to barristers who had been Members of Parliament in the ranks of the ruling party.[20] Conservatives vied with Liberals to get their appointees on the Bench, with an eye not only to past services rendered in political life but also to future services to be rendered in judicial life. The results of this selection process were manifest in trade union and workmen's compensation cases, where judges tended to divide according to former political allegiance as pro-employer or pro-employee, their decisions having considerable political impact in the country.[21] In the case of the male monopoly litigation, the judicial manoeuvring was found to be unnecessary, since all the judges – whether Conservative or Liberal – accepted the same male-orientated approach. Only in Lady Rhondda's case was there the kind of manoeuvring that had characterised the trade union cases, but by now it represented a belated action by a defeated and aged fraternity, stripped of its power, to retain at least its ethos.

To combat what he regarded as the obstructive influence of past political appointees on the Bench, Lord Sankey encouraged the elevation of career lawyers rather than lawyer-politicians to the judiciary, hoping to reduce the conflict produced by judges of one political generation adjudicating on the legislation of politicians of a later generation. In exchange for loss of influence on public life, the judges were offered greater salaries and additional public esteem. The honour accorded to them was thus inversely proportionate to their political power; the more innocuous they became, the more their majesty was praised.

With the decline in the judges' political influence went a decline in the use of the common law as a means of superimposing the judges' views on those of Parliament. The problem was not simply a constitutional one. Parliament at that time was becoming to some extent responsive to the demands of newly enfranchised working men, while the judiciary on the whole reflected the interests and values of the landed and commercial classes.

The main instrument that the judges had been using to assert the interests of men against women and of employers against workers was the common law. The common law tradition has so frequently been associated with concepts of fundamental right and justice that it is at first startling to find that it was used as the main doctrinal justification for preventing the advancement of working people of both sexes, notably in conspiracy cases, and of women of the middle and upper classes, primarily in the male monopoly cases. In the seventeenth century the common law had been yoked to a principle of the fundamental rights of the people of England as a weapon to challenge the divine rights of the Kings of England. It drew its doctrinal strength from a claim to have existed since time immemorial, having its roots in an antiquity that predated the prerogative rights of the kings. In order to establish this ancient origin, a history was invented by the judges. This retrospectively created history was almost entirely fictional, but so strong was the need of the judges to assert the supremacy of the common law and the concomitant idea of uninterrupted custom, that contrary facts were simply ignored or treated as irrelevant. Essentially this fictionalised history represented a projection into the past of the current world-view of the judges. Coke was the leading exponent of this asserted antiquity, and it was Coke's manufactured views that were relied upon for the next three centuries as having set out immemorial custom. In the 'persons' cases, it was in fact his pronouncements on the public disabilities of women that were seized upon by the judges to reject the women's claims; yet his assumption of permanent legal subordination of women had as little historical foundation as another claim of his to the effect that Parliament had met before the Norman conquest. In reality Coke was not averse to bending the law to assert his values, and his statements on the legal status of women must be particularly suspect in view of what was by common account his disastrous domestic life. (His second wife wrote after his death: We shall never see his like again, praises be to God.)[22] Thus the anti-feminism of one generation of judges was carried by the common law to the anti-feminism of another generation. Attempts by counsel to suggest that Coke's writings on the public rights of women might have been influenced by his personal experiences were peremptorily brushed aside by nineteenth- and twentieth-century judges who essentially agreed with his opinions. In other cases, however, statements by early judges with which these judges no longer agreed, to the effect that husbands might castigate insubordinate wives with rods, were held to be manifestly archaic and no longer representative of the common law.[23]

Counsel for the women in the public rights cases laboured assiduously to prove that in reality women in ancient times had voted and had held public office, but the facts that they established turned out to be weaker than the spurious historiography that asserted an inveterate usage to the contrary. The very circumstance that the notion of immemorial usage was based on fiction rather than proof made it a particularly pliable tool in the hands of the judges. In the seventeenth century, the common law judges used the common law to justify challenges to established authority, while in the nineteenth century they used it to resist attempts at reform. What maintained continuity between the idea of the common law over the centuries was that it continued to be the instrument of the judges and to express in a vigorous if indirect form the interests of the social group with whom the judges were associated. The fundamental rights of the English people thus amounted to little more than the fundamental rights of the judges, and chief amongst these was the right to determine how social claims should be legally classified and what procedures should be followed for their enforcement.

This is an appropriate point at which to make a few comments on the English judicial style, which emerged so characteristically in the 'persons' cases. The theory of judicial precedent, in terms of which judges are bound by the decisions of their predecessors, played an important role in giving an appearance of technical propriety to what today we would consider manifestly partisan and oppressive decision-making. In the absence of a written constitution or any fundamental code, the theory is that the judges look only to the words of a particular Act of Parliament and to the decisions of earlier judges when declaring the law. This process is seen as largely deductive, involving the extension by analogy of principles gathered from previous decisions to the circumstances of new cases.[24] It expressly excludes examination of the social or political importance of the issue in hand.

It is adherence to this doctrine that gives to English legal argument its unusually close and tangled character. Where other legal systems promote undue rhetoric, the English legal system engenders extra-ordinary pedantry. Great forensic battles are fought over the precise meanings of words such as 'building', 'place', 'use' and 'and'. There is little scope for lofty statements or appeals to fundamental concepts of right when the issue in a case is whether the word 'and' only means 'and' or whether it can also mean 'or'. The modes of reasoning employed in the most technical of matters are exactly the same as those used for issues of manifest constitutional importance. Thus, when determining a matter such as whether women should be included in the category of 'persons' for purposes of voting, the judges deployed exactly the same format or argument as they did in deciding whether a wooden hut was a 'building' for purposes of planning permission.

This special emphasis on the word rather than the concept, on the fact rather than the sentiment, on the cited instance rather than the overarching principle, is usually attributed by defenders of the common law to the peculiarly pragmatic character of the English people. The survival of the common law as expressed through a multitude of cases, rather than through a unified code, is said to reflect a native genius for building up doctrine on the basis of concrete responses to the dealings of practical men, and has been seen as an inheritance to be guarded with the utmost care. In other societies, to be rigidly systematic might be regarded as a virtue, but in England it is counted as a serious intellectual fault, inviting the appellation 'doctrinaire'. This self-contained inward-looking character of English lawyers was exemplified by a joke put about in the law journals of the last century, that a jurist was someone who knew something about the laws of all countries except his own. Yet references to virtues allegedly unique to the English are at best descriptive rather than explanatory. Unless one attributes national character to some biological essence or relies on a crude geographical determinism, one is forced to ask why a certain intellectual style developed amongst lawyers in England, as opposed, say, to those in continental Europe. Max Weber has suggested that the answer lies in the success of the English legal profession in keeping legal education under its control and out of the hands of the Universities.[25] Rather than regarding native genius as an explanation of the character of legal reasoning, he sees the legal profession as the creator of the concept of native genius, which it used as a weapon in defence of its group interest. Thus it was in the interests of the legal profession to assert the superiority of their indigenous practical wisdom over the imported speculations of the University professors, and this led to a continuing emphasis on the virtues of English case-law. So successful have the professions been in this respect, that not only do they to this day continue to control the qualifications for legal practice, but they have even succeeded in getting the Universities, which they have so frequently humiliated, to extol their virtues.

One consequence of this has been the evolution of a peculiarly aloof judiciary and complacent legal profession, unused to critical debate of their own functioning. Evaluations of the Bench and the profession as institutions are almost invariably construed as attacks on judges, barristers and solicitors as individuals, bringing into question their subjective sincerity. In reality, the question of collective bias, such as that expressed in favour of male monopoly, is totally separate from the question of personal integrity, which will vary from individual to individual. Thus, to accuse the judges of anti-feminist partiality is not to say that they were necessarily hypocritical or corrupt. The days when the judges clandestinely auctioned themselves to the wealthiest litigant had long passed. English law was far too pedantic and the Bar far too disciplined and inward-looking to manifest that gross hypocrisy which characterised the legal professions in some other jurisdictions. Such corruption as there was, operated not through bribes but through 'legitimate' patronage and through subtle economic and status pressures. For public officials to have attempted to bribe judges who already shared their way of looking at things, would have been a gross waste of taxpayers' money.

If legal academics were not inclined to challenge the judicial posture of neutrality, however, the same could not have been said of the feminist activists. Scores of suffragette women indicated by their conduct in court that, to put it at its politest, they had withdrawn any legitimacy which they might formerly have accorded the judiciary. They shouted till they were hoarse, and some when they could shout no more hurled books, chairs, shoes and ink-bottles at the magistrates. In prison, they refused to abide by the rules, and went on prolonged hunger-strikes. They were deliberately disputing the notion that, where women were challenging the dominion of men, they could expect male judges, lawyers, policemen, prison officers and doctors to function impartially. The women declared in word and action that they would not be bound by a constitution that refused to accord to them the status of being persons in public life. To submit to being tried by a body established by the constitution was to concede its legitimacy in advance. The issue was whether men should decide whether women could decide.

The violence effected and the suffering endured by the suffragettes was largely demonstrative in nature. As young girls they had been brought up to tolerate rather than inflict suffering, and they converted this capacity into a weapon. They achieved autonomy by courting the violence of the male protectors of the male-dominated state, and then enduring whatever was inflicted on them. Having risked death themselves by extending their daring and endurance to the point of dying, the pro-war section of the movement was later able with special passion to spur on young men to death in the trenches.

The resoluteness with which the women pursued their aims was seen not as proof of consistency but as evidence of hysteria. Modes of struggle that had been determined by their social situation – no guns, no industrial power, no vote – were attributed to their biological condition. The intense feminism represented by Christabel Pankhurst proved peculiarly embarrassing, and neither female nor male historians appear even to this day to have been able to come to terms with it. The feminism expressed by her sister Sylvia was related to male radicalism and socialism, but Christabel's cannot be integrated into any such tradition. This is not because the women's battle, in contrast with that of the workers, has already been won, but because it has hardly got under way; historically the feminist revolt must be regarded as still underdeveloped.

As far as the judges and magistrates were concerned, the suffragettes were merely a particularly annoying set of defendants, whose actions disturbed the dignity of the courts and made it more difficult to plan the list of cases. The major instrument of judicial self-defence against the feminist assaults was to assert judicial neutrality. In case after case, the presiding officers stressed that political questions, including the justice of the women's claims, were no concern of the courts, whose function it was merely to uphold the law. In no case does there appear to have been the slightest expression of judicial sympathy for the suffragettes, and the one judicial pronouncement that stands out is the description by a Lord Chief Justice of hunger-striking by women prisoners as 'this wicked folly'.[26] Yet as far as the women defendants and their supporters were concerned, the concept of judicial neutrality was a myth. In their eyes it was impossible for male-exclusive courts applying laws laid down by male-exclusive institutions to be impartial when the very issue at stake was male-exclusiveness. To uphold the law when it was being challenged was necessarily to take sides. Moreover, as the test cases on male monopoly showed, the judges were not reluctant enforcers of laws they knew to be bad, but dogged defenders of male supremacy. Where they did have a choice on a matter of legal principle, they exercised it against the women, and where they did feel free to make a comment on the women, they did so in terms that were hostile to the claims for equality.

As far as the judges were concerned, land could be apportioned, money distributed, and reputations adjusted, but sex was indivisible. Either women were entitled to vote, or take a seat on a council, or study medicine, or practise as lawyers, or they were not. Male domination could survive the entry of one or two women into the disputed domains, but male-exclusiveness could not. The battle-lines were thus drawn over questions of principle and the struggle was a political one between bitterly hostile groups whose aims were totally antagonistic. This is not to say that the contestants were identifiable solely by sex. There were men who supported the women's struggles, just as there were women who opposed them. But the contest was over gender, and because of the way in which the issue was categorised there could be no compromise, only victory or defeat for one side or the other. Today the essence of the contest remains the same, but the formulation of the issues has changed considerably. As the matter was then projected in terms of a rigid and legally enforced sex bar, the interests could not be adjusted or reconciled. The judges were called upon, within the narrow area of choice permitted them by the English legal system, to support one set of combatants against the other. Writing in her middle age shortly after Lord Sankey's judgment, Sylvia Pankhurst spoke of the efforts that had been made before her birth by her father in his capacity as counsel for the women in the first franchise case:

If women were to be excluded from the vote by virtue of irremediable defect of mental power, he had argued they were excluded as much by the word 'person' as 'man'. To his hearers his contention perhaps sounded exaggerated; but actually this was the ruling which the Courts were presently to give; women were not to be regarded as *persons* in respect of public rights and functions. It was bad law, but upheld by the prejudices of the time and maintained for half a century.[27]

It is understandable that Sylvia Pankhurst, as all other feminists, should have considered the decisions in the male monopoly cases to be bad law upheld by prejudice, just as their opponents considered it to be good law maintained by neutrality. Rebels are less likely to accept the impartiality of judges than are those whose authority the judges uphold. Members of the women's movement were not inclined to regard as neutral judges who in a series of cases refused to allow women to enrol as lawyers, who failed to uphold the right of women to petition the Prime Minister in person, and who gave their approval to the use of forced-feeding against women hunger-strikers. At the height of the militant campaigns, the courtrooms became battle arenas, in which female defendants created uproar as part of their challenge to the right of the state to prosecute them for demanding the vote. Judges, juries, prosecutors, policemen and prison officers were seen as part and parcel of a single apparatus designed to repress their struggles. The fact that the personnel of the courts were entirely male intensified the feeling of the defendants that they were being judged by men for challenging the institutions of men. Here again the analogy holds with blacks in a white supremacy court. Nelson Mandela, African rebel against white domination in South Africa, challenged the jurisdiction of the court trying him with the following words:

> The white man makes all the laws, he drags us before his courts and accuses us, and he sits in judgment over us .... I feel oppressed by the atmosphere of white domination that lurks all around in this courtroom .... I have grave fears that this system of justice may enable the guilty to drag the innocent before the courts.[28]

Deleting the word 'white' where appropriate, this denunciation expressed precisely the opposition of the suffragettes, especially at the height of their campaign, to the male-exclusive courts.

There is no scope for impartiality over questions of power and violence. Women could either vote or not vote, and the violence they did and the violence they had done to them had either to be condoned or punished. The judiciary refused them the vote, penalised them for the violence they committed against property, and sanctioned the violence done to them by prison doctors.

The women correctly perceived that their main battle was a political one directed at Parliament rather than a legal one directed at the judges. And in defence of the judges against present-day criticism, it can be said that the politically sensitive issue of gender discrimination was appropriately one for decision by Parliament rather than the courts. Nevertheless, had the judges favoured the substance of the women's claims, had they attached as much force to the concept of a developing democracy as they did to the idea of an ancient differentiation, they could in good judicial conscience have found for the women. If they had chosen this course, their judgments would have been denounced by some of their contemporaries as being contrary to the spirit of the common law and the constitution of England (Scotland), and hailed by most subsequent commentators as exemplifying the spirit of the common law and the constitution of England (Scotland). The judgment of Lord Mansfield's court outlawing the holding of slaves on English soil is famous;[29] the many judgments rejecting women's claims to equality of treatment are not even known. Posterity too has its biases.

What emerges from a perusal of the male monopoly cases, then, is that the judges serenely ignored not only the natural meaning of the word 'person' but also factual and historical evidence which demonstrated that the legal status of women was one of subordination rather than elevation. One of the characteristics of judicial pronouncement in England, particularly noticeable in these cases, was its lack of selfconciousness or strain. The judges asserted the law with what Karl Mannheim in another context has called a 'somnambulistic certainty with regard to truth'.[30] As Mannheim has pointed out, when a conceptual apparatus is the same for all the members of a group, the presuppositions underlying the individual concepts never become perceptible; human beings do not theorise about the actual situations in which they live as long as they are well adjusted to them. The judges were accordingly content to adopt modes of classification without questioning the assumptions about power, property and sex that underlay them. Mannheim points out that ruling groups can in their thinking become so intensively interest-bound to a situation that they are simply no longer able to see certain facts which would undermine their sense of domination. Collectively and unconsciously certain groups in their thinking obscure the real condition of society both to themselves and to others so as to stabilise that society, just as utopian groups on the other hand hide aspects of reality that would shake their belief or paralyse their desire to change things. The term 'ideology' may thus be used to signify some systematic world view that describes, explains and justifies a particular form of social ordering. The rationalisation that is implicit in ideology need not be logical; it is enough that it be plausible. Nor need it be expressed systematically or even consciously entertained. In Britain, where it is the height of political insult to accuse an opponent of being ideological, a person's ideology is likely to be an inarticulate conglomerate of opinions held together by what is termed 'common sense'.

Thus we may accept that judges, like other people, are moved more by what they believe than by what they know. Shared beliefs shape reality and explain phenomena, and depend for their credibility not on empirical verification but on antiquity and reiteration. Their tenacity is attributable to the manner in which they serve social needs and not to their capacity to reveal social truths. If an individual's consciousness is at variance with demonstrable reality, he is called mad and locked up. If, however, a whole social group shares a distorted consciousness, they attribute to their consciousness a special virtue and elevate it to a region above ordinary experience.

The function of fallacious truism, then, is precisely to disguise social reality, or rather, to describe the world in terms favourable to the position of a particular group. It helps to explain what would otherwise be non-understandable and to justify what would otherwise be non-acceptable, transmuting hard conflict into soft poetry, sharp fact into hazy metaphor, the unpleasant evident into the palatable self-evident. If the interest it served could be revealed, it would dissolve. But it cannot be disposed of by disputation, since belief structures evidence far more firmly than evidence structures belief. The reality projected by the feminists and sustained by the very fact of the litigation, was easily subordinated by the judges to their shared ideology as males.

The expression 'male ideology' should thus not be seen as connoting that the judges viewed women's position in terms of some systematic philosophy traceable to the writings of any particular political philosopher. In the days before the social survey was established as the final authority for any pronouncement, it was usually quotations from the Bible and the Classics that served to validate any significant social statement, but these were used more as ornaments and indicators of cultured dialogue than as sources of doctrine. Nor in suggesting that the judges articulated male ideology is it contended that they were particularly misogynistic, or in any way conspiratorial; those who wielded power normally had no need to resort to deviousness, since they could more easily and safely achieve their purposes by relying on the values and agencies fashioned to sustain their power. On the contrary, the more sincere the judges were in their beliefs, the more effectively could they act upon them.

Male ideology denied the existence of inequity in the treatment by men of women, and rationalised legal disabilities imposed on women in terms of each sex having dominium in its separate sphere. In the context of actual and legal male domination, however, the theory of complementarity was merely a gracious way of explaining female subjection. This rationalisation was not something invented by upper-class Victorian males. There was any amount of literature on which the judges and others could draw to testify to the subordination of women through the ages. The specific contribution they made was to place a halo over domesticity, granting to it a special virtue, and pushing it to an extreme.

The final jurisprudential question that arises from a perusal of the 'persons' cases, is whether the issue of judicial bias is really the one around which discussion of the judicial function should revolve. The notion of impartiality is not itself neutral. It is a value-laden concept that presupposes that it is both feasible and desirable for the machinery of state to operate in a neutral manner 'without fear or favour'. In this context the very idea of neutrality presupposes social inequality. To say that judges should be unbiased between rich and poor, white and black, male and female, is to accept that these are enduring social categories. It is the procedural right to a proper hearing in court that then purports to equalise the unequal. In fact, together with the concept of a democratically controlled legislature, the notion of a fair trial is crucial to the legitimation of rule in modern Western states. It is more than simply a mechanism for adjusting disputes between individuals and resolving conflicts of interest between groups. For millions of individuals who never enter a court, the knowledge that the judges are there is what matters. The judiciary stands as a symbol of order in what otherwise might be regarded as a chaotic society.[31] The judges demonstrate that citizens are governed by the rules of the many rather than the ambitions of a few. This is why the principle of equality before the courts is so important. The possessed and the dispossessed are equally entitled to a hearing and equally bound by a judgment; by asserting the principle of equality of access, the courts do not eliminate inequality, they merely render it more tolerable. Thus the myth of judicial neutrality continues to flourish in Britain, and all historical evidence inconsistent with it is either explained away or, more frequently, simply ignored.

THE MYTH OF MALE PROTECTIVENESS

The male monopoly cases reveal the existence of a second major myth, the myth of male protectiveness. Women were variously described as refined, delicate and pure, quite as worthy and noble as men, but different. One judge said he shared the widely held view that women were intellectually inferior to men, and in particular were incapable of severe and incessant work, while another judge expressly left open the question of whether women were fickle in judgment and liable to influence. But the general view of those who spoke of the unfitness of women for public life was that their incapacity should be seen as an exemption flowing from respect rather than a disability based on inferiority. Men and women were different but complementary, rather than separate but equal.

The judges, particularly when setting out to justify their refusal to allow women to vote or attend mixed classes, were quick to stress how much they respected women. They did not actually say that they counted women amongst their best friends, but they were assiduous in their emphasis on how 'courteous, tender and reverent' they felt towards females. The words that constantly recur in describing their attitudes towards women are decorum, respect and propriety. In their view, this respect for women did not hold women back, but shielded them from the harsh vicissitudes of public life. Male judges and male legislators were at one in holding that male veneration surrounded and upheld the delicacy of women, and, far from debasing or oppressing women, elevated them to a superior position. One Member of Parliament declared that a man would be ennobled by possession of the vote, but a woman would be degraded by it, since she would lose the admirable attributes of her sex, namely her gentleness, affection and domesticity. In his opinion, and he spoke as a lawyer, the very disabilities of women taken as a whole showed how great a favourite the female sex was to the laws of England.[32] A Lord Chief Justice declared without any sense of irony that a statute dealing with abduction had been passed 'to protect women against themselves'.[33]

The most striking aspect of the judicial and other pronouncements on female delicacy is that what was asserted as incontrovertible fact was in reality nothing more than fallacious abstraction. Very few of the women whom the judges knew, whether they were litigants, or cleaners of the courtroom, or servants in the home, actually corresponded in any way to the judicial representation. At the time when the judges were speaking, more than a million unmarried women alone were employed in industry, while a further three quarters of a million were in domestic service. The judges had only to read the *Edinburgh Review* to discover a 'horrifying' analysis by an anonymous feminist of the nature, pay and conditions of women's work.[34] For the great majority of Victorian women, as for the great majority of Victorian men, life was characterised by drudgery and poverty rather than by refinement and decorum. Applying the judges' criteria, then, most women were simply not women. And, if John Stuart Mill can be accepted, far from men being the natural protectors of women, husbands battered their wives at least as frequently then as they do today. Mill told Parliament that he should like to have a Return of the number of women who were annually beaten, kicked or trampled to death by their male protectors, and to contrast the sentences imposed, if any, with the same punishments by the same judges for thefts of small amounts of property. 'We should then have an arithmetical estimate', he declared, 'of the value set by a male legislature and male tribunals on the murder of a woman, often by torture continued through years.'[35]

The sexual myth in fact fitted in neatly in practical terms with the myth of judicial neutrality, though logically they should have been incompatible. In all the public rights cases except the last one, the effect of the judgments was to deny the women's claims and to maintain male supremacy. The judicial myth justified this on the grounds that the judges were merely the impartial instruments of the law precluded from investigating the desirability or otherwise of women being allowed to do the things they wished to do. The sexual myth, on the other hand, justified the judgments on the grounds that the exclusion of women from public life was a mark of special respect rather than a sign of special disregard. Thus the notions were simultaneously advanced that the judges were entirely non-partisan and that the judges were protecting the women for their own advantage. These apparently contradictory myths were reconciled in intention if not in logic, since they both served the same end of giving the appearance of justice to what otherwise would have been manifest inequity.

The myth of male decorum was most strongly expressed by Judge

Willes in the Manchester Voters' case and by the judges in the Sophia Jex-Blake case. Willes was in fact one of the most admired judges of his day, and his sentiments on women were singled out for approbation by many judges during the next half century. Responding to the claim by counsel for the women that to deny them the vote purely on grounds of sex when they fulfilled all other qualifications was to hold that women were to be treated on a par with imbeciles, he expressly protested against it being thought that the legal incapacity of women arose from any underrating of the sex either in point of intellect or of worth. As appears from the summary of the Manchester Voters' case already given, he declared that such an approach would be inconsistent with one of the glories of civilisation – the respect and honour in which women were held. In his view, the exclusion of women from public office was to be seen as an exemption founded upon motives of decorum, and to be regarded as a privilege rather than a disability. Women were excused rather than prohibited, not because of any unfitness but out of a sense of decorum. He quoted extensively from early writers on the law and the constitution to the effect that at least since the days of Coke at the turn of the seventeenth century this had been the approach of English lawyers. Similarly in Scotland the judges framed their generalised references to women in terms of respect for female delicacy. The claims by Sophia Jex-Blake and her colleagues that they should in every way be treated on the same basis as men, aroused horror in virtually all the judges, whose concepts of womanhood were grossly offended by the notion of female students studying anatomy in mixed classes, and, even worse, carving presumably nude cadavers in the presence of male students. The more extreme anti-feminist view as expressed by Lord Neaves was that women should be kept out of University altogether, since the weaker mental constitution of female students would inevitably hold back the rest of the class, just as the admission of women to the medical profession would threaten its high standards. As has been seen, he contended that the instruction necessary for mastering household and family affairs, as well as the ornamental branches of education that aided social refinement and domestic happiness, would distract from University studies, while conversely the lack of feminine arts and attractions would hardly be supplied by the sort of knowledge gained at a University.

The more sympathetic judicial view was that women could be allowed to qualify as doctors, and yet not cause sexual embarrassment, by means of attending separate classes. Lord Deas felt that for a small group of women to be shut up with an overwhelming majority of men would have caused the women such unease that they might have felt a greater sense of grievance than they did at being excluded altogether. For their own sake, therefore, it was a reasonable policy to exclude them from mixed classes. Lord Ardmillan, on the other hand, stressed that much as he admired intelligent and virtuous women, he could only be shocked by the thought of their 'promiscuous attendance' with men at dissection or during clinical exposition. In this opinion such an activity would imperil their delicacy and purity – the very crown of womanhood – and react on the courtesy, reverence and tenderness of manhood.

These views were expressed with the authority of persons who were certain that they were enunciating the sentiments of all good-thinking people. Yet not only were these ideas clearly in contradiction with generally available information about working women in Edinburgh, but they were inconsistent with the facts of the particular case being tried. The myth of femininity was stronger than the evidence of the real females actually before the court. Sophia Jex-Blake was robust in temperament rather than delicate; she could be impeded by men, but certainly not be embarrassed by them. One female commentator even wrote later that her brilliance and ambition put back the cause of female doctors by fifty years. The male students at Edinburgh, on the other hand, far from being tender and reverential towards the women, had subjected them to riotous and drunken abuse, apparently at the instigation of the professor of medical jurisprudence. The men had attempted to terrorise the women rather than protect them, even though all that the women sought to do at the time was to sit in the same examination room. The masculine respectfulness asserted by the judges in support of segregating or excluding women was in reality represented by an incessant campaign of intimidation and insult, which extended beyond the women to their male supporters. When the University authorities intervened, they did so not to assist the harassed women but to help the harassing professors, imposing on the women endless indignities culminating in their total exclusion.

The judicial suggestion that a partition be erected down the middle of the anatomy room similar to the one that segregated male prisoners from female in the Pentonville Prison chapel, gives a clue to the kind of male/female relationships comprehended in the dominant ideology of the time. What was needed was a screen not between the women's eyes and the nude corpses, but between the women's eyes and the men's eyes. Men might watch women at work on corpses, but these men had to be superiors, such as professors supervising students, or doctors supervising nurses. Sexual companionship was seen to be inconsistent with work, and work on a basis of equality to be incompatible with sexual companionship. The destiny of middle-class women was to be middle-class wives, or, if they failed to marry, middle-class nurses, but it was not to be middle-class doctors. They were to complement men, not compete with them. Where the ethic of individual endeavour conflicted with the concept of the male-dominated family, it was the latter that was to prevail.

Universities claimed to be the centres of reason, doctors the upholders of science and judges the guardians of logic. The combined wisdom of all three should have produced truths of the most formidable degree. Instead it produced academic mythology reinforced by professional mythology reinforced by judicial mythology. The myth of sexual complementarity shrouded the enforced subordination and exclusion of women; the myth of judicial neutrality masked judicial support for male domination; and the myth of professional integrity veiled economic and domestic self-interest.

The medical profession was determined to prevent its ranks from being diluted by the entry of females. In this respect the doctors were no different from any other craft group that had a legal monopoly over payment for the performance of certain types of work. They fought as tenaciously to resist threats to their income and status from a new class of competitors as skilled artisans did to exclude semi-skilled operatives from certain forms of employment. The exclusion of women from medical practice was thus associated more with professionalism than with prudery. Science and university training were the instruments whereby the doctor was elevated above the empirical healer or midwife. In Britain, as in other countries, women had been prominent as healers in the community: 'the unlicensed doctors, anatomists and pharmacists of western history'.[36] Their remedies were dismissed by the male professionals as superstitious lore, to be contrasted with the scientific treatment of qualified practitioners. Women might continue to heal, but only in the ancillary role of nurses under male instruction.[37] The fact was well known that it was primarily women who washed bodies, dressed wounds and attended to the personal needs of injured and diseased patients of both sexes. Furthermore, what passed for science then did as little to cure patients as Victorian prisons did to rehabilitate convicts. In fact, at that time the treatment by leeching and purgatives offered by the male doctors was probably worse than the less drastic ministrations of the female folk healers. Opium was freely prescribed and became the religion not of the masses but of the middle classes. As the physician Oliver Wendell Holmes senior put it: 'if all the medicines used by all the doctors were thrown into the sea, then so much the better for mankind and so much the worse for the fishes'.[38] Then, as now, conveniently for medical science, patients died of the diseases as known to the doctors, and so confirmed diagnosis by death. Even in the sphere of child-bearing, male doctors asserted that the forceps they used was a mark of scientific skill to be contrasted with the amateur hands of the female midwives, and thereby secured control over the pregnancies and deliveries of wealthy women. The profession of obstetrics and gynaecology was accordingly established to consolidate the position of the learned male as opposed to the merely experienced female.

What is so striking is how illiberal the so-called liberal professions were. The male doctors successfully lobbied Parliament to prevent females from entering their ranks, while male professors and male lawyers had relatively little difficulty in persuading male judges that women should be excluded from the campus and the courtroom. Yet this was always done under the claim not of protecting themselves but of protecting the women. The professional men asserted that they wished to save female students from going against their natures, and male students from giving in to theirs. They declared that they sought to secure the Universities against a drop in standards and the public against incompetent healers, but in fact they were mainly shielding male purses from female competition.

This, at least, was one of the allegations made by feminists, who could see no reason in logic or in policy why women of proved ability who wished to become doctors should be debarred from doing so. Replying to this argument, Lord Deas said in his judgment that it would be absurd to suggest that the entry of women into medicine was objected to on grounds of economic jealousy. He declared that opponents of the women conscientiously believed that to let females into the profession would diminish the delicacy that surrounded women in well-bred society. It appears, however, that he was well aware of the spuriousness of this attitude when set against women's actual role in attending to the ill, but instead of refuting the myth of female refinement, which would have distressed his male hearers, he reaffirmed it by asserting that when it came to severe suffering and danger to health, nature itself threw a veil over delicacy and preserved it uninjured.

Underlying all the judgments, it is possible to discern the central theme of domesticity. In the minds of the judges, the graciousness of an accomplished hostess would be totally undermined by the combative intellectuality thought appropriate to a professional person. Middle-class men did not share the objection of many of the members of the nobility to work, in fact they prided themselves on their industriousness, nor did they object to women working, since they employed women to clean and cook in their homes, as well as to milk and reap on their farms and spin in their factories. What they did object to with a vehemence indicative of a special interest, was to their own wives working. Women of the middle class were expected to run households in which the menfolk could eat, be clothed, entertain and sleep in comfort. Secondly, they were to produce sons for business, the professions, the military and the church, and daughters for good marriages. Thirdly, they were to display in their households a graciousness, refinement and sentiment, lacking in the hard world of business, which would mark off the reputation of their families and maintain the esteem of their class. It was this third requirement that distinguished the middle-class woman from her working-class cousin. Working-class women were also required to look after the home and reproduce sons and daughters, but they were expected not to attempt graces above their station. A degree of spending that would indicate taste and refinement in a middle-class woman, would be castigated as reckless and profligate if gone in for by a working-class woman. In terms of male ideology, the model working-class wife was pious and thrifty, qualities which were not inconsistent with work outside the home, while the prototype middle-class wife, on the other hand, was ornamental and decorous, attributes which were incompatible with outside employment.

Superficially it might have seemed that the actions of the legislators in keeping working-class women out of the coalmines were of a pattern with those designed to exclude middle-class women from the professions. In both cases the argument was used that women should be spared unseemly kinds of employment. But even if the language of justification used in both situations was similar, the interests at stake were entirely different. The fact that millions of women, both married and single, worked in paid employment outside the home, showed that there was no overwhelming biological or cultural aversion to women working for cash. There was nothing intrinsic to the female condition, no special frailty, that the male legislators and judges were bent on respecting.

The phrase used at the time was that employment would 'un-sex' women, to the manifest disadvantage of both sexes. This phrase was not used in a literal sense, otherwise there would have been difficulty in explaining the notoriously high number of children of their masters born to women in domestic service. What was envisaged was femininity rather than sexuality, that is, female manners rather than female eroticism. Feminist writers could not contain their indignation at what they considered male hypocrisy in deliberately ignoring the extent to which millions of women were in reality employed away from their homes, often in laborious and poorly paid jobs. 'In Staffordshire', wrote one such writer, '[women] make nails; and unless my readers have seen them, I cannot represent to the imagination the extraordinary figures they represent – black with soot, muscular, brawny – undelightful to the last degree.'[39] Elsewhere, she wrote, there had been a factory strike, with letters, speeches and placards, and a liberal expenditure of forcible Saxon language. Who had been these people gathered together in angry knots on the corners of streets? – Women! It was industry and not small committees in London, she declared, which should answer the charge of un-sexing women.

The great battles to exclude women from underground mining and certain sectors of heavy industry had nothing in common with the efforts to keep middle-class women out of the professions. The attacks on female employment in industry were waged largely as Parliamentary counter-offensives against the emergent industrialists by the landed interests, with the aristocracy and landed gentry using the language of humanitarianism to assert the values of rural paternalism against the ethic of unrestricted industrial enterprise.

The extraordinary emphasis on proper dress, decorum and etiquette for Victorian ladies was tied to attempts by the industrialists to surpass the gentry not only in economic and political power, but in manners and self-esteem as well. Leisure for women became a mark of status just when the dignity of labour was being contrasted with the indolence of the aristocracy and the laziness of the poor.[40] It has been said that by the mid-nineteenth century the wife's idleness was the most sensitive indicator of social standing, because through her the income of the husband was translated into symbols of respectability. In these terms the inanity of female existence in prosperous Victorian homes could become comprehensible if seen as the wife's contribution to the social esteem of the whole family.[41] The courts gave express recognition to this principle when they defined 'pin money' as an allowance made by a husband to his wife for the purchase of dresses and ornaments 'in order that his dignity in society may be maintained'.[42]

In England the life-style of the industrial middle-class household was governed by conflict and competition not so much with the lower classes as with the upper, in particular with the landed aristocracy and gentry. The courage and endurance which the gentleman might have manifested by chasing after foxes, the entrepreneur instead exhibited in risking his capital and working to see it augmented. An ornamental wife was proof of credit-worthiness both on earth and in heaven, since only the financially secure could afford the expense of such a wife, and only those favoured by Providence could be financially secure. Reputability depended not merely on the display of fortune, but on the ability to demonstrate sets of manners and codes of conduct superior to those of the country lords and squires. By cultivating through his wife new refinements even more useless than those of the country gentleman, the city tradesman was able to claim social superiority. It was not he who was seen as a ruthless moneygrabber, but the country gentleman who was converted into a silly bumpkin. As far as the man from the new industrial and commercial class was concerned, his work routine kept him at home alongside his wife in the evenings and at week-ends. In contrast to the males of the landed gentry who devoted considerable spare time to vigorous physical sports such as riding, shooting, drinking, whoring and soldiering, he spent his regular hours at home maintaining the decorum of the household. Whereas the rural gentleman cultivated a conception of Manhood that emphasised spontaneity, courage and bearing, the wealthy towns-man elevated self-control and spirituality into the prime virtues of his sex. At the same time, the increasingly manifold and increasingly useless accomplishments of the townsman's wife were symbols of his increasingly high social status.

Yet the emphasis on the elaborate clothing, cultivated speech and social refinement of the urban ladies should not be taken as proof that the role of the middle-class wife was purely ornamental or symbolical. In addition to being required to display social delicacy, she had to manage what was in effect a large economic and political enterprise, namely the household. She had to hire and fire servants, bargain with tradesmen, control children and attend to the mul-titudinous needs of her husband. Whether regarded (as by Mill, Engels and Veblen) as a head servant, or else as a manager, her tasks were detailed and multifarious, requiring what today would be called great skills in home economics, personnel management and interpersonal relations. As Mill told Members of Parliament, women whose chief daily business was the laying out of money so as to produce the greatest results with the smallest means, could give lessons to his hearers who contrived to produce such singularly poor results with such vast means.[43]

The vaunted complementarity of the sexes, invariably expressed in semi-mystical terms, had practical roots in a division of labour in respect of which the husband supervised minions at work and the wife supervised minions at home. Different attributes were required for the performance of their respective tasks, and these attributes were given exaggerated reflection in the culture of the times. It is suggested, then, that the main reason why Victorian men resisted the entry of middle-class women into public life and the professions was their interest in ensuring that their wives remained housekeepers. Mill certainly hinted as much, adding that it was a reason that men were ashamed to advance because of its manifest injustice.

If correct, this hypothesis helps to explain two otherwise puzzling phenomena. The first is that the middle-class sections of the suffragette movement aroused far greater antagonism from middle-class men than did the working-class section. One might have anticipated that middle-class men would have assented more readily to the vote being granted to their mothers, wives, sisters and daughters, who were likely to share their values and allegiances, than to working-class females who were socially and politically distant from them. Yet the enfranchisement of propertyless working women appears to have been looked on with greater equanimity than the enfranchisement of propertied ladies. This is evidenced by the fact that when Prime Minister Asquith chose, in what is generally regarded as the turning point in the campaign for votes for women, to receive a deputation of suffragettes, he selected working-class women from the East London Federation headed by Sylvia Pankhurst rather than women from the larger middle-class suffrage groups. The second apparent paradox clarified by this hypothesis is that middle-class women increasingly entered the professions at a time when the number of domestic servants was declining. It seems that possession of servants, far from freeing middle-class women from domesticity, tied them to their homes. Supervising servants became a career in itself which acted to exclude all other careers. Middle-class men accordingly shared an interest in keeping their wives at home and away from professional work and in preparing their daughters for similar domestic vocations.

Although the issue of women in the professions presented itself to the men as a projected assault on all that was decent and proper in society, underlying their sense of spiritual shock was a fear that the satisfactory ordering of their own material lives would be shattered. These men had a direct, material stake in keeping their wives at home running their households, attending to their comforts and providing the ambience necessary for the furtherance of their careers. This fitted in with the ethic which said that sentiment should be kept out of business, where it was inconvenient for trade, and kept in the home, where it was useful for domesticity; sentiment was feminised, and women were sentimentalised over. Charitable activity confined to suitable hours was one form of work that was not incompatible with the kind of service that middle-class men sought from their wives, and it also became possible for the many women who were not going to marry, to enter newly established public service occupations such as teaching and nursing, provided they did so subject to the tutelage of men.

It may be interpolated here that during most of the nineteenth century there was literally a great shortage of husbands in England – in the mid-Victorian period differential mortality and large-scale emigration of males contributed towards the position whereby one-third of marriageable women remained spinsters. One influential writer has even contended that it was a superfluity of women rather than a revival of the ideas of the French Revolution that provided the thrust for the women's movement of that period.[44] Some emphasis on demographic and occupational factors is perhaps needed as a corrective to histories that attribute the rise of the emancipation movement purely to the leadership of individual personalities, but it would seem to do a disservice both to the feminists and to the recording of history to play down the significance of conscious activity on the part of politically aware women. A number of facts point away from the demographic explanation: the population imbalance preceded the mass campaigns by a full half century; the women's movement was not confined to Britain and was strong in countries like New Zealand where the shortage was of wives and not of husbands; the campaigns for reform of family law were led by married women since it was they who suffered most under patriarchy; the fiercest fights were over political questions such as the vote and not over economic questions such as entry into the professions; and married women were active alongside unmarried at all levels of the emancipation struggle. In fact, undue emphasis on demographic factors comes close to being a sophisticated variant of the notion that the genesis of the women's movement lay not in a political consciousness that accurately reflected women's social oppression, but in an hysteria that deviously gave vent to their emotional frustration. It entirely overlooks the fact that women participated alongside their menfolk in the general democratic campaigns that preceded the Reform legislation and went on to demand that rights being extended to men be accorded to them as well. The vigour of the campaigns against male monopoly needs to be understood in terms of male obduracy rather than of female destructiveness, and research should be directed at the husband's actual self-interest rather than the spinster's alleged rage. It is not, of course, suggested by this that male stubbornness flowed from some constitutional or biological characteristic, but rather that it arose out of the material and social advantages that flowed from possession of a male biology.

The relative shortage of marriageable men intensified anxiety that daughters would be left without spouses. An unmarried daughter seeking a husband had to do more than manifest the allure of sex, money or rank; she needed to hold out the skills and accomplishments of general manager of the household. Alliances between families to consolidate fortunes and cement reputations were dependent on good marriages being arranged, since husbands and wives were to be complementary to each other in perpetuating the family fame and fortune. The wife's contribution was expected to be partly ornamental – the more useless her accomplishments the more they added to her status – and partly practical – and the more useful her skills the more they added to her husband's comfort. Sexual fidelity on the part of the wife was important not only to prevent disputes over inheritance, but also to maintain constancy towards the household. The way in which a wife was expected to love, honour and obey her husband was to look after his house properly. Even when she manifestly hated and despised him, she was expected to stay at his side.

Far from speaking of women as subordinate to men, however, the judges asserted that females were generally in a superior position, the mechanism of their elevation, according to Lord Ardmillan, having been Christianity. In fact, changes in the institutions of Christianity in Britain contributed substantially to a decline in the status of women in public life. The digests of arguments addressed by counsel on behalf of the women in the nineteenth-century male monopoly cases indicated that prior to the English Reformation women's religious orders had played a prominent role in church and hence public life, and that abbesses and prioresses had had a respected place in councils of government. In the period before the end of the sixteenth century, women had voted in Parliamentary elections, acted as attorneys, held leading positions in trading guilds, and even occupied high military office. It would seem that although in feudal times the law of succession had favoured elder sons, it had not excluded women from inheriting titles to land and succeeding to family position in the absence of a male heir. Thus the public position of women had been stronger in the sixteenth century than it was at the time when the judges were speaking in the nineteenth.

Three factors seem to have contributed to the decline over the centuries, the first being the destruction of the nunneries, accomplished during the period of extension of Royal power when Church treasure was used to finance the national army and navy. As one sardonic writer put it, the exclusion of abbesses from Parliament completed a process of political inequality begun with the expulsion of Eve from paradise.[45] It is notable that even today the position of women in the Church in Britain continues to be weaker than it was five hundred years ago; only the armed forces can approach the ministry for the rigidity with which they exclude women.

A second reason for the decline in women's public position was the growth of Parliament and the replacement of hereditary office by appointed office. In this sense, the development of Parliament was profoundly undemocratic in that at the very time when it denounced the principle of hereditary supremacy it entrenched the principle of sexual supremacy. The only hereditary public office that survived was that of the monarchy. It is more than a little paradoxical that during the period under review it was possible for a woman to hold the highest office in the land but not the lowest. It was Queen Victoria who summoned the legislators and in whose name the judges acted, yet both Parliament and the judiciary refused to acknowledge a general right of women to hold public office. Presumably from the sixteenth century onwards it was regarded as preferable to have a Protestant woman from a British family on the throne than a Catholic man from a French or Spanish one.

The third factor which diminished women's position in public life was the growth of the professions and the establishment of the Universities. The separation of knowledge from production and of work from the home drastically weakened the economic and political situation of women. In the mediaeval artisan and trading guilds, women were normally subordinate to their fathers and husbands, but not necessarily to their sons. Widows frequently took over control of the family tools and the running of the family enterprise, and exercised correlative influence in the guilds. The Universities were residential in character, however, and accordingly from the outset favoured men, who could more easily live away from home than women. Britain in fact appears to be unique amongst industrialised societies in the extent to which single-sex education has persisted, and the males-only principle is most strongly maintained in the oldest schools and colleges, which either exclude females altogether or else admit only a tiny quota. Oxford and Cambridge were in fact the last rather than the first Universities to admit women to degrees, Cambridge resisting until 1948. Universities claim to be the inheritors of truth and the upholders of merit, yet as far as women were concerned they were manifestly citadels of intolerance. Similarly, the professions controlled entry into their ranks by requiring extensive training either at University or in a form of apprenticeship away from home. A widow could not inherit a husband's legal or medical practice, because law and medicine were early converted into professions requiring knowledge of Latin and philosophy, neither of which were particularly helpful in healing or in resolving disputes, but both of which were of great assistance in displaying the special sort of learning that entitled its possessor to a special fee.

Whether in the Church, Parliament or the law, then, male protectiveness as proclaimed by the judges was mythical rather than real — what was in truth being protected was the right of upper-middle-class men to have their wives working for them and for them alone.

2 *United States:* Are Women Citizens?

I should like to thank Professor Elizabeth Defeis of Seton Hall Law School and Professor Herma Hill Kay, University of California Law School, Berkeley, for reading the American portions of this work. J.H.W.

INTRODUCTION

'Register now', Susan B. Anthony read in the Rochester, New York, morning newspaper on November 1, 1872. 'If you were not permitted to vote, you would fight for the right, undergo all privation for it, face death for it.'[1] With these words firmly in mind, Anthony walked down to the local registration office and after considerable argument convinced three inexperienced male inspectors that she should be allowed to register as a Republican. Her bold and well publicised action prompted approximately fifty other women to register to vote in Rochester and on November 5 fourteen of them, including Anthony, actually did cast ballots. Twenty-three days later on Thanksgiving all fourteen were arrested under a provision of the federal Civil Rights Act of 1870 which was designed to prevent white voters from cancelling out black votes by voting more than once. Obviously the 1870 law was never intended to apply to women trying to vote only once. Its enforcement against these women was a clear indication of the political nature of their arrests. Still another indication was the ever watchful presence at Anthony's subsequent trial in June, 1878, of President Ulysses S. Grant's political aide and Senator from New York, Roscoe Conkling. An avowed opponent of women's suffrage, Conkling moved freely in and out of the judge's chambers throughout the trial.

The Anthony case never reached the United States Supreme Court because of two legal technicalities – both beyond her control. First, since she had been briefly imprisoned after voting she would have been able to take her case directly to the Supreme Court by writ of *habeas corpus* if her counsel had not independently decided over her protests to pay her bail of one thousand dollars. Likewise, presiding Judge Ward Hunt later refused to enforce his judgment against her which carried with it the fine of one hundred dollars plus court costs. Prevented in this manner from going to jail a second time, she could not seek direct Supreme Court review of the adverse decision.

The legal system was thus manipulated in a way which allowed the judges to avoid making a proper determination on the issue: to what extent were women to be regarded as full citizens in the eyes of the Constitution? This was an important period in American politico-legal history. The bitter Civil War to determine the character of the American state had only recently ended in victory for the North. The

Reconstruction amendments had explicitly ended slavery and granted rights of citizenship to blacks. Anthony's challenge, if accepted, would have compelled the Supreme Court to rule on a matter which to this day it has not been willing to adjudicate, namely, the constitutionality of sex discrimination per se. Instead, they evaded the issue, and when in a series of other cases, the question of rights for women cropped up, they invariably gave decisions which favored male supremacy. To understand the inter-action of law, politics and the women's movement at that time, a brief exposition of colonial and early post-Revolutionary legal history is required.

THE LEGAL STATUS OF WOMEN IN COLONIAL AMERICA

A review of the early colonial period suggests that the legal position of women was stronger then than it was to be in Anthony's day; the two centuries which separated their period from hers might have been centuries of constitutional progress for men, but they were centuries of decline for women. A period of some progress until the middle of the eighteenth century was arrested rather than enhanced by the Revolution. Whatever Independence and the new Con-stitution might have done to strengthen the rights of women as against the British Crown, they did nothing to strengthen their rights vis-à-vis their own menfolk. On the contrary, the post-Revolutionary period was one of declining legal status for women, brought about either by the increase of citizenship rights for men without an equivalent grant to women, or by the actual cutting down on or eliminating of rights which colonial women had exercised. Legislatures, judges and the legal profession all made their con-tribution to this decline, as the following pages will show.

The early colonial period in the New World was characterised by an absence of strict adherence to common law because of the primacy of local customs or ecclesiastical rulings. This generally meant greater leniency than had previously existed in the colonising nations for married women, widows, and children in terms of inheritances, economic rights, and guardianship provisions. It also appears to have resulted in more liberal decisions involving per-manent marital separations than existed at the time in England or Europe, although absolute divorce remained difficult to obtain. The relative scarcity of women, in addition to the absence of a pro-fessional class of lawyers in the seventeenth and first half of the eighteenth centuries, permitted a humanising of New World laws for all classes of free women in general and for married women in particular.[2]

From the beginning of the colonial period as English common law was modified to fit New World conditions, these modifications were most apparent in commercial areas where married women were declared *'feme-sole traders'* – a title that gave them the right to sue, conduct businesses, be sued, enter into contracts, sell real property, and have the power of attorney in the absence of their husbands. Whether single or married, seventeenth- or eighteenth-century women could not act as attorneys-at-law, but they often were attorneys-in-fact. This power-of-attorney was not always conferred by a colonial court or legislature; necessity or prominence sometimes allowed wives to assume such legal power when their husbands were incapacitated or unavailable. Nonetheless, no individual married woman (*feme couverte*) ever obtained equal legal status with the single or widowed woman (*feme sole*).

Prior to 1776 some middle and upper middle class married women did take advantage of equity jurisprudence[3] to prevent property and possessions they had brought with them to marriage from falling under the exclusive control of their husbands. In fact, there is evidence that there had been a gradual but steady merging of the two systems of equity and common law jurisprudence in American legal practice, which generally resulted in relatively liberal treatment of wealthier, free white women. Nonetheless, legal penalties remained more severe for black, native American, and white female indentured servants than for this small privileged class, and all female laborers, regardless of class or race, received approximately twenty to thirty percent less for their labor than men by 1776.

Yet throughout the colonial period there is an impressive array of women workers and entrepreneurs because of the general labor shortage and the resulting circumvention of common law restrictions on female activities. In Philadelphia, for example, women engaged in roughly thirty different trades ranging from essential to luxury services. They included female silversmiths, tin-workers, barbers, bakers, fish picklers, brewers, tanners, ropemakers, lumberjacks, gunsmiths, butchers, milliners, harnessmakers, potash manu-facturers, upholsterers, printers, morticians, chandlers, coach-makers, embroiderers, dry cleaners and dyers, woodworkers, stay-makers, tailors, flour processors, seamstresses, netmakers, braziers, and founders. It is this diversity of female labor in Philadelphia and other colonial towns that has led to the conclusion that work for women was much less sex-stereotyped in the seventeenth and eighteenth centuries than it was to become in the nineteenth. There is no doubt that women were lawfully engaged in these activities. But it must be remembered that they often found themselves in these essential and nonfamilial roles, not because the colonial period was less patriarchal, but because they were substituting for dead or absent husbands or other male relatives. It was simply not considered 'inappropriate' according to prevailing socio-economic norms for women to engage in this wide variety of occupations, carry on the family business if widowed, or become a skilled artisan while still married or if single.

This relatively lenient legal treatment of women was beginning to change, however, by the end of the eighteenth century, largely as secular law practices came to prevail over local and theological ones and as increased mercantile specialisation demanded greater economic stability and hence a closer application of the more conservative aspects of English common law. While bar associations and professional training for lawyers were evident before the Revolution, they increased in influence, contributing to the development of even greater legal conservatism, after 1776 with respect to women, save for indentured servants, whose numbers decreased. This decline in female legal status also resulted in part from an increasing reliance upon Blackstone's *Commentaries* as a guide both in training professional lawyers and in codifying American law. Not only were free white women more stringently prevented from acting as attorneys-in-fact because of the greater professionalisation of law following the Revolution, but the new law codes also explicitly barred practices which, though not formally authorised previously, had not been expressly forbidden.

The loss in legal functions for the vast majority of women who were married or widowed was not entirely precipitated by the Revolution. Some legal losses for both sexes were inevitable given the legal conservatism that prevailed before, during, and after the break with England, especially for women whose enhanced legal status had never been made secure by adequate political rights. The leniency of the laws toward early colonial women had reflected the necessity for them to be as productive (economically and biologically) as possible. Naturally, as their numbers increased, this need declined, and with it women's legal and socio-economic standing.

Even before the Revolution, a regressive change in the legal status of women was in progress. It can be traced primarily through property and probate records. One of the major legal functions in which women had participated from the beginning of the colonial period was the writing of wills and acting as the beneficiaries of wills, dowries, or dowers. Under common law, widows could not be heirs, that is, they could not be accorded full property rights of their deceased husbands as head of the household. But they could be named sole executrixes of their husbands' property and were often accorded dower rights that were 'interpreted by the courts in a manner which was in many instances at variance with common law rules'. In this fashion they exercised considerable control over the transmission of property from one colonial generation to another. Consequently, despite the fact that widows were 'considered a community responsibility' and were technically unable to sell any real property that they had not already possessed at the time of marriage (and protected through an equity trust), in practice both their proprietary and contractual rights were expanded in the course of the seventeenth and first half of the eighteenth centuries in order to provide them with greater economic independence.[4] The Revolution does not appear to have fostered these legally liberating colonial trends.

In Virginia, for example, throughout the seventeenth century men clearly favored their wives as executrixes and often provided them with more than one-third of their estates as dower law required. Because of the initially higher male mortality rates, southern wills generally favored women more than those written in New England. Increasingly, however, in both geographical areas eighteenth-century wills began to relegate widows to share part of a house with the surviving son who, as executor, also received the bulk of the inheritance. This trend developed even though there is some indication that widows wanted to administer their husbands' estates and would have preferred (as today) to live with their daughters and sons-in-law. It may have reflected a distinct, yet tacit, disagreement between husbands and wives over patrilineal or matrilineal inheritance. If so, this was a basic disagreement over power (in terms of property inheritance) that women lost in the course of the eighteenth century.

This loss became most noticeable statistically in the decades immediately preceding and following the American Revolution, according to a recent study of Hingham, Massachusetts by Daniel Scott Smith. Prior to 1720 no less than twenty-seven percent of colonial wives with adult sons were named sole executrixes of their husbands' property. This figure dropped to six percent between 1761 and 1800 with eighty-five percent of the male wills naming sons as executors. Also, before 1700 in Hingham 98.5 percent of all families with three or more daughters named one after the mother. By 1780 this had dropped to 53.2 percent, and the practice was to decrease even more by the end of the nineteenth century, although less rapidly for boys than girls because of the potential inheritance value of having the same name as one's father or other close male relative. If these percentages turn out to be representative, they would indicate a significant loss in the legal and economic status of eighteenth-century middle and upper class women, who had more commonly exercised such responsibility and power in the seventeenth century.

Similarly discouraging statistics can be found in South Carolina where between 1726 and 1787 there were approximately 1,930 recorded cases of women renouncing their dower rights. At common law in England a widow was entitled to a life interest in one-third of the land held by her husband at any time during the marriage. In colonial America, however, dower rights were generally abrogated or limited to one-third of the property held by the husband at the time of his death. Unless there was considerable wealth in the family the dower rights of most widows were not adequate for their support. Yet in South Carolina during the years covering pre-Revolutionary activity, the War for Independence and the drafting and ratifying of the new Constitution, that is, from 1761 to 1787, fifty-two per cent of all the recorded renunciations of dower took place.

All of these conveyances were made, according to the official records, without undue duress or physical intimidation. Whether this is true or not, these transactions represent a drastic decline in the property controlled by wealthier women in South Carolina by the end of the Revolutionary period. Again, if these figures prove representative for other colonies and states they indicate a general decline in female economic power through perfectly legal means. There is strong indication that many of the large South Carolinian estates controlled by men were built on the basis of these renunciations, or in the case of the Loyalists, preserved from confiscation by transference of ownership to those not suspected of disloyalty to the Revolutionary cause. Moreover, landmark court decisions in the first quarter of the eighteenth century in all of the states significantly undermined the right of dower itself in order to facilitate land speculation and improvement in what was then a rapidly developing American economy.[5]

A final example of loss of legal status among women can be

found in the differences between female and male colonial wills. They indicate not only lower levels of literacy among women, but also, and most importantly, because they had so little that they could legally leave, the wills of married women (as opposed to those of widows) were of necessity 'expressive' or 'affective' and in the form of personal property, rather than 'instrumental' in the form of real property. In addition, what they did leave was more often to their daughters or other female relatives (even though they could only do this through their sons-in-law or other male members of the family) rather than to their sons. Naturally part of this female intergenerational transmission along other than direct male blood lines was dictated by the nature of the willed items themselves and the individual woman's knowledge and/or actual control over her possessions. But it should also be noted that widows of property also tended *not* to make their sons their heirs to the degree that men of property did – another indication that women did not endorse the slowly emerging smaller family unit based on preference for male children-as-heirs, to the degree that their husbands did.

What limited political rights women had possessed before 1776 were also specifically denied them or implicitly discouraged under the new state constitutions. Throughout the colonial period, even though unmarried women with enough property technically had been able to qualify to vote on local issues, few had exercised this right except for a handful of strongly independent Dutch, English, or Quaker women in Massachusetts, New York, New Jersey, Rhode Island, and Pennsylvania. Without formal political rights colonial women had obviously been quite limited in exercising political influence and had fulfilled any civic aspirations vicariously through their husbands or other male members of their families. In any event, none of the new state constitutions granted women the right to vote with the exception of New Jersey. In that state, unmarried women worth fifty pounds could and did vote until that right was rescinded in 1807 as the result of an amendment introduced, interestingly enough, by a *liberal* Republican member of the state legislature. New York was the first state in 1777 to disfranchise women voters by inserting the word 'male' into its constitution, and the other original eleven states soon followed suit by specifically forbidding women or actively discouraging them from voting.[6]

Even with these conscious acts of disfranchisement, it cannot be said that the political status or power of women deteriorated drastically as a direct result of the Revolution, because it must be remembered that few had voted or stood for office in the colonial period or even requested such political rights. The significant decline in the political position of women came a few decades later when the franchise was extended to virtually every white male regardless of property holdings. The precedents set in the new revolutionary constitutions only prepared the way for the Jacksonian era of the 1820s and 1830s, which 'witnessed the completion of the retrograde and anti-democratic tendency that had commenced a half century earlier', as far as female suffrage was concerned. This period ended with what Harriet Martineau described as the 'political nonexistence of women'.

WOMEN IN THE FIRST HALF OF THE NINETEENTH CENTURY

In general, the greatest societal setback for women, which was a direct result of the Revolution, came with new private and public laws of the United States in the first three decades of the nineteenth century. Morton J. Horwitz has noted that from 1780 to 1820 a new rationale for common law had to be worked out in the United States because the Revolution had undermined its legitimacy. American judges began to abandon the eighteenth-century, natural-law concept of law and to view it as an instrument to achieve policy goals. Horwitz argues that 'an instrumental perspective on law did not simply emerge as a response to new economic forces in the nineteenth century. Rather, judges began to use law in order to encourage social change...'. At the same time lawyers began to play a more important role than juries in private law-making through their influence over state legislatures and judicial decisions that 'defeudalised social relations among men but left inter-gender social relations feudal'.[7] This legal reform of first private and then public law was considerably less liberalising for female than for male citizens, especially in the area of contractual relationships, although American women continued to have a better legal status than their counterparts in England and Europe. During the course of post-Revolutionary legal reforms, natural law was abandoned as a theoretical base for reforming American law. This increased the likelihood that women's legal rights would not be given much attention by post-Revolutionary lawyers or judges because only natural-law philosophical theories of the Enlightenment, which had played such an important role in justifying rebellion against the Crown, had also allowed such writers as Condorcet and Mary Wollstonecraft to argue for equality of the sexes.

At first glance the regression in the legal status of women so evident by the end of the first half of the nineteenth century appears to have been caused primarily by the codification of American law beginning in the 1820s and 1830s. This codification process reflected a movement in the direction of public law based on state statutes and a more strict application of common law to women in private litigations now that they were not numerically scarce and had become a marginal part of the labor force. Codification also consolidated the gradual erosion of their legal status that had become evident by the middle of the eighteenth century. The process was both subtle and complex. There was a stage between the end of the Revolution and the beginning of codification in which private contract law in particular began to reflect the breakdown of customary law and conduct. At this same time there was a concerted effort to rid the United States of feudal vestiges of English law such as equity trusts to protect the property of married women. Most important, there was also increased commercialisation and the beginning of industrialisation in the United States during the period. As private law began to reflect a conscious tendency on the part of early United States federal judges and lawyers to use the law as a means of reform, it conveniently facilitated the needs of early American entrepreneurs.

Regardless of the exact motivation of legal practitioners, the results were the same – customary, extralegal circumventions or lax applications of common law for both men and women became a less likely means of settling disputes, especially those involving property, as the courts literally began to make new private laws. Since women had lost so many property rights by the time of the Revolution they were even less involved in this process after the Revolution. Under Jacksonian democracy a popular antipathy developed toward both the legal profession and its manipulation of common law in the courts. This sentiment gave rise to the codification movement. Instead of democratising American contract law or the legal system in general, all codification did was freeze or institutionalise the process where it was around 1850.[8] While the power of judges and lawyers to influence private law through court decisions may have been reduced by the codification process, the result was that laws in the form of state statutes misleadingly appeared impartial and above petty political and economic interests. In fact, this *public law* simply institutionalised the existence of a legal and economic elite that had already been created by the early post-Revolutionary changes in *private law*. Rather than achieving a redistribution of wealth or even more proprietary rights for women, Jacksonian codification concretised existing inequalities between rich and poor men and between men and women in general.

Some of the original post-Revolutionary moves to reform property law in New York, for example, actually made the laws governing the property of married women more complex and uncertain. Especially in the area of uses and trusts, equity procedures were restricted or eliminated without replacing them with other proprietary or contractual rights. When New York legal codifiers defeudalised and commercialised property in 1828 and again in 1836, with specific state laws governing transactions between white males, they inadvertently made inter-gender property relations more ambiguous than they had been under equity. The incompleteness of property reform, the virtual elimination of dower rights through court decisions, and the growing demand and concern of a number of men and women in a burgeoning industrial society for stable and clear-cut inheritance procedures led to the Married Women's Property Acts in various states both before and after (but not during) the American Civil War.

Some legal historians have maintained that most of these acts were no more than codification of equity jurisprudence, which had never provided a parity of legal status between men and women in any case. Judge Joseph Story accurately summarised this function of equity courts between the American Revolution and the Civil War when he wrote in his *Commentaries on Equity Jurisprudence:*

> And here, on the subject of married women as well as in the exercise of the jurisdiction in regard to infants and lunatics, we cannot fail to observe the parental solicitude with which Courts of Equity administer to the wants and guard the interests, and succor the weakness of those who are left without any other protectors, in a manner which common law was too rigid to consider or too indifferent to provide for.[9]

Other legal historians have maintained that equity was too complicated to codify and that at best some of the first Married Women's Property Acts, like that of 1848 in New York, actually protected common law property rights of fathers who were worried that their sons-in-law might squander their daughters' dowries or inheritances. They were usually not designed to shelter any wages or gifts women might acquire independently during marriage or to give women functional control over the property obtained by dower or inheritance.

Of the nine Married Women's Property Acts passed by states

before the Civil War (beginning with Mississippi in 1839) none significantly expanded the legal rights of wealthier women from what they had been under equity trusts. Since property reform under the direction of post-Revolutionary lawyers often severely limited the application of trust and since this was the major legal vehicle whereby women had held property separate from their husbands under equity jurisprudence, something had to fill the void left by the first generation of reformers. A few isolated voices like that of New York Judge Thomas Herttell made strong arguments for equalising the property rights of men and women. Most state legislators, however, voted for Married Women's Property Acts on the basis of conservative economic reasoning designed to protect, not to liberate women. Unlike the equity procedures which they replaced, these acts did not explicitly classify women with lunatics and infants; but neither did they do anything to alter or reform prevailing gender-based custom and stereotypic attitudes. While establishing simpler statutory procedures for protecting married women's separate property, they changed 'as little as possible the underlying institution of marriage'. They also strictly adhered to traditional ideas of patriarchy by denying women the right to sell, sue or contract without their husbands' or other male relatives' approval. As one ardent supporter later remarked in 1888 after such acts had become law in all the states *and* in England: 'There is recognition in these acts of the inherent incapacity of women, as a rule, to deal judiciously with their own property or to act with even ordinary wisdom in the making of contracts.' This type of legislation left all non-economic privileges of husbands completely intact and restrictive judicial interpretation of these laws minimised increases in women's rights.[10]

At no time in the course of the nineteenth century were Married Women's Property Acts liberally interpreted by the lower courts. The importance of these very legally limited and narrowly interpreted acts lies in the fact that reform of American law through state legislation was a major instrument whereby the legal status of women could be improved following independence from England. By 1900 this type of legislative reform constituted the most significant means of advance for women with respect to marital property rights. We must remember that by the middle of the nineteenth century a debate over which of various traditional forms for achieving legal change should predominate had been in progress for two hundred years. Besides state legislation, the other two basic instruments of such change since the colonial period were equity jurisprudence and legal fictions. The debate over these three means to legal reform intensified after 1800 as post-Revolutionary members of the legal profession began to influence private law and to codify the public laws of the new nation. By the end of the nineteenth century it was clear that the dominant agents of law reform in the United States would be statutes passed by state legislatures, new amendments to the federal Constitution, and subsequent judicial interpretation of these state laws and of the Constitution.

Although twenty-five of the thirty-three states admitted to the Union before 1860 at some time allowed for the exercise of equity jurisprudence or equity procedures, and eighteen of these twenty-five states at some time had constitutions which called for the establishment of special Chancery Courts, equity was on its way out as a separate form of jurisprudence in the United States. Also, the major legal fiction applied to women had been the debilitating one of the unity of the wife within the husband. This particular legal fiction was at the heart of Blackstone's famous common law dictum about the civil death of married women.[11] Two other related legal fictions gained prominence in the course of the nineteenth century. First, there was the assumption of the inherently inferior or unfit position of women due to their biological make-up and function as childbearers. Second, there was the assumption of the inherently superior or pedestal position assigned to women because of their moral purity, feminine delicacy, and sense of civil propriety. These were opposite sides of the same coin and both were ascribed to women by men on the basis of what is now called gender discrimination. Of these three traditional means of achieving legal reform only the first – legislation at the state level – was truly a viable alternative. The victory of reform through legislation was in large measure the result of the codification of public law in the first half of the nineteenth century. In adapting private law to the economic needs of those white males who had benefited most from the War for Independence, reformers on the state level began to commercialise and simplify the law of real property. This was certainly a step forward for a young nation that was rapidly becoming industrialised. Married Women's Property Acts represented a necessary afterthought in the ensuing codification process based on protection, not equality for females.

Despite the failure of the Property Acts to enhance women's constitutional status, wherever the first women's rights movement was particularly active, property reforms affecting women, though quite limited, were more comprehensive than where there were no organised female activists. New York, Ohio, New Jersey, Massachusetts, Pennsylvania, Indiana, Wisconsin and Kansas eliminated most common law and equity restrictions on the right of women to hold property and in some cases control their wages before the Civil War, while Connecticut, Delaware, New Hampshire, Vermont and West Virginia made no changes in the law of marital property until after 1865. The same is true of most southern states except for Mississippi. This contrast suggests a connection, however tenuous, between the emergence of new marital property laws and the early women's movement.

The basic problem faced by this first generation of women's rights advocates remained the same for the rest of the nineteenth century and some would say down to the present day. It is the problem of gender discrimination, or what a 1973 Supreme Court decision called 'romantic paternalism' and this work refers to as the myth of male protectiveness. It is based on a patriarchal view of women's prescribed or expected position in society rather than on any shared set of logical, judicial determinations. Therefore, despite the existence of the Married Women's Property Acts, simple legal rights taken for granted today, such as the ability to take out a life insurance policy, were denied to American women. After much litigation the first one was issued in 1850 to Caroline Ingraham, whose occupation was listed as 'woman'.

AMERICAN WOMEN AND THE CIVIL WAR

By the middle of the nineteenth century most of the major female abolitionists in the United States such as Lucretia Mott, Sarah and Angelina Grimke, Lucy Stone, Sojourner Truth, Antoinette Brown, Susan B. Anthony, and Elizabeth Cady Stanton, were simultaneously working for the emancipation of blacks and of themselves as women. By 1850 women constituted a majority in northern abolition societies and were the leading organisers of antislavery petition drives. Unfortunately, but not too surprisingly, most male abolitionists both before and after the Civil War opposed women taking up their own cause along with that of blacks. This sexism was to have disastrous effects on the women's movement after the Civil War when its leaders, having subordinated the cause of women to fighting the war at the behest of their male colleagues in the abolitionist movement, tried to return to the work of their own emancipation.

Prior to the war, however, this small group of women leaders successfully combined the two issues, asserting their own right as well as that of slaves to equal and humane treatment under the laws of the land. The famous 'Declaration of Sentiments' and resolutions passed at the Seneca Falls Convention in 1848 represented, therefore, not the beginning but the climax of several decades of work on the part of the first women's movement. What is important about the meeting is not simply that the major statement was patterned after the Declaration of Independence, or that one of the resolutions called for the enfranchisement of women. This was, by the way, the only resolution which was not passed unanimously because almost half of the one hundred men and women attending feared that a demand for the right to vote would defeat the more rational resolutions by making the convention look ridiculous. While the right to vote may have been the most emotionally controversial at this 1848 meeting, it was not necessarily the most significant.

What were the other more rational and presumably more important demands made at Seneca Falls? First, there was the general assertion that since women were created equal to men, they deserved equal treatment as citizens under the law and equal participation with men in educational and religious institutions and in the 'various trades, professions and commerce'. All of the more specific grievances cited dwelled not on the question of enfranchisement, but on legal and social questions concerning dependence within the family, wife-beating, dual standards of morality, divorce, child-custody, and control over property and wages — all problems stemming from the institution of marriage as it had evolved by the middle of the nineteenth century. Both Anthony and Stanton and other radical feminists reasserted for the remainder of the century that 'marital bondage' was 'woman's chief discontent'. As their militant newspaper, *The Revolution*, proclaimed on October 27, 1870:

> But we are not dreamers or fanatics; and we know that the ballot when we get it, will achieve for woman no more than it has achieved for man. . . . the ballot is not even half the loaf; it is only a crust — a crumb. The ballot touches only those interests, either of men or women, which take their root in political questions. But woman's chief discontent is not with her political, but with her social, and particularly her marital bondage. The solemn and profound question of marriage . . . is of more vital consequence to woman's welfare, reaches down to a deeper depth in woman's heart, and more thoroughly constitutes the core of the woman's movement, than any such superficial and fragmentary question as woman's suffrage. (p. 264)

This, therefore, is the lasting significance of the Seneca Falls

Convention. It reflected the most radical brand of feminism then, as today, because of its attack on the institution of modern marriage and the stifling domesticity fostered by the appearance of the small nuclear family and the rise of the cult of true womanhood with industrialisation and urbanisation. These original feminists were demanding their complete emancipation in the name of justice and humanity. Later generations of female activists before 1920 settled for the single right to vote in the name of motherhood and the family. Women have yet to achieve the comprehensive equality of treatment as human beings demanded at Seneca Falls in 1848.

Behind this delay and the narrowing of feminist goals was the legal and political impact of the Civil War on women reformers. In retrospect there is no doubt that the war effectively killed the broadly based humanitarian aspects of the first women's movement. First, the women's movement split in 1868 into two wings represented by the National Woman's Suffrage Association (NWSA) and the American Woman's Suffrage Association (AWSA). Ostensibly this division, which remained for twenty years, was caused by the dispute over whether or not women, as well as black males, should be granted the right to vote. It involved much more: strategy, socio-economic tensions within the movement, commitment to humanistic feminism, and the conflict between radical and status quo reform of American society.

Second, of the leading male abolitionists before the war, only four – Samuel J. May, Robert Purvis, Parker Pillsbury and Stephen S. Foster – remained even minimally loyal to women's rights after the war by insisting on their enfranchisement. All the rest including Wendall Phillips, George William Curtis, Thomas Wentworth Higginson, Horace Greeley, William Lloyd Garrison, Gerrit Smith, Theodore Tilton, Frederick Douglass and the brothers Samuel and Henry Blackwell did not want any aspect of the 'Women's Question' to complicate their work of putting the country back together. Thus the Republican party expediently made the Fourteenth and Fifteenth Amendments[12] keystones of their reconstruction program for the nation. Together these two amendments and the initial litigation arising from them legally humiliated postwar feminists.

To understand their outrage, we must appreciate the contributions of women to the Civil War. Having supported war at the expense of their own movement and other reforms, leading feminists, such as Anthony, Stanton and Lucy Stone, did expect that women would be rewarded for their war efforts with the vote if nothing else. Instead, they found out that the war had been fought to preserve the union, to free the slaves, but not at all to enhance women's rights. As in the American Revolution and the War of 1812, women were called upon in even greater numbers, particularly in the South, to carry on with farm work and feed and clothe soldiers. They also entered mills in the North in greater numbers than ever before and made significant contributions in the fields of teaching and retail trading while the fighting continued. For the first time they began to work in the offices of federal government and some of them were even permitted because of the male labor shortage to take up occupations that only their female colonial ancestors had been privileged to engage in, such as those of innkeeper, steamboat captain, teamster and mortician.

Approximately 400 women actually served as soldiers on both sides during the Civil War. Some, like Sarah Emma Edmonds, used male names and dress in order to engage in combat, but most served without disguising their sex in the roles of spies, saboteurs, scouts and couriers – blowing up bridges and arsenals and helping prisoners and slaves to escape. A few such as Harriet Tubman and Anna Ella Carroll devised military strategy and suggested battle plans (Tubman for Colonel James Montgomery and his 300 black soldiers in the campaign along the Combahee River in South Carolina and Carroll for Grant's Tennessee campaign which was one of the turning points in the war). Most women on both sides, however, served behind the lines: 3200 became nurses, despite the hostility of army doctors; others raised over fifty million dollars in the North for training more nurses, for care of the wounded and for hospital supplies. Women worked in myriad capacities in all medical facilities. Finally, Susan B. Anthony personally organised the Woman's National Loyal League in New York working for $12 a week during the duration of the war and facing the sporadic violence of racist draft riots that occurred in the city. Under her dogged leadership, by August 1864 this organisation had collected approximately 400,000 signatures on petitions for the unconditional emancipation of the slaves which was finally achieved with the passage of the Thirteenth Amendment in 1865.[13]

Surely such efforts were worthy of more than oratorical recognition: at least a small group of postwar feminists thought so. Much to their shock, anger, and dismay their 'rewards' turned out to be the Fourteenth and Fifteenth Amendments. It was, they were told by Republicans, 'The [male] Negroes' hour' – a claim Elizabeth Cady Stanton repeatedly and eloquently denied in vain. Again and again in her speeches on reconstruction, Stanton returned to the Declaration of Independence as she had at Seneca Falls in 1848. What had gone

wrong with the Declaration of Independence, she insisted, had been
the drafting of the federal Constitution:

> Our Fathers declared all men equal, then placed the power in the hands of
> the few. They declared no just government could be formed without the
> consent of the governed, then denied the elective franchise to men without
> property and education, to clergymen, women and negroes. They declared
> taxation without representation tyranny, then taxed all these dis-
> enfranchised classes. Through a century of discord, friction and injustice,
> these violations of the republican idea have culminated at last in a four
> years bloody war. And now we stand once more debating with ourselves
> the fundamental principles of government. From the baptism of this
> second revolution, with a century of added experience, shall we repeat the
> blunder of the Fathers and build again on the old foundation whose corner
> stone is class and caste?[14]

And in opposing Republican Reconstruction legislation and
amendments she noted that they were all too little, too sectional, and
too partial, saying:

> This is not reconstruction, it is whitewashing, it is patching, it is propping
> up what cannot stand. This is not the negroes' hour. We have passed from
> him to the broader question of the life of the Republic. In the discussion of
> his rights we have gone back to first principles and learned that the safety
> and durability of a nation demand that the least right of the humblest
> citizen be secured . . . . The demand of the hour is equal rights to all, that the
> ideal republic of the Fathers be now made a fact of life.[15]

Stanton's negative prediction proved all too correct. Positive
application of the Fourteenth Amendment to women took many
years and is still not complete. Its initial application to women was
largely negative because of the Supreme Court's narrow interpretation of the privileges and immunities clause and its adherence to
procedural due process, that is, due process applied strictly to the
enforcement of laws. It was not until substantive due process subsequently supplemented procedural due process that the Fourteenth
(and Fifth[16]) Amendments offered greater hope against arbitrary
state regulations. Under substantive due process all federal and state
legislation is judged by how 'reasonably' it furthers a legitimate
governmental objective. Originally, however, women and occupational groups failed to obtain a broad or substantive interpretation
of the privileges and immunities clause of section one covering all
citizens and the entire spectrum of civil rights, including the right to
choose one's occupation freely and to vote. The Supreme Court in
the *Bradwell v. Illinois* and the *Slaughter-House Cases* of 1873
limited the privileges and immunities of United States' citizens to

only those rights which owed their existence to the federal government, its national character, its Constitution, or its laws. Hence, the right to choose and follow one's occupation and the right to vote were not held to be privileges and immunities of federal citizenship and accordingly could be cut down or eliminated by state legislation.

This narrow, procedural interpretation of section one of the Fourteenth Amendment implied that the states had the broadest kind of power to enact laws governing the health, welfare, safety, and morals of the public – as interpreted by each state legislature. Due process was viewed simply in terms of the means used to enforce the laws of the land. Substantive due process, the concept which was to override states' rights in this century, only entered the legal scene after 1900 and was of no benefit to the original generation of feminists, although their immediate descendants tried to use it to obtain protective legislation for all workers – men, women and children. No longer widely applied to invalidate state legislation, substantive due process has recently been applied in cases involving marital privacy and the right to have an abortion. (See pp. 162–6 below.)

To the female activists of the late 1860s, however, the initial significance of the Fourteenth Amendment was that it specifically stated in section two that the states could not deny the right to vote to any 'male' citizen over twenty-one, and that the Fifteenth Amendment underscored that right for blacks by stating: no citizen could be denied the right to vote because of 'race, color or previous condition of servitude'. These women had unsuccessfully employed every effort to get Republican leaders to eliminate the word 'male' from the former and to add the word 'sex' to the latter. Taken together these two amendments implied that women were not citizens of the United States and female activists wasted no time testing both in the courts. In a very real sense, therefore, passage of the Fourteenth and Fifteenth Amendments forced all postwar women reformers – whether they considered themselves radicals or moderates – to concentrate on what had never been their primary prewar goal: suffrage.

THE CASE OF *UNITED STATES OF AMERICA V. SUSAN B. ANTHONY*

Between the time of her release on bail in November 1872, and her trial on June 18, 1873, Susan B. Anthony made numerous speeches on her own behalf in Monroe and Ontario counties, trying to influence prospective jurors. It was perspicacious of her to have done this because, as it turned out, she was not allowed to testify in her own defense. In approximately fifty pretrial talks her theme remained the same: 'Is it a crime for a United States citizen to vote?' This and most of the other legal questions that Anthony raised before her trial were not considered by the United States Circuit Court of New York that heard her case, nor were they dealt with by any American court in a sex-neutral fashion until the last half of the twentieth century. The Circuit Court ignored questions such as whether the Fourteenth Amendment included women as citizens and therefore as persons; whether women had the right to a jury of their peers; and whether women should continue to submit to taxation without representation?

Her basic argument against the crime of having voted was the following.

> For any State to make sex a qualification that must ever result in the disfranchisement of one entire half of the people, is to pass a bill of attainder, or an *ex post facto* law, and is therefore a violation of the supreme law of the land. By it, the blessings of liberty are forever withheld from women and their female posterity. To them, this government has not just powers derived from the consent of the governed. To them this government is not a democracy. It is not a republic. It is an odious aristocracy: a hateful oligarchy; the most hateful ever established on the face of the globe. An oligarchy of wealth, where the rich govern the poor; an oligarchy of learning, where the educated govern the ignorant; or even an oligarchy of race, where the Saxon rules the African, might be endured; but surely this oligarchy of sex, which makes the men of every household sovereigns, masters; the women subjects, slaves; carrying dissension, rebellion into every home of the Nation, can not be endured.[17]

She defended this position by resorting primarily to the first section of the Fourteenth Amendment, which specifically stated: 'No State shall make or enforce any law which shall abridge the privileges or immunities of citizens of the United States; nor shall any State deprive any person of life, liberty or property, without due process of law; nor deny to any person within its jurisdiction the equal protection of the laws.' Anthony logically raised the rhetorically simple question about this historic section of the Fourteenth Amendment: *Are women persons?* Her answer was equally simple and rhetorical.

> I hardly believe any of our opponents will have the hardihood to say they are not. Being persons, then, women are citizens, and no State has a right to make any new law, or to enforce any old law, that shall abridge their privileges or immunities. Hence, every discrimination against women in

the constitutions and laws of the several States, is to-day null and void, precisely as is every one against negroes. Is the right to vote one of the privileges or immunities of citizens? I think the disfranchised ex-rebels, and the ex-state prisoners will all agree with me, that it is not only one of them, but *the one without which all the others are nothing*.

Anthony even anticipated a revival of the infamous *Dred Scott v. Sandford*, 60 u.s. 394 (1857) decision in which Justice Taney, called upon to decide the citizenship rights of blacks taken into free territory, had placed women and children in a 'special category' of nonvoting citizens. Ignoring that portion of the majority decision which had excluded blacks from even this type of second-class citizenship, she focused on the section which stated: 'The words "people of the United States" and "citizens", are synonymous terms, and mean the same thing. They both describe the political body, who, according to our republican institutions, form the sovereignty, and who hold the power and conduct the government, through their representatives.' She vehemently denied that *Dred Scott* should be used 'against the women of the entire nation, vast numbers of whom are the peers of those honorable gentlemen themselves, in morals, intellect, culture, wealth, family – paying taxes on large estates, and contributing equally with them and their sex, in every direction, to the growth, prosperity, and well-being of the Republic'.

She further buttressed her point of view by pointing out that at least two United States Judges had recently asserted that the Fourteenth Amendment did indeed grant women the right to vote. Anthony believed that if the Fourteenth Amendment did not grant *all* citizens the right to vote, then it had no purpose because black males were already entitled to all other constitutional privileges and immunities of the Constitution under the terms of the Thirteenth Amendment which had granted them (and black women) freedom from slavery.

Thus, you see, those newly-made freed men were in possession of every possible right, privilege, and immunity of the Government, except that of suffrage, and hence, needed no constitutional amendment for any other purpose. What right, I ask you, has the Irishman the day after he receives his naturalization papers that he did not possess the day before, save the right to vote and hold office? And the Chinamen, now crowding our Pacific coast, are in precisely the same position. What privilege or immunity has California or Oregon the constitutional right to deny them, save that of the ballot? Clearly, then, if the xiv. Amendment was not to secure to black men their right to vote, it did nothing for them, since they possessed everything else before. But if it was meant to be a prohibition of the States to deny or abridge their right to vote – which I fully believe –

then it did the same for all persons, white women included, born or
naturalized in the United States, for the amendment does not say all male
persons of African descent, but all persons are citizens.

At this point, however, Anthony had to face up to the existence of the
last of the three famous Reconstruction Amendments following the
Civil War, namely, the Fifteenth Amendment. This one simply stated
that 'the right of citizens of the United States to vote shall not be
denied or abridged by the United States or by any State on account of
race, color, or previous condition of servitude'. On the surface this
amendment seemed to contradict her arguments about the Fourteenth Amendment conferring the franchise on all citizens. She
explained away this apparent contradiction by interpreting the
language of the amendment to her rhetorical advantage. 'How can
the State deny or abridge the right of a citizen,' she asked, 'if the
citizen does not possess it?' Then she proceeded to attribute the
passage of this amendment to purely partisan reasons. Since the
southern states under the domination of the Democratic party were
not honoring the Fourteenth Amendment it was necessary for the
Republican party of President Grant to compel compliance (in order
to insure his re-election in 1872) with 'this positive prohibition of the
Fifteenth Amendment'.

Finally, in the event that none of the above arguments convinced
her audiences, Anthony carried her case to its logical extreme by
saying that women in general, and married women in particular,
despite the passage of some Married Women's Property Acts, existed
in a state of servitude.

But if you will insist that the xv. Amendment's interdiction against
robbing United States citizens of their right to vote, 'on account of race,
color, or previous condition of servitude,' is a recognition of the right,
either of the United States or any State, to rob citizens of that right for any
or all other reasons, I will prove to you that the class of citizens for which I
now plead, and to which I belong, may be, and are, by all the principles of
our Government, and many of the laws of the States, included under the
term 'previous condition of servitude.'
    First. – The married women and their legal status. What is servitude?
'The condition of a slave.' What is a slave? 'A person who is robbed of the
proceeds of his labor; a person who is subject to the will of another.' ...
There is an old saying that 'a rose by any other name would smell as
sweet,' and I submit if the deprivation by law of the ownership of one's
own person, wages, property, children, the denial of the right as an
individual, to sue and be sued, and to testify in the courts, is not a
condition of servitude most bitter and absolute, though under the sacred
name of marriage?
    Does any lawyer doubt my statement of the legal status of married

women? I will remind him of the fact that the old common law of England prevails in every State in this Union, except where the Legislature has enacted special laws annulling it. And I am ashamed that not one State has yet blotted from its statute books the old common law of marriage, by which Blackstone, summed up in the fewest words possible, is made to say: 'Husband and wife are one, and that one is the husband.'[18]

Thus may all married women, wives, and widows, by the laws of the several States, be technically included in the xv. Amendment's specification of 'condition of servitude', present or previous. And not only married women, but I will also prove to you that by all the great fundamental principles of our free government, the entire womanhood of the nation is in a 'condition of servitude' as surely as were our revolutionary fathers, when they rebelled against old King George. Women are taxed without representation, governed without their consent, tried, convicted, and punished without a jury of their peers. And is all this tyranny any less humiliating and degrading to women under our democratic–republican government to-day than it was to men under their aristocratic, monarchical government one hundred years ago?

Having proven women's condition of servitude to her own satisfaction, Anthony left no stone unturned in her public defense of herself. She went on to attack the presence of masculine pronouns in all American state and federal statutes. If the legal profession insisted on a literal interpretation by sex then consistency would dictate that women would be exempt from all the tax laws among others. 'There is no she, or her, or hers, in the tax laws', she provocatively told her listeners. She also noted that all the pronouns in the section of the Civil Rights Act she was charged with having violated were male. Then she cited that 1868 Supreme Court Case of *Silver v. Ladd* in which it had been held that the words 'single man' and 'unmarried man' should be interpreted in a generic sense. In this case involving a widow's right to land under the Oregon donation law of 1850, the Court said that 'embraced within the term single man [was] an unmarried woman'.

Most of her speeches before her trial ended with two appeals – one to women and one to judges.

We no longer petition Legislature or Congress to give us the right to vote. We appeal to the women everywhere to exercise their too long neglected 'citizen's right to vote'. We appeal to the inspectors of election everywhere to receive the votes of all United States citizens, as it is their duty to do. We appeal to United States commissioners and marshals to arrest the inspectors who reject the names and votes of United States citizens, as it is their duty to do, and leave those alone who, like our eighth ward inspectors, perform their duties faithfully and well. We ask the juries to fail to return verdicts of 'guilty' against honest, law-abiding, tax-paying United States citizens for offering their votes at our elections; or against intelligent, worthy young men, inspectors of election, for receiving and counting such citizens' votes. We ask the judges to render true and unprejudiced opinions of the law, and wherever there is room for a doubt to give its benefit on the side of liberty and equality to women, remembering that 'The true rule of interpretation under our National Constitution, especially since its Amendments, is that anything for human rights is constitutional, everything against human rights unconstitutional'.

Her closing words warned that if the legal system did not respond women would battle for the ballot and other kinds of remedial legislation in order to bring about the day 'when all United States citizens shall be recognized as equals before the law'. Anthony never lived to see this 'complete triumph', as she called it, and neither has any generation of American women.

None of Anthony's pretrial statements was heard in court because of several questionable procedural decisions by the presiding judge. First, Judge Hunt refused her the right to testify on her own behalf; then he delivered a previously prepared written opinion immediately following three hours of argument by her attorney; finally, he summarily instructed the all male jury to bring in a verdict of guilty. When Anthony's lawyer protested this unconstitutional procedure, Judge Hunt simply discharged the jurors and denied a motion for retrial. In the opinion he had written before hearing the defendant's case, Judge Hunt ruled that the Fourteenth Amendment could not be used as a basis for defense because of the recent Supreme Court ruling in *Bradwell v. Illinois* (see below pp. 97–8) in which it had been determined that 'the rights referred to in the fourteenth amendment are those belonging to a person as a citizen of the United States and not as a citizen of a state. . .'. He further argued that even if Anthony honestly believed that she had the right to vote, such a belief did not excuse the act. Judge Hunt relied almost exclusively on the District Attorney's opening remarks which said that when Anthony voted on November 5, 1872, 'she was a woman. I suppose there will be no question about that'. Therefore, being 'a person of the female sex' the act of voting was automatically 'against the peace of the United States of America and their dignity'. Judge Hunt simply echoed this circular reasoning in his summary when he said only 'two principles apply here: First, ignorance of the law excuses no one; second, every person is presumed to understand and to intend the necessary effects of his own acts. Miss Anthony knew that she was a woman, and that the constitution of this state prohibits her from voting'.

Anthony's attorney, Henry R. Selden, had pointed out in his brief that he had personally told her 'that she was as lawful a voter as I am, or as any other man is, and advised her to go and offer her vote'.[19] He argued, therefore, that she had the right to vote, believed she had the right to vote, and that female voting was not a crime under the Civil Rights Act of 1870. Most of his defense of the first point was based on recent improvements in the legal status of women under some Married Women's Property Acts. In making this argument, however, he was using these acts in a manner that contradicted Anthony's pretrial statements about them. Selden also used a standard male interpretation of this specific kind of legislation and of the right to vote in general, which was anathema to Anthony's brand of radical feminism. There is no documentary evidence indicating how she reacted when she heard her attorney tell the court:

> On the one hand it is supposed by some that the character of women would be radically changed – that they would be unsexed, as it were, by clothing them with political rights, and that instead of modest, amiable, and graceful beings, we should have bold, noisy, and disgusting political demagogues, or something worse, if anything worse can be imagined. I think those who entertain such opinions are in error. The innate character of women is the result of God's laws, not of man's, nor can the laws of man affect that character beyond a very slight degree. Whatever rights may be given to them, and whatever duties may be charged upon them by human laws, their general character will remain unchanged. Their modesty, their delicacy, and intuitive sense of propriety, will never desert them, into whatever new positions their added rights or duties may carry them.
>
> So far as women, without change of character as women, are qualified to discharge the duties of citizenship, they will discharge them if called upon to do so, and beyond that they will not go. Nature has put barriers in the way of any excessive devotion of women to public affairs, and it is not necessary that nature's work in that respect should be supplemented by additional barriers invented by men. Such offices as women are qualified to fill will be sought by those who do not find other employment, and others they will not seek, or if they do, will seek in vain.

Selden also employed elaborate constitutional and historical arguments about the positive implications for women of the Fourteenth Amendment, but by the time he argued the case the *Bradwell* decision had legally foreclosed most of them. His primary defense remained, therefore, that his famous client had acted in 'perfect good faith, with motives as pure and impulses as noble as any which can find place in your honor's breast in the administration of justice ...'. To condemn her as a criminal for voting when she had been advised it was legal 'would only add another most weighty reason to those which I have already advanced, to show that women need the aid of the ballot for their protection'.

In a final attempt to defend herself Anthony tried to speak in court before being sentenced. Although her remarks were ultimately cut short by Judge Hunt, she did manage to question whether she had indeed been tried by her peers and to express her defiance of the entire male dominated legal system. The exchange that took place between the judge and the feminist is dramatic enough to be quoted at length.

May it please the Court to remember that since the day of my arrest last November, this is the first time that either myself or any person of my disfranchised class has been allowed a word of defense before judge or jury –

Judge HUNT: The prisoner must sit down; the Court can not allow it.

Miss ANTHONY: All my prosecutors, from the 8th Ward corner grocery politician, who entered the complaint, to the United States Marshal, Commissioner, District Attorney, District Judge, your honor on the bench, not one is my peer, but each and all are my political sovereigns; and had your honor submitted my case to the jury, as was clearly your duty, even then I should have had just cause of protest, for not one of those men was my peer; but, native or foreign, white or black, rich or poor, educated or ignorant, awake or asleep, sober or drunk, each and every man of them was my political superior; hence, in no sense, my peer. . . . Precisely as no disfranchised person is entitled to sit upon a jury, and no woman is entitled to the franchise, so, none but a regularly admitted lawyer is allowed to practice in the courts, and no woman can gain admission to the bar – hence jury, judge, counsel, must all be of the superior class.

Judge HUNT: The Court must insist – the prisoner has been tried according to the established forms of law.

Miss ANTHONY: Yes, your honor, but by forms of law all made by men, interpreted by men, administered by men, in favor of men, and against women; and hence, your honor's ordered verdict of guilty, against a United States citizen for the exercise of 'that citizen's right to vote', simply because that citizen was a woman and not a man. . . . As then the slaves who got their freedom must take it over, or under, or through the unjust forms of law, precisely so now must women, to get their right to a voice in this Government, take it; and I have taken mine, and mean to take it at every possible opportunity.

Judge HUNT: The Court orders the prisoner to sit down. It will not allow another word.

Miss ANTHONY: When I was brought before your honor for trial, I hoped for a broad and liberal interpretation of the Constitution and its recent amendments, that should declare all United States citizens under its protecting aegis – that should declare equality of rights the national guarantee to all persons born or naturalized in the United States. But failing to get this justice – failing, even to get a trial by a jury *not* of my peers – I ask not leniency at your hands – but rather the full rigors of the law.

Judge HUNT: The Court must insist – (Here the prisoner sat down.)

Judge Hunt: The prisoner will stand up. (Here Miss Anthony arose again.) The sentence of the Court is that you pay a fine of one hundred dollars and the costs of the prosecution.

Miss Anthony: May it please your honor, I shall never pay a dollar of your unjust penalty. All the stock in trade I possess is a $10,000 debt, incurred by publishing my paper – *The Revolution* – four years ago, the sole object of which was to educate all women to do precisely as I have done, rebel against your man-made, unjust, unconstitutional forms of law, that tax, fine, imprison, and hang women, while they deny them the right of representation in the Government; and I shall work on with might and main to pay every dollar of that honest debt, but not a penny shall go to this unjust claim. And I shall earnestly and persistently continue to urge all women to the practical recognition of the old revolutionary maxim, that 'Resistance to tyranny is obedience to God.'

Judge Hunt: Madam, the Court will not order you committed until the fine is paid.

Anthony's words continued to ring in the ears of later generations of American feminists down to the present. Matilda Joslyn Gage, who had made seventeen pretrial talks on Anthony's behalf, later predicted: 'In the near future these trials of women under the Fourteenth Amendment will be looked upon as the great State trials of the world; trials on which a republic, founded upon the acknowledged rights of all persons to self-government, through its courts decided against the right of one half of its citizens on the ground that sex was a barrier and a crime.' Attorney Selden reacted to Judge Hunt's interpretation of the 1870 Civil Rights Act by saying: 'The war [between the states] has abolished somethings besides slavery, it has abolished jury trial.'

A *nolle prosequi* was entered for the other thirteen women who voted with Anthony and the charges against them were dropped, but the three male inspectors stood trial under the same Civil Rights Act. Unlike Anthony, these men were allowed to testify on their own behalf. She was called as witness for the defendants, but as soon as she asserted that she had presented herself at the voters' registration *not* as a female, but as a citizen with the right to vote, she was summarily dismissed from the witness stand by the same Judge Hunt. The three registration inspectors were found guilty and fined twenty-five dollars each. Their attorneys advised against payment and after a nine-month delay they were sentenced to jail in February 1874. Ironically it was Anthony who secured their release by indirectly appealing to President Grant through the New York Senator, A. A. Sargent. Grant officially pardoned them on March 3, 1874.[20] In the intervening days hundreds of Rochester people visited them in the local jail and the fourteen women who had voted, including Anthony, brought them daily meals.

Although she never paid her own fine, she was not sentenced to jail and so the Anthony case ended anticlimactically for a number of reasons. Most important was the fact it never reached the United States Supreme Court because of the legal technicalities mentioned in the Introduction. No doubt this was a great disappointment to her. She had anticipated that the post-Civil War cases involving the right of women to vote would set a new constitutional precedent. Right after she had voted on November 5, 1872, Anthony wrote her old friend, Elizabeth Cady Stanton: 'Well, I have been and gone and done it! Positively voted the Republican ticket – straight – this A.M. at seven o'clock. . . . How I wish you were here to write up the funny things said and done. . . . If only now *all the Woman Suffrage women* would work to *this* end of *enforcing the existing Constitutional supremacy of National law* over State law, what strikes we might make this very winter!'[21] Many years later, however, she realised that her own test case had only set a negative precedent. Subsequently she commented in the *History of Woman Suffrage* that all such trials of women who had tried to vote under the Fourteenth Amendment added up to the same thing: 'making sex [i.e. being female] a crime in the eye of United States laws.'

WOMEN LAWYERS AND THE AMERICAN BAR, 1865–1920

The case which most damaged the arguments of Anthony's attorney was that of *Bradwell v. Illinois*. This had a double significance. In the first place, it dealt with the extent to which the individual states could abridge the privileges and immunities of local citizens, including women. Secondly, since it concerned the question of the right of women to practice as lawyers, it indicated the degree of willingness of the legal profession and judiciary to have women in their ranks.

At the same time when the first of the 'persons' cases were being argued in England, women were attempting to enter the legal profession in the United States. They soon discovered that state laws and courts revealed erratic patterns on this subject. A few allowed women to practice as attorneys, but most required a court decision, an act of the legislature, or *both* before a woman could be admitted to the bar. Although women had been granted power-of-attorney in colonial times, post-Civil War judges went to great lengths to ban them from the legal profession and other 'gainful occupations' that they had practiced a century earlier. Sometimes it was argued that this was in keeping with traditional common law which did not recognise married women as legal entities. These state courts also argued that statutes setting up requirements for admission of attorneys were never intended to apply to women. But then, neither the federal Constitution nor the Fourteenth Amendment were specifically 'intended' to apply to women.

This argument about the intention of the founding fathers or the drafters of a constitutional amendment or of state legislators was obviously a *non sequitur* because attitudes change over time, and original intentions of one generation, even when possible to determine, constitute a questionable basis for action several generations later. The intention of the framers of the Constitution in 1783 concerning blacks was clearly questioned and superseded by the Thirteenth, Fourteenth, and Fifteenth Amendments, which freed and technically granted all constitutional rights to this segment of the population. By 1920, a similar reversal of popular and legal opinion had occurred and all states were then routinely admitting women to the bar. By that time the American Bar Association also allowed female members.

It was not until 1957, however, that the Supreme Court officially disallowed certain state regulations of bar admissions.[22] Female participation in the legal profession remained at a token level from 1920 until the present despite recent increases in the number of practicing women lawyers. The long struggle of female attorneys to advance from exclusion to tokenism is not atypical of the fight by American women to gain entrance into other professions which have systematically discriminated against them, such as medicine, higher education, engineering, and the ministry.

In 1869 the first woman was admitted to the practice of law in the United States. This occurred in the state of Iowa when Arabella A. Mansfield applied for a law license. Under the Iowa Code of 1851 admission to the bar had been specifically limited to 'any white male person'. The Iowa Supreme Court ruled in the case of Mansfield that 'the affirmative is not any implied denial of the right of females'.[23] As a result of this precedent, the Iowa Code of 1873 deleted the words 'white male' as a bar admission requirement. Apparently, however, the deletion occurred fortuitously and should not be viewed as consciously favoring women's liberation. The same thing occurred later in 1964, when the word 'sex' was added to the Civil Rights Act (see pp. 210–11 below). In this instance a Republican member of the Iowa state legislature had recommended that the word 'white' be eliminated in the bar admission bill and a Democrat sarcastically suggested that the word 'male' should be removed as well.[24] It cannot be said that the intent of the legislature was to strike a blow against either racism or sexism within the legal profession. But it was the unexpected result.

In the same year that Mansfield was admitted to the Iowa bar, women were admitted to study law at the St. Louis Law School. This was the first law school in the United States to accept students regardless of sex. Mansfield had obtained her legal knowledge essentially through an apprenticeship system by studying in a law office. Of the two women who matriculated that year one, Lemma Barkaloo, became the first woman to try a case in an American court in 1870. Ironically, Barkaloo had earlier been turned away from Columbia University Law School. In 1870 when Columbia denied admission to three more female applicants, one male member of the Board of Trustees of the Law School exercised his prerogative of protective paternalism when he reportedly said: 'No woman shall degrade herself by practicing law in New York, especially if I can save her. ... I think that the clack of these possible Portias will never be heard in Dwight's Moot Courts.'[25]

It was also in 1870 that Ada H. Kepley became the first American woman to receive an accredited law degree. It was from Union College of Law in Chicago. All of these legal pioneers had studied law privately before attempting to enter such schools. Around the same time similarly qualified women in Connecticut, California, Colorado, and Indiana were being denied admission to schools of law and to the bar. Sometimes states would deny admission only to reverse this opinion a few years later by new statutes. Such reversals avoided the question of women's constitutional rights. Perhaps the best example of this kind of capricious reversal occurred in Wisconsin when Lavinia Goodell was denied admission to the bar in 1875 and then granted a license to practice by that same state in 1879. In this four-year period the Wisconsin Supreme Court completely reversed itself. In 1875 Chief Justice C. J. Ryan had carried the day with the argument that to construe the masculine pronoun in the state law governing bar admissions to include women would constitute a 'judicial revolution'. Speaking for the entire court he furthered argued:

Nature has tempered woman as little for the judicial conflicts of the court room as for the physical conflicts of the battlefield. Woman is modeled for gentler and better things. ... [Our] ... profession has essentially and habitually to do with all that is selfish and extortionate, knavish and criminal, coarse and brutal, repulsive and obscene in human life. It would be revolting to all female sense of innocence and sanctity of their sex, shocking to man's reverence for womanhood and faith in woman on which hinge all the better affections and humanities of life, that woman should be permitted to mix professionally in all the nastiness of the world which finds its way into the courts of justice. ... Discussions are habitually necessary which are unfit for female ears. The habitual presence of women at these would tend to relax the public sense of decency and propriety. If these things are to come, we will take no voluntary part in bringing them about.[26]

In 1879 after state law specifically forbade this sex barrier Chief Justice Ryan continued to dissent, but now the majority opinion read:

We are satisfied that the applicant possesses all the requisite qualifications as to learning, ability, and moral character to entitle her to admission, no objection existing thereto except that founded upon her sex alone. Under the circumstances, a majority think that objection must be disregarded. Miss Goodell will therefore be admitted to practice in this court upon signing the roll and taking the prescribed oath.[27]

This same sporadic and often capricious pattern continued until by 1920 only Delaware and Rhode Island did not admit women to the bar. Both relented after the passage of the Nineteenth Amendment granting the suffrage to women that year. The issue of women's right to practice law was accordingly a keen one, and the constitutionality of state prohibitions on such a right reached the Supreme Court soon after the adoption of the Fourteenth Amendment.

Married Women Cannot be Lawyers

From 1865 to 1920 only two cases involving the exclusion of women from the practice of law reached the Supreme Court of the United States. The best known one was *Bradwell v. Illinois*, 83 U.S. 130 (1873). Myra Colby Bradwell specifically sought the benefit of the privileges and immunities clause of the first section of the Fourteenth Amendment. An avowed suffragist and champion of women's legal rights, she had passed the Illinois bar examination in 1869 only to be denied admission to that bar because she was married. Her husband was Judge James B. Bradwell. Despite the precedent that had been set earlier in the year by the Mansfield case in Iowa, the lower court based its refusal to allow her to practice law on Blackstone's idea that a married woman was not competent to perform such duties as making contracts which an attorney would have to do. This argument about her common law disabilities was totally inapplicable because Myra Bradwell had been making contracts and acting in other official, legal capacities as president of a publishing company in Illinois and as founder and editor of the most important legal publication in the west and mid-west, the *Chicago Legal News*. In fact, the state had granted her a special charter to engage in such legal activities. Yet the Illinois Supreme Court said she was not qualified to act in a similar capacity as a lawyer.

When the case came before the Supreme Court of the United States, Justice Miller simply ignored the lower court decision and held that the right to practice law was not a privilege and immunity of citizenship. He based his position on the well-known *Slaughter-House Cases* decision delivered the day before on April 14, 1873. This decision placed such severe limitations on the scope and meaning of the privileges and immunities clause of the Fourteenth Amendment that it has been virtually unused since. While this majority opinion was bad enough as far as Bradwell's right to practice law was concerned, the concurring opinion of Justice Bradley was even more damaging because of the overtly sexist language and attitudes it contained. In the Blackstone tradition Bradley insisted that women had no legal existence separate from their husbands despite the passage of a number of Married Women's Property Acts. His opinion stated:

> The civil law, as well as nature herself, has always recognized a wide difference in the respective spheres and destinies of man and woman. Man is, or should be, woman's protector and defender. The natural and proper timidity and delicacy which belongs to the female sex evidently unfits it for many of the occupations of civil life. The constitution of the family organization, which is founded in the divine ordinance, as well as in the nature of things, indicates the domestic sphere as that which properly belongs to the domain and functions of womanhood. The harmony, not to say identity, of interests and views which belong or should belong to the family institution is repugnant to the idea of a woman adopting a distinct and independent career from that of her husband. So firmly fixed was this sentiment in the founders of the common law that it became a maxim of that system of jurisprudence that a woman had no legal existence separate from her husband, who was regarded as her head and representative in the social state.

He conceded that many women were unmarried and not affected by any of the duties, complications, and incapacities arising out of the married state, but these were exceptions to the general rule. 'The paramount destiny and mission of women [was] to fulfill the noble and benign offices of wife and mother,' according to Bradley. 'This is the law of the Creator. And the rules of civil society must be adapted to the general constitution of things, and cannot be based upon exceptional cases.'

The humane movements of modern society, which had for their object the multiplication of avenues for woman's advancement and of occupations adapted to her condition and sex, had his heartiest concurrence. But he was not prepared to say that it was one of her fundamental rights and privileges to be admitted into every office and position, including those requiring highly special qualifications and demanding special responsibilities. In the nature of things it was not every citizen of every age, sex, and condition that was qualified for every calling and position. It was the prerogative of the legislator to prescribe regulations founded on nature, reason, and experience for the due admission of qualified persons to professions and callings demanding special skill and confidence. So he concluded:

> This fairly belongs to the police power of the state; and, in my opinion, in view of the peculiar characteristics, destiny, and mission of woman, it is within the province of the legislature to ordain what offices, positions, and callings shall be filled and discharged by men, and shall receive the benefit of those energies and responsibilities, and that decision and firmness which are presumed to predominate in the sterner sex.

It is worth noting several inter-relationships between the *Bradwell* and *Slaughter-House Cases*. First, they were both argued in January, 1872, and the two opinions were scheduled to be announced on the same day in April, 1873. It has been suggested that 'because the cases were *sub judice* during the fourteen-month period of decision' the narrow interpretation of privileges and immunities with respect to choice of occupations in *Slaughter-House* was probably 'influenced by the court's realisation that a broad interpretation would necessarily change the status of women'.[28] While this may be true, much more was involved in this decision. The *Slaughter-House Cases* involved an attempt by butchers in Louisiana to obtain federal protection under the privileges and immunities clause from state legislation, which had created a private monopoly of the slaughter-house trade. The majority opinion, however, did not limit itself to denying butchers the right to choose an occupation under the privileges and immunities clause. It also addressed itself to the equal protection clause of the Fourteenth Amendment and said that it could only be applied to class distinctions based upon race. The exact wording of the majority opinion was: 'We doubt very much whether any action of a state not directed by way of discrimination against the negroes as a class, or on account of their race, will be held to come within the purview of this provision.'

Justice Bradley's position on these two cases is also noteworthy. In a dissenting opinion he argued *against* Myra Bradwell's right of choice of occupation but he was in the majority when he argued *for* the butchers having that same right. In the *Slaughter-House Cases* Bradley said that 'a law which prohibits a large class of citizens from adopting a lawful employment ... does deprive them of liberty as well as property, without due process of law. Their right of choice is their liberty; their occupation is their property. Such a law also deprives these citizens of the equal protection of the laws ...'. He held to a diametrically opposing viewpoint in *Bradwell*.

Matthew Carpenter, one of the best known advocates of the day, also took similarly irreconcilable positions in these two cases. He was, unlike Bradley, arguing *against* the butchers and *for* Bradwell as her attorney. His positions were as inconsistent as Bradley's, albeit for different legal reasons. Nonetheless, both men used standard *sexist* arguments. Carpenter, for example, tried in *Bradwell* to trade the right to follow an occupation for the right to vote by assuring the court that if they granted women their choice of profession it would not lead to granting them suffrage. For this was simply a political right which could be infringed or abridged while an occupation was a right of citizenship. Furthermore he assured the court of this by noting that 'female suffrage ... would overthrow Christianity, defeat the ends of modern civilisation and upturn the world', and no one wanted this – except Myra Bradwell and her feminist supporters.

Such inconsistencies on the part of Carpenter and Bradley were never seriously questioned by the Court or any lawyer or legal historian until recently. Was her case simply considered less important because of prevailing 'natural male dominance' theories of the time? Did the general political climate of the Reconstruction Era play a more important role than sexism in the *Bradwell* and *Slaughter-House* decisions? It should be remembered that this was a time of political and constitutional uncertainty as northern Republicans tried to assert federal authority over southern Democrats and the power of individual states in general. The Supreme Court ended up the referee in this sectional and constitutional struggle between congressional and state power. In any case, Myra Bradwell apparently was not taken very seriously by her contemporaries. A recent history of the United States Supreme Court has suggested: 'While Chicago lawyers could not fail to respect "our Myra's" remarkable attainments ... her serious effort to win recognition as a lawyer was commonly treated as somewhat whimsical.'[29] She did not again apply for admission to the bar, even though the Illinois legislature passed an act in 1872 giving all persons, regardless of sex, freedom in selecting an occupation. However, in 1890, four years before her death, the Illinois Supreme Court admitted her to the practice of law; two years later Bradwell was admitted to practice before the Supreme Court of the United States.

Myra Bradwell never practiced law, although most of her professional and political activities were closely related to the law and she remained an outspoken advocate of women's rights. When she heard of the negative and arbitrary decision in the Anthony case she wrote in her newspaper the *Chicago Legal News* that Judge Hunt 'violated the Constitution of the United States more, to convict her of illegal voting, than she did in voting, for he had sworn to support it, she had not'.[30] Perhaps there is some poetic justice in the fact that both her daughter and son became attorneys. Even in death, however, Bradwell could not escape the same male condescension that had greeted her earlier attempt to be recognised as a lawyer. Thus, according to a memorial in the *American Law Review* in 1894, she was described as 'a gentle and noiseless woman, her tenderness and refinement making her character all the more effective, Mrs. Bradwell was one of those who live their creed instead of preaching it. She did not spend her days proclaiming on the rostrum the rights of women but quietly, none the less effectively, set to work to clear the barriers.'[31]

One point of immediate interest that emerges from Myra Bradwell's case is that, despite the great differences in the constitutional situation in the United States and England, the judges in both countries were expressing roughly similar sentiments and arriving at substantially the same results, even though the technical routes they followed were considerably different. The major differences were that the United States judges articulated policy issues far more freely than did their English counterparts, for the United States Constitution encouraged them to do so. Consequently, the inconsistency and judicial confusion created by such decisions as the *Slaughter-House Cases* and *Bradwell v. Illinois* were readily apparent and they did not bode well for a broadening of women's legal rights in the early post-Civil War years. This was true not only with respect to choice of occupation, but also, as the Anthony decision already demonstrated, with respect to the franchise. In both *Bradwell* and *Anthony* the New State Circuit Court and the Supreme Court had respectively admitted that women were 'citizens' under the Fourteenth Amendment. The all important question that remained to be answered was – were they also 'persons' in the language of that amendment?

ARE AMERICAN WOMEN 'PERSONS'? – THE RIGHT TO VOTE

The only case to reach the Supreme Court out of all the attempts women made to vote in the 1870s was *Minor v. Happersett*, 88 U.S. 162 (1875). Virginia Minor tried to vote at the same time that Anthony did in the fall of 1872. Unlike Anthony, however, she was not allowed to register to vote in St. Louis, Missouri and so never did cast a ballot. But she and her husband first filed suit against the local registrar, then appealed the case to the Missouri Supreme Court, and finally to the United States Supreme Court in 1874. The Minors' brief began with an elaborate argument based on practical, political grounds that 'there can be no half-way citizenship' under the Federal Constitution. This was dismissed by the Court out of hand. It entertained only those arguments based on the rights of citizens to vote under the First Amendment (voting was a form of free expression), the Thirteenth Amendment (not voting was a form of involuntary servitude), and the Fourteenth Amendment (voting for officials of the federal government was a privilege and immunity of national citizenship, rather than simply state citizenship because these positions would not exist if the federal government did not).

The Supreme Court chose only to consider whether voting was a privilege and immunity of citizenship. It most noticeably failed to address the question of why voting for *national* officers did not constitute a form of *national* citizenship that could not be abridged arbitrarily by individual states. Instead, the Court used historical arguments to prove that it had never been the 'intent' of the framers of the federal or state constitutions to enfranchise women. 'For nearly ninety years the people have acted upon the idea that the Constitution when it conferred citizenship did not necessarily confer the right of suffrage. . . . Our province is to decide what the law is, not to declare what it should be.' Rather than simply relying on the narrow interpretation of the *Slaughter-House* definition of national citizenship under the Fourteenth Amendment, Chief Justice Waite proceeded to discuss the constitutional merits of the case in a sweeping fashion. He began by noting that 'disputes have arisen as to whether or not certain persons or certain classes of persons were part of the people at the time [of the adoption of the Constitution of 1787]', but there was never any question of their being citizens. This set the stage for the next part of that historic decision. The Court had already held that 'there is no doubt that women may be citizens' because 'sex has never been made one of the elements of citizenship in the United States. In this respect men have never had an advantage over women.' Like children, Chief Justice Waite had argued that women were also 'persons', because they were counted as part of the total population.

Then, using parallel reasoning to the *Dred Scott* decision, the *Minor* court declared that historically women constituted a special category of citizens whose inability to vote did not infringe upon their rights as citizens or persons. Thus it avoided the constitutional question raised by the Minors of whether voting for national officials was a privilege and immunity of national citizenship. The *Minor* decision, like the *Dred Scott* one twenty years before, could only be over-ruled by constitutional amendment. In other words, it took the Thirteenth Amendment to abolish the special category of slavehood for blacks by granting them citizenship, and it finally took the Nineteenth Amendment to abolish in part the special category of citizenship for women by granting them the right to vote. What is curious here is that the *Dred Scott* decision has for some time been considered a blot on constitutional law, but the *Minor* decision and the related *Bradwell* one have yet to receive the same deserved castigation by the legal profession. Again the question must be asked – Why? Is it because of the Reconstruction politics or the Victorian sexism involved in both cases? It has been suggested that Justice Waite had Justice Taney's infamous *Dred Scott* decision before him when preparing the *Minor* one and that this was no mere coincidence. It was, according to this theory, absolutely essential for judges to deal as summarily and as harshly as possible with the question of increased legal rights for women following the Civil War in order that they might proceed to reverse the newly gained legal status of the freed black slaves.[32]

Once second-class citizenship had been unequivocally established for women, the white, male-dominated judiciary could then use this as a legal model to build a rationalisation for Jim Crow laws. Just as advances in civil rights for blacks in the 1960s gave women a model with which to fight for greater legal rights, it is possible that one hundred years earlier the reverse had taken place. Sex bias paved the way for increased racial bias within the American legal system, in the last quarter of the nineteenth century. In each instance of discrimination, judges could and did argue as in *Minor* that 'if the law is wrong, it ought to be changed; but the power for that is not with us. . . . No argument as to women's need of suffrage can be considered. We can only act upon her rights as they exist. It is not for us to look at the hardship of withholding [privileges and immunities of citizenship]. Our duty is at an end if we find it is within the power of a State to withhold'.

Feminists reacted to this 1874 Supreme Court decision upholding the disfranchisement of women with a volley of angry letters-to-the-editor and articles. One read in part:

> As long as there were no women who demanded the ballot, and by tacit consent it was relinquished, the fraud practiced by debarring them from it was merely of a negative character – but the privilege should have been left open; but from the moment that one woman demanded it, an outrage was practiced upon her by the entire people in denying it her, and the pleas that it is not woman's sphere . . . is the most subterfuge of any, for it is not for men, but for woman alone, to determine what the sphere is, or is not.[33]

All such protests were to no avail. The Supreme Court of the United States had not only upheld the police power of the states through the most narrow interpretation possible of the privileges and immunities clause of the Fourteenth Amendment, but it had also placed women on the confining pedestal known as 'special category of citizen', largely on the basis of historical precedent. In addition, the *Minor* court tacitly upheld the 'intent' of the drafters of the Fourteenth Amendment, for the Congressional debates of late 1860s made it clear that Congress had not intended to enfranchise women with the passage of the Fourteenth Amendment.

The Supreme Court continued to issue decisions for the remainder of the century based on arguments which muddied constitutional waters more than they cleared them because of the resulting legal inconsistencies between cases involving women and those that did not. Ten years later, for example, in *Ex parte Yarbrough*, 110 U.S. 651 (1884), a voting case involving personal intimidation of a black male, the Court ruled that the right to vote for a member of Congress did have its origins in the Constitution and therefore could not be abridged by the states. Later decisions interpreted this to mean that voting for a national official was, therefore, a privilege and immunity of national citizenship. This was the question the Court had refused to address when the Minors had raised it in 1874. While the *Yarbrough* decision did not technically overrule the position taken by the *Minor* court, by any logical determination it was overruled *sub silentio.* Yet the Court argued unconvincingly that *Yarbrough* could be distinguished from *Minor* because private actions of intimidation were involved, not state qualifications for voting, and because somehow the requirement by states that electors be male was a lawful state qualification for voting and not an abridgement of the rights of females to vote. Thus, the crucial, if questionable, distinction that the Courts made between *Yarbrough* and *Minor* was based in part on the difference between the right of a state to set qualifications for voting and the actual abridgement of a citizen's right to vote. A sex qualification was by implication not an abridgement.

As if *Yarbrough* had not confused matters enough the Supreme Court then proceeded in 1886 to declare that corporations were 'persons' under the Fourteenth Amendment. This possibility had been raised during the original Congressional debates over the amendment and at the time a majority of Congressmen had clearly indicated that it was not their 'intent' to have businesses qualify as persons. Two decades later a burgeoning corporate structure prevailed over Congressional 'intent'. Finally, twenty-one years after *Bradwell*, the Supreme Court's contradicting array of decisions over women as persons, women as voters, and women as lawyers reached a logical extreme with *In re Lockwood*, 154 u.s. 116 (1894). This was the only case other than Myra Bradwell's to reach the Supreme Court because of a state's refusal to license a woman lawyer.

Belva A. Lockwood's legal career had a stormy history long before her appeal to the Supreme Court in 1894. As one of the first women to complete her law studies at National University Law School in Washington, D.C., she was denied her degree until she protested to President Ulysses S. Grant, who was *ex officio* president of the law school as well. 'You are, or you are not the President of the National University Law School,' she wrote in 1873. 'If you are its President I wish to say to you that I have been passed through the curriculum of study of that school, and am entitled to, and demand my Diploma.'[34] Her imperious manner was dutifully rewarded by Grant that same year when Lockwood was forty-three years old. While she was then admitted to the bar of the District of Columbia, in 1876 she was denied permission to practice before the Supreme Court of the United States. She overcame this obstacle by lobbying for federal legislation enabling all women lawyers the right to appear before the Supreme Court. In 1879 she became the first woman to benefit from the passage of this landmark statute. An avid suffragist, she ran for President of the United States as a candidate of the National Equal

Rights Party in 1884 and 1888.

Against this formidable background and reputation, the state of Virginia denied her the right to practice law, although she had already been admitted to the bars of several other states in addition to the District of Columbia and the Supreme Court. The state's bar admission act indicated that any 'person' who had been licensed to practice in any other state or in the District of Columbia could practice in Virginia. In this instance the Supreme Court of Appeals of Virginia decided that 'person' meant 'male' even though the Court had stated that women were both 'persons' and 'citizens' in *Minor*. It affirmed this position by refusing to issue a writ of *mandamus* ordering the state to admit Lockwood to practice. As in *Bradwell*, there was no mention of equal protection and *Bradwell* had already ruled against the privileges and immunities argument. The historical and legal importance of *Lockwood* lies in the fact that the Supreme Court chose to allow states to confine their definition of a 'person' to males only. This, of course, was exactly the same question that Anthony had first posed in Rochester, New York, when she had voted in 1872. From 1894 until 1971[35] states could maintain that women were not legally 'persons' by virtue of this single Supreme Court decision.

Three years after her 'persons' case had made Supreme Court history, negative as that was, Belva Lockwood, at the age of sixty-seven, enigmatically responded when asked if she considered herself a 'new woman'.

> As a rule I do not consider myself at all. I am, and always have been a progressive woman, and while never directly attacking the conventionalities of society, have always done, or attempted to do those things which I have considered conducive to my health, convenience or emolument, as for instance: Attended college and graduated when the general sentiment of the people was against it, and this after I had been a married woman. [Cites legal battles]. ... I was the first woman to ride a wheel [bicycle] in the District of Columbia, which I persisted in doing notwithstanding newspaper comments. ... I do not believe in sex distinction in literature, law, politics, or trade; or that modesty and virtue are more becoming to women than to men; but wish we had more of it everywhere. I was new about 60 years ago, but did not then appreciate my privileges.[36]

Despite these later reservations about her own accomplishments, Lockwood's life clearly represented a 'new way' for American women at the turn of the century. However, only the hardiest could follow in her footsteps.

LEGACY OF THE RECONSTRUCTION AMENDMENTS FOR BLACKS AND WOMEN

The *Lockwood* decision clearly indicated that judicial neutrality had not prevailed in post-Civil War gender cases. As women attempted to improve their legal status through various interpretations of the Reconstruction amendments, their efforts were thwarted by a series of overtly sexist decisions. Also, by interpreting the broad language of the Fourteenth Amendment so that it extended to only one of two groups normally denied equal rights under the law – blacks and women – the Supreme Court insured continuation for almost a century of the artificial distinction between the legal status of women and the legal status of blacks.[37] Both groups were now accorded citizenship but not equality before the law in fact, or even equality with each other. The passage of the Fourteenth and Fifteenth Amendments figuratively as well as literally separated the rights of women and the rights of blacks and contributed to the split within the women's movement in 1869. Indeed, they had been separate political issues all along even though they were logically and morally very similar. After all, the existence of slavery had caused a Civil War; the women's question was never accorded such status or intensity of feeling in the nineteenth century except on a personal, private level.[38] It was one thing for northern male abolitionists to free southern slaves – little would change in their personal lives as a result. It was entirely another matter for them to free their own women.

Male opposition to female rights following the Civil War is probably one of the major reasons behind the still incompletely explained split in the first women's movement in 1869 because some married women refused to oppose their husbands during the turbulent Reconstruction years. This split led to the formation of the National Woman Suffrage Association (NWSA) and the American Woman Suffrage Association (AWSA) – a division that lasted until 1890. Another reason for the disagreement among postwar female activists was the degree to which they personally felt legally humiliated by the Fourteenth and Fifteenth Amendments. These two Reconstruction amendments convinced some that the right to vote was through state level political activity. AWSA women preferred this more moderate form of activity compared to earlier court battles and agitation against the federal government.

The more militant women of NWSA, led by Anthony and Stanton, continued to reject all male politicians as turncoats when it came to the rights of women. They also continued to fight for a broad range of female rights in the courts as well as in the political arena. Because they opposed these two Reconstruction amendments and the presumably liberal Republicans who supported them, they left themselves open to the charge of racism, as more recently did the women who turned from the male dominated civil rights and antiwar activities of the 1960s to join the current women's movement. The more moderate post-Civil War female reformers, and most of their male colleagues, on the other hand, were more than willing to place the vote for black men ahead of the vote for women – black or white. This charge of racism against Anthony and Stanton reeked of hypocrisy. Their uncompromising stand was grounded in principle and received support by several prominent black leaders such as Sojourner Truth and Robert Purvis, whereas both Reconstruction amendments, historians have long agreed, were predicated more on political expediency than any belief in the equality of the races. Most simply stated, the northern-based Republican party saw the political potential of two million black male votes in the South and had no intention of letting the controversial women's question stand in the way of creating a power base in the formerly rebellious states.

Few, if any, Americans could rise above the prevailing racism of the day and this included the former male abolitionists, the suffragists, and the legal profession. Moreover, nations like the United States which possess written constitutions giving the courts powers to assert prescribed fundamental rights, have seen massive social, sexual, and racial subordination maintained by the judges under the rhetoric of equality. The English common law system, on the other hand, has flourished with equal vigor in the contexts of liberal democracy at home and slavery and colonial absolutism abroad. The greatest asset of law to rulers is that it converts great social issues relating to power into a series of *ad hoc* disputes concerned with rights, while maintaining at all times the appearance of procedural justice.

This is certainly what American women found to be true between 1865 and 1920. These years mark the first time that women systematically tried to obtain equality of treatment in the courts under the United States Constitution. While they did not succeed, in retrospect their attempts are interesting for a number of reasons. First, the few cases of major significance involving women clearly indicate the overwhelming legal obstacles that the several generations of women of these years faced almost regardless of the issues being discussed. Second, judicial patterns or preferences that emerged by 1920 from these cases lingered for many years – some down to the present. Third, there was also a subtle interaction between the political and legal activities of women reformers during this period. Their relationship has been largely ignored by both legal historians and historians of women's history.

It is now possible to trace how these two types of activity on the part of women varied in intensity *according to their perception of their legal status at any given time*. In fact, it can be argued that to the degree the courts discouraged female legal reform, women took political action as a form of compensation. Such compensatory political actions were often more conservative in nature than their initial court cases were. A similar but possibly less obvious relationship continues to exist today because women have still not found adequate legal means for obtaining equality of treatment.

So the legal and political implications of the Reconstruction amendments for the first women's movement were enormous. The Civil War itself had disrupted the momentum of the movement women had organised for their own fights since 1848. When the postwar political efforts of the more militant reformers, like Susan B. Anthony, failed to expressly include women in the Fourteenth and Fifteenth Amendments, they immediately began the first of a series of systematic attempts by several generations of women to use the courts to improve their legal and political status – first through the privileges and immunities clause, then through the due process clause, and finally, continuing down to the present, through the equal protection clause. To date, none of these attempts to apply these portions of the Fourteenth Amendment to women has been completely successful.

THE FIRST WOMEN'S MOVEMENT REACTS TO JUDICIAL DISCRIMINATION

Although the first women's movement in the United States is usually said to have begun with the Seneca Falls Convention of 1848, women did not effectively organise on behalf of their own rights until after the Civil War. They were only marginally involved in the passage of the Married Women's Property Acts in the 1840s and 1850s. In New York, for example, marital property legislation was passed in 1848 three months *before* the gathering at Seneca Falls. Elizabeth Cady Stanton later recalled that debate over the New York Married Women's Property bill first gave 'rise to some discussion of women's rights' and that its passage 'encouraged action on the part of women'.[39] Immediately following the Civil War women energetically took their campaign for rights to the courts. Many of them either were married to lawyers, were attempting to become lawyers, or like Susan B. Anthony were personally well-versed in the law. Consequently they quickly understood the enormity of their defeats in court within a decade following the war. As a result, they began to organise more and more along political rather than legal lines in the 1870s and 1880s.

One of the turning points in this realignment of the women's movement occurred at the centennial celebration of the American Revolution in 1876. After being refused a place on the program, Anthony and four other NWSA women insisted on formally presenting a 'Women's Declaration of Rights' during the official proceedings and passing out copies to the centennial audience. Beginnning with the words: 'The history of our country the past hundred years has been a series of assumptions and usurpations of power over women, in the direct opposition to the principles of just government', it called for the impeachment of all American leaders. With this declaration the original generation of women reformers turned more and more to political activities in part out of the realisation that they had failed to improve their legal status through the courts.

Their reorientation is reflected in the contrasts between the 1876 declaration and 1848 Seneca Falls one. By the time of the centennial, women no longer had to demand the right to speak in public or to participate in most religious and educational institutions. Consequently, the 1876 declaration stressed political and civil rights. In particular, disfranchisement, trial without a jury of peers, taxation without representation, the inequity and divergence of laws pertaining to married women in the various states and the inconsistencies in recent Supreme Court decisions pertaining to women were all underscored. Other social and cultural issues such as the double standard of morality, male dominance in marriage, inequitable divorce and child-custody settlements were all mentioned, but not given the prominence they had been accorded at Seneca Falls in 1848.

Clearly this was a sign of the times. It was becoming increasingly evident even to these militant reformers that they could not oppose the prevailing Victorian standards of morality and socio-economic mores, especially those associated with industrialisation and the modern nuclear family. By 1890 when the American and National leaders finally settled their differences and formed the National American Woman Suffrage Association (NAWSA) the right to vote was the single concern of this new organisation. This meant, among other things, that the question of married women's legal status received less and less attention by the turn of the century. When women finally achieved the right to vote in 1920, little had been done to improve the legal status of married women beyond the nineteenth-century Married Women's Property Acts. Questions of personhood, credit, wages, domicile, divorce settlements, child custody – even the right to a birth name – all had remained neglected or ignored in the fight for suffrage. A second women's movement would not emerge to take these issues up until the 1960s.

Nonetheless, there was some middle ground between the old radicalism of the first generation of women reformers and the conservatism of most second generation suffragists prior to 1920. It lay with a handful of women who were leaders in the progressive reform movement of the early twentieth century in addition to being suffragists. Some of them consciously attempted to link the social welfare wing of Progressivism with suffrage. These were the same women, like Jane Addams, Alice Hamilton, Lillian Wald, Grace and Edith Abbott, and Florence Kelley, who also tried to keep avenues of communication open between working and middle class women, and who resisted the anti-immigrant ethos so prevalent at the turn of the century. Moving from individual urban reform projects like settlement houses, such women soon realised that they needed political power to build better neighborhoods and to improve the deplorable working conditions of the urban masses. And so they formed or supported numerous national organisations dedicated to securing state legislation to make modern society more livable for all classes of people. Specifically, they supported protective labor legislation for *all* workers – men, women and children.

WOMEN AND PROTECTIVE LEGISLATION

Women, who particularly suffered under the factory system, had tried unsuccessfully since the 1820s to organise themselves in the face of discrimination not only by male employers, but by male trade unions as well. NAWSA did little that was practical to aid women workers although beginning in 1893 its annual convention platforms called for equal pay for equal work,[40] and encouraged working women to protect themselves by obtaining the right to vote. It is worth noting that when working women did begin to support the right to vote after the turn of the century, they did so as a means to an end – that is, to improve their economic plight, not as an end in itself as so many middle class women did.

Not until 1903, however, when the National Women's Trade Union League (NWTUL) formed, did middle class women collectively begin to assist working women in organising themselves within the existing sex segregated labor market and male dominated trade unions. Led by middle and upper class women, they organised support for strikes by women workers and occasionally made the American Federation of Labor (AFL) consider more seriously its discriminatory practices against female laborers. By seldom questioning or attacking male dominance within the union system or the capitalist system, the NWTUL never became a radical force in American labor history. While the NWTUL made no attempt to end the sex stereotyping of two-thirds of all the types of work women performed then, it should be noted that the same percentage of 'female' jobs exists today despite recent efforts to eradicate gender differentiation in the job market. Probably the most valuable contribution of the NWTUL to the plight of working women was the support it gave to obtaining protective labor laws. Two other middle class women's organisations participated in the protective law effort: the General Federation of Women's Clubs and the National Consumers' League (NCL) – the latter being the major force behind lobbying for protective legislation.

By 1908 there were nineteen laws setting maximum hours for women and/or prohibiting night work for women. However, the constitutionality of such legislation was in question because three years earlier in *Lochner v. New York*, 198 U.S. 45 (1905), involving a limit on working hours for male bakers, the Supreme Court had invalidated state protective legislation on substantive, rather than procedural due process grounds. The decision stated in essence that this kind of protective restriction could not be imposed by the state on these men because it violated the constitutional rights of personal liberty and the liberty of contract. The court's *Lochner* decision clearly stood in the way of protective legislation for women as well as men, and so in the next protective legislation case to reach the Supreme Court, which involved a woman, a new defense had to be devised. The case turned out to be *Muller v. Oregon*, 208 u.s. 412 (1908). Prior to this decision a number of state Supreme Courts had issued decisions both validating and invalidating protective legislation for women. The NCL as co-counsel with Oregon state's Attorney General and represented by Louis D. Brandeis could have argued its case against *Muller* (who had been convicted of requiring a female employee to work more than ten hours in violation of state law) in one of two ways. It could have tried to displace the 'common understanding' argument in *Lochner* about the lack of health dangers in bakeries or any industrial job by using empirical, sociological evidence to show that any such job performed steadily for more than ten hours a day was dangerous to a worker's health *or* it could have argued that because women were involved there was reason to make an exception to the *Lochner* doctrine of liberty of contract on the grounds that women needed 'special protection' because there was 'something special or different' about them.

FROM BRANDEIS TO BANISHMENT

Theoretically the famous 113 page 'Brandeis brief' combined both approaches by presenting statistical and sociological data from non-judicial sources collected primarily by female volunteers like Josephine and Pauline Goldmark. In actuality, however, the brief (and later the decision) focused primarily on the physical differences between men and women and in particular on women's biologically reproductive, rather than her economically productive, role in society. Thus, the majority opinion did not really consider the individual working woman involved in the case in terms of either her working conditions or her performance on the job. Instead, the Court concentrated on her procreative functions and those of all American working women.

In ruling in favor of the state the Supreme Court used language and attitudes reminiscent of the *Anthony*, *Bradwell* and *Minor* cases. In addition, it incorporated the *Dred Scott* argument that the 'women as citizens' constituted a special category. Thus, the Court agreed with Brandeis and the NCL that limitations could be placed on a woman's right to contract in the interest of the 'future well-being of the race' and avoided any direct confrontation or contradiction of the *Lochner* doctrine. Specifically the *Muller* decision said:

That woman's physical structure and the performance of maternal functions place her at a disadvantage in the struggle for subsistence is obvious. This is especially true when the burdens of motherhood are upon her. Even when they are not, by abundant testimony of the medical fraternity continuance for a long time on her feet at work, repeating this from day to day, tends to injurious effects upon the body, and as healthy mothers are essential to vigorous offspring, the physical well-being of women becomes an object of public interest and care in order to preserve the strength and vigor of the race.

Still again, history discloses the fact that woman has always been dependent upon man. He established his control at the outset by superior physical strength, and this control in various forms, with diminishing intensity, has continued to the present. As minors, though not to the same extent, she has been looked upon in the courts as needing especial care that her rights may be preserved ... even with the consequent increase of capacity for business affairs it is still true that in the struggle for subsistence she is not an equal competitor with her brother. Though limitations upon personal and contractual rights may be removed by legislation, there is that in her disposition and habits of life which will operate against a full assertion of those rights. ... Differentiated by these matters from the other sex, she is properly placed in a class by herself, and legislation designed for her protection may be sustained, even when like legislation is not necessary for men and could not be sustained.

The impact of the 1908 *Muller* decision on the history of protective legislation for working women was immediate and should not be underestimated. Some states which had taken anti-protective stands now reversed themselves; others began to extend the doctrine of sex differences to obtain all kinds of protective and often excessively restrictive laws governing work hours for women; still others tried to extend the doctrine to uphold minimum-wage laws for women or for women and minors. This attempt to establish minimum wages was struck down by the Supreme Court fifteen years later in *Adkins v. Children's Hospital*, 261 U.S. 525 (1923). Again, the National Consumers' League was involved as an *amicus curiae* and used the 'Brandeis approach'. Only this time, because wages and not hours were involved, the Court appeared more concerned with freedom of contract of the employers than with the welfare of the employees.

In the nineteenth century women had been treated differently from men by the courts primarily on the basis of divine insight which judges apparently received directly from the 'Creator' they so often cited. In the first half of the twentieth century they began to 'protect' women because of their presumed physiological deficiencies with barely more evidentiary foundation than existed one hundred years before. Judicial neutrality unclouded by male bias and corporate favoritism could have dictated in *Adkins* that substandard wages and accompanying malnutrition would damage a woman's procreative potential as much, if not more, than working too many hours as *Muller* had proclaimed. Instead, the collective 'common sense' of the Court found in *Adkins* that while it was unconstitutional to have women work long hours because it would inhibit their ability to produce healthy children, it was equally unconstitutional to force employers to pay a minimum wage to insure the continued health of mothers and their offspring. In *Muller* women had to pay an economic price for future generations; in *Adkins* employers did not. Ironically the Court acted not only on the basis of judicial common sense in *Adkins*, but also apparently under the influence of the Nineteenth Amendment granting equal voting rights to women.[41] The judicial denial of minimum wages both to men and women was not reversed until 1937 by *West Coast Hotel v. Parrish*, 300 U.S. 379 (1937), when judicial neutrality fell victim to the Great Depression and New Deal labor legislation.

By that time, however, the discriminatory application of protective legislation against women was a fact of American economic life largely due to lower court decision with the encouragement and approval of most former suffragists and male union leaders. Beyond any doubt *Muller* opened the door to gender bias in protective legislation. At the time, however, the decision was welcomed by progressive reformers in general because it did improve some of the worst conditions women faced in an unregulated factory system. Moreover, further protective legislation that followed in the wake of *Muller* convinced a number of female activists that their needs were being met by the courts. This belief actually lulled them into a state of complacency. Only a handful of the most militant feminists in 1908 saw the future danger of the *Muller* decision: it could be used to keep women from advancement on the job and out of some occupations altogether. This is, of course, exactly what happened over the years. The AFL almost immediately reversed its initial support of protective legislation for men, women and children and proceeded to use the biological differences between men and women as the basis for reducing competition from women and children in certain industries. It officially banished women from so-called 'men's jobs' such as streetcar conducting, printing, and bartending; it sanctioned unequal pay for men and women even when the work was equal; and it established separate lists for men and women. From 1908 until the present, all such exclusion tactics have successfully been used by the AFL and other male dominated unions to keep women from competing in the labor market on an equal basis with men.

In retrospect, therefore, despite the constitutional breakthrough it represented at the time, it is possible to question the wisdom of the Brandeis approach in *Muller*. Women have continued to experience economic discrimination because the Supreme Court presumed to establish policy on the basis of quasi-scientific data and its own 'common knowledge' about the nature of women. However needed protective legislation was at the time to ameliorate the worst features of the capitalist factory system in the United States, we can now easily perceive the anti-feminist and reactionary legal and economic implications of the *Brandeis* brief. As has been the case so many times before in the history of the women's legal and political reform, what appeared to be such a great improvement ended up a mixed blessing at best.

It is also worth noting that the famous *Muller* decision based on the *Brandeis* brief actually represented an exception to the general run of Supreme Court decisions. Generally Justices refused to accept empirical data of a nonjudicial nature and expressed extreme skepticism about so-called expert witnesses. In other words, from around the turn of the century until the 1937 *West Coast Hotel* decision, the *Lochner* precedent prevailed in theory if not in fact, except in cases involving nonminimum wage protective legislation for women. Lawrence Tribe has pointed out that 'While the Supreme Court invalidated much state and federal legislation between 1897 and 1939 [approximately 197 cases], more statutes in fact withstood due process attack in this period than succumbed to it'. Under the influence of the Progressive movement, the Court held almost three times fewer state police power statutes unconstitutional between 1889 and 1918 than it did between 1920 and 1930.[42] However interpreted, '*Lochnerism*' is less significant a constitutional concept where women are concerned than where men are because of the exceptional precedent set by *Muller*.

THE DEMISE OF THE FIRST WOMEN'S MOVEMENT

Another interesting aspect of *Muller* is its indirect impact on the first women's movement. Most women political activists had concentrated their efforts in the first two decades of the twentieth century on obtaining suffrage. The movement in general had not attempted to influence state or federal court decisions on protective legislation, although individual women reformers supported such legislation. After its political triumph in 1920 with the passage of the Nineteenth Amendment, the first women's movement once again succumbed to internal divisions. Some of these were already evident before and during the First World War with the establishment of the radical National Woman's Party. In the 1920s total disintegration occurred over the Equal Rights Amendment. Just as many 'pure' or radical feminists had refused to accept suffrage as a simplistic panacea for women's and society's ills, so had they fought the sexist implications of protective legislation that applied only to women. But their voices had been drowned out before the First World War by a sea of respectable suffragists and female social welfare Progressives. Expediency and suffrage had prevailed and when women did not vote as a bloc to produce the utopian society promised, the right to vote came to be regarded as a hollow victory by even its staunchest supporters. In fact, in the course of the 1920s suffrage came to be looked upon in many circles as a major moral failure – not unlike the attitude of many toward the classic attempt to legislate morality in that decade – Prohibition.

Progressives like Jane Addams and Florence Kelley, who had worked so hard for both suffrage and protective legislation for women, refused to support the Equal Rights Amendment when it was introduced in the 1920s by the militants in the National Woman's Party led by Alice Paul. Support of complete legal equality with men would have negated the recently hard-won victories of these moderates and would have forced them to reconsider the crucial question of working within established capitalist parameters. This they were not prepared to do. It was indeed a confusing time for women. They still did not have true economic independence, equal social expectations, political experience, or even the educational and professional training necessary for obtaining leadership in politics. At the same time they were faced with the post-First World War reaction against socio-economic change disguised under the superficially liberating glitter of the Jazz Age and Freudian theories on sexuality. Finally women were confronted by a depression in 1929 that turned 'Flappers' back into 'Gibson Girls' overnight, as traditional values were once more reasserted and men given preference for jobs. The first women's movement could hardly have survived even had it not been plagued by similar internal divisions over strategy and tactics and personality between the radicals and the moderates – very similar to those that had plagued the original generation of female reformers after the Civil War.

Certain limited political, legal, educational, and economic objectives had been obtained. But, as in the past, radical feminists of the 1920s discovered that full emancipation still lay ahead and recent achievements had been too little, too late. Women obtained the right to vote, not in the nineteenth century when it would have been truly significant in terms of the grassroots legacy of Jacksonian politics, but in the twentieth century at the very time when electoral politics in the United States was breaking down into a meaningless choice between Tweedle-dum and Tweedle-dumber. This was due largely to the manipulation of public opinion through new developments in mass media communication and the pluralist assumption that 'packaged' candidates and campaigns are necessary for the smooth and efficient operation of the American economic and political system. It now looks as though women are at long last going to receive equal pay for work and equal opportunity to compete for positions with men in a declining job market.

A handful of militants in the 1920s like Alice Paul, Anne Henrietta Martin, and Burnita Shelton Matthews, saw that the vote was at best an inefficient tool and that all inequalities in the law pertaining to jury service, property rights, marriage, divorce, and work had to be eradicated before women could truly exercise the right to vote in any meaningful manner.[43] Above all, the vote had not eliminated sex discrimination in American life. But in the 1920s there were too few women liberated enough to appreciate this argument or to use the vote effectively and there were too few former suffragists who were militant enough to carry on endless legal battles against male bias in the name of justice and humanity.

Their descendants in the 1960s and 1970s have taken up where the militants of the 1920s left off with the Equal Rights Amendment and the old Seneca Falls arguments against 'marital bondage', pointing out the remaining economic and legal disabilities of women within the nuclear family. Once again white middle class women are leading this second women's movement because, as in the past, they were the first to benefit from and hence respond to the contradictions and frustrations of changing socio-economic and political conditions in the United States. After thirty years of quiescence they were awakened from the post-Second World War dream of the 'feminine mystique' by the civil rights movement, counter culture, further educational and post-educational advancement, the war in Vietnam, and rising but not yet equal, social expectations among women. Two hundred years after the American Revolution and one hundred and twenty after Seneca Falls, the struggle continues. Will it end with too little, too late, as it has so many times in the past?

THE CONSTITUTIONAL RIGHTS OF FEMALE BARTENDERS AND JURORS

To the degree that the federal Constitution of the United States was based on eighteenth-century common law as the ideal of liberty and justice, it created an exclusively masculine system of justice. Since most of the increases in the legal rights and socio-economic liberties of women 'have been in derogation of common law', [44] they have been made in spite of, not because of, the American Constitution. Before 1900, for example, none of the amendments to, or interpretations of, the Constitution enhanced the legal status of women. The Nineteenth Amendment of 1920, which granted the franchise to females, remains the only successful attempt to include women by sex in the Constitution. The successful passage of the Equal Rights Amendment would represent the second. As late as 1934 a Maine court reiterated that under the Fourteenth Amendment 'the liberty thus assured' is 'to enjoy those privileges long recognised at common law as essential to the orderly pursuit of happiness by free men'.[45] To this day American women have not been included in the Constitution through judicial interpretation in an unambiguous way that guarantees them equal protection under the law. The reason for this is primarily male bias reinforced by the fact that English common law did not originally accord liberty and equality to women.

Discrimination based on sex is not yet *unconstitutional* in the United States. Sex discrimination is *illegal* under certain prescribed conditions by virtue of federal legislation and presidential Executive Orders of the 1960s and 1970s (see pages 210–11 below). Generally speaking, for the past two decades judicial interpretations of the Constitution have consistently lagged behind some state and most federal legislation in guaranteeing equality before the law to women. Two or three recent exceptions notwithstanding, United States Supreme Court decisions based on stereotypic views of women have not changed substantially in the last century despite the existence of two separate women's rights movements. This is not to say that the Justices remain unaware of changing public opinion, but they have proven more impervious to new societal values on the question of sex than on those related to race or national origins. It has been the American Congress which has recently led the way in trying to overcome sex discrimination – not the American judicial system, excepting again a handful of federal or state court decisions.

Before the 1960s, however, Congress, as well as the Supreme Court, deferred to state legislatures in matters involving sex discrimination. Under the Constitution states have the right to pass statutes based on gender and other class or group distinctions if it is deemed in the public interest. When the Fourteenth Amendment says that states cannot 'deny to any person within its jurisdiction the equal protection of the laws', it does not mean that states cannot discriminate among categories of individuals. Technically there has to be a reasonable connection (or 'rationale') between a blanket classification and the public policy or purpose for which any law has been enacted. In most instances the burden of proof rests with the person who charges that any particular classification discriminates unfairly between different groups of people. Blue-eyed people cannot be prevented from driving cars, but people with poor eye-sight can be required to wear glasses because the latter is considered a reasonable classification, while the former is not.

Another test of state legislation involves those few actions that the Supreme Court has designated as fundamental or basic rights, such as voting, interstate travel and reproductive freedom. In these cases the state must show some 'compelling interest' why it is differentiating among classes of individuals. This is referred to as 'strict scrutiny' and a state cannot simply argue that its discriminatory classification is reasonable. This traditional 'reasonable generalisation' standard based on fundamental rights explicitly or implicitly guaranteed by the Constitution, is not the one that is applied to discrimination based on race, religion, or national origin. Here the question is not what *rights* people have to engage in certain fundamental activities, but *who* these people are. Sex would seem to be similarly qualified for suspect categorisation.[46] To date, it has not been held by any majority of Supreme Court Justices to be a 'suspect classification' which would automatically subject all state laws discriminating on the basis of sex to active review, that is, strict scrutiny. Consequently state legislative power remains more pervasive in the area of sex discrimination than in any other broad categorisations of citizens by inherent physical and cultural characteristics over which they have no conscious or voluntary control.

Therefore it is not surprising that the interpretation by state legislatures of public policy did little to improve the legal position of women before 1900, except minimally through a variety of Married Women's Property Acts. In any case, an expansion of the legal rights of women through legislative statutes at the state level *does not enhance their constitutional rights*. When such state statutes reflect changing public opinion, they do contribute to a gradual under-mining of views about women embodied in eighteenth-century interpretations of common law. By themselves, however, they do not give women the necessary constitutional rights to protect themselves from future sex discrimination by state legislatures, Congress, or the Supreme Court. Arguments have been used successfully in the past to prevent females from practicing medicine and law, from tending bars and serving on juries. Such arguments were not valid for white males because it was assumed that they had all possible constitutional rights, particularly those under the first section of the Fourteenth Amendment. Women and minorities have had to fight political and legal battles for over a century to begin to obtain these same rights under the federal Constitution.

In 1948, for example, the Supreme Court upheld a state statute that denied women the right to be bartenders unless they were wives or daughters of male tavern owners.[47] Although state and federal judges have ignored or attempted to differentiate this opinion forbidding 'all women from working behind a bar', as recently as 1970 the Supreme Court again approved its 1948 position.[48] The most direct challenge issued to the Supreme Court to reconsider its sex based discrimination in the area of liquor sales came in 1971 in a California case, *Sail'er Inn, Inc. v. Kirby*. In a most far-reaching decision the state Supreme Court declared:

> Today most bars, unlike the saloons of the Old West, are relatively quiet, orderly and respectable places patronized by both men and women. Even if they were not, many bars employ bouncers whose sole job is to keep order in the establishment. ... Women must be permitted to take their chances along with men when they are otherwise qualified and capable of meeting the requirements of their employment. ... We can no more justify denial of the means of earning a livelihood on such a basis than we could deny all women drivers' licenses to protect them from the risk of injury by drunk drivers. Such tender and chivalrous concern for the well-being of the female half of the adult population cannot be translated into legal restrictions on employment opportunities for women. ... Laws which disable women from full participation in the political, business and economic arenas are often characterized as 'protective' and beneficial. Those same laws applied to racial or ethnic minorities would readily be recognized as invidious and impermissible. The pedestal upon which women have been placed has all too often, upon closer inspection, been revealed as a cage. We conclude that the sexual classifications are properly treated as suspect, particularly when those classifications are made with respect to a fundamental interest such as employment.[49]

The Supreme Court of the United States has not shown any

inclination to take up the gauntlet of *Sail'er*, although under Title VII most of this type of discrimination is now illegal (see pages 210–18 below). It has finally, however, revised its views on the right of women to serve on juries. Under common law jury duty in colonial America was exclusively the preserve of white males. Then in 1879 the Supreme Court held that the exclusion of blacks from juries denied them equal protection and due process under the Fourteenth Amendment.[50] In this same decision, however, the Justices specifically said that states could continue to 'confine selection [of jurors] to males'. Clearly, the Fourteenth Amendment did not apply to sex – only to race. In 1884 a female defendant, who had been indicted by a grand jury in the Territory of Washington, charged that the presence of married women in that body was unconstitutional. The territorial Supreme Court ruled to the contrary saying that since women could vote in the area and control property under the local Married Women's Act, they were indeed both 'qualified electors' and 'householders'. Judge Turner so strongly dissented that three years later the same court overruled its original decision and barred women from jury duty, as was the common practice in most states and territories at the time.

In light of subsequent decisions Judge Turner's dissenting opinion represented a milestone in the history of male bias in judicial decisions. He argued that married women could not be either 'householders' or jurors despite the 'advanced ideas of the nineteenth century' because they were

> unfitted by physical constitution and mental characteristics to assume and perform the civil and political duties and obligations of citizenship. . . . The liability to perform jury duty is an obligation not a right. In the case of a woman, it is not necessary that she should accept the obligation to secure or maintain her rights. If it were, I should stifle all expression of the repugnance that I feel at seeing her introduced into associations, and exposed to influences which, however others regard it, must, in my opinion, shock and blunt those fine sensibilities, the possession of which is her chiefest charm [*sic*], and the protection of which . . . is her most sacred right. . . . The husband was not only the head of the family at common law, because under the law he had the right to be obeyed by all the family, including the wife, but because of inherent and acquired differences between himself and wife in mental and physical constitution. . . . I believe that the facts I have mentioned obtain to this day, and that they operate and will continue to operate to give the husband paramount authority in the household . . . until an upheaval of nature has reversed the position of man and woman in the world. Legislative enactment would not make white black, nor can it provide the female form with bone and sinew equal in strength to that with which nature has provided man. No more can it

reverse the law of cause and effect, and clothe a timid, shrinking woman, whose life theater is and will continue to be and ought to continue to be, primarily the home circle, with the masculine will and self-reliant judgment of a man.[51]

Not until after the First World War and the passage of the Nineteenth Amendment did the question of female eligibility for jury service again appear in numerous litigations. By then women could vote and consequently it appeared that they were finally 'qualified electors' under most state statutes. However, most state legislatures did not follow this logic, nor did the Supreme Court. In a series of cases in the 1930s and 1940s the Court held that when a state assembly 'used the word "person" in connection with those qualified to vote [or] to describe those liable to jury service, no one contemplated the possibility of women becoming so qualified. . . . No intention to include women can be deduced from the word male'.[52] And so it went. By 1942 only twenty-eight states permitted women to serve on juries and fifteen of these allowed them to claim exemption because of their sex. Twenty other states disqualified female jurors summarily. By 1962 despite the passage of the Civil Rights Act of 1957 insuring the right of women to sit on *federal* juries, twenty-one states still did not permit them to serve on lower level juries equally with men. By 1973 women could sit on juries in all fifty states, but in nineteen they were singled out for special exemptions, ranging from pregnancy and minor children to embarrassment and simple request as a female. Very often the rationale for these exemptions was based on *Fay v. New York*, 332 U.S. 261 (1947) and *Hoyt v. Florida*, 368 U.S. 57 (1961). In *Fay* the Supreme Court implied that women did not have a constitutional right to serve on juries, saying:

> The contention that women should be on the jury is not based on the Constitution, it is based on a changing view of the rights and responsibilities of women in all phases of life. . . . Woman jury service has not so become a part of the textual or customary law of the land that one convicted of crime must be set free [if the jury does not include women].

In *Hoyt* the Court ruled that a state law was constitutional when it automatically exempted women from jury duty unless they expressed an affirmative desire to serve. The female defendant in this 1961 case, unlike the woman in 1884, insisted that she was entitled to a jury made up of both men and women. She had been convicted by an all male jury of murdering her husband with a baseball bat. The Supreme Court viewed the Florida statute as one based on reasonable classification. Realising that this would mean under-representation of women on juries, the Court nonetheless maintained such a sexual imbalance 'in no way resembles those involving race or colour' because in *Hoyt* there was 'neither the unfortunate atmosphere of ethnic or racial prejudices ... nor the long course of discriminatory administrative practice ...'. Because he did not acknowledge the existence of an 'unfortunate atmosphere' created over the years by gender discrimination, Justice Harlan employed language reminiscent of Judge Turner seventy-seven years earlier when he said:

> Despite the enlightened emancipation of women from restrictions and protections of bygone years, and their entry into many parts of the community life formerly reserved for men, woman is still regarded as the center of the home and family life.

Although at least one federal court in Alabama declared in 1966 that the exclusion of women juries was a violation of the equal protection clause of the Fourteenth Amendment, state courts did not follow suit, nor has the Supreme Court so ruled. Two 1970 opinions issued by New York courts once again upheld the exemption of women from jury duty as a reasonable practice. In fact, one opinion was very much in keeping with the sexist ideology of both Judge Turner and Justice Harlan because it was based on assumptions about prescribed roles for women that go back to antiquity and have no 'reasonable' place in the modern legal system except to perpetuate male bias. It said:

> Granted that some women pursue business careers, the great majority constitute the heart of the home, where they are busily engaged in the 24-hour task of producing and rearing children, providing a home for the entire family, and performing the daily household work, all of which demands their full energies. Although some women now question this arrangement, the state legislature has permitted the exemption in order not to risk disruption of the basic family unit. Its action was far from arbitrary.[53]

Not until 1975 did the Supreme Court of the United States overrule *Hoyt*. In *Taylor v. Louisiana*, 419 U.S. 522 (1975) it held that a statute denying a male defendant (ironically in this case accused of rape) trial by a jury composed of a cross section of the community violated his rights under the Sixth Amendment. *Taylor* did not specify that women had the right to serve on juries on equal terms with men. However disappointing this decision was because it *did not* make sex a suspect classification under the Fourteenth Amendment it nevertheless had the effect of invalidating all remaining state laws restricting jury duty on the basis of gender.

Such unexpected and often circuitous victories over sex discrimination have multiplied in recent years. In retrospect, it is clear that despite the existence of the federal Constitution the technical arguments offered by American judges to uphold female exclusion from juries differed from those employed by the British judges, but the results were remarkably similar, as were the rationalisations used. From a formal point of view, the American judges were deciding on the constitutionality of provisions that for the most part expressly excluded women, whereas British judges were determining the precise meaning in law to be given to words in allegedly ambiguous statutes. Yet similar conceptions of womanhood led both British and American judges to use what judicial power their respective legal systems granted them to rule in favour of male monopoly and against female advancement. A recent survey made of judicial decisions in gender-based cases in the United States concludes with the observation that male dominated courts in that country historically followed male dominated legislatures in exhibiting the belief that women were and ought to be confined to the social roles of homemaker, wife and mother.[54] From the litigant's point of view it mattered little that British judges acknowledged their subordination to Parliament whereas American judges claimed the power to strike down unconstitutional legislation. Both sets of judges were induced by their general view of womanhood to find technically appropriate means of affirming male supremacy.

FEMALE LITIGANTS AND THE AMERICAN CRIMINAL JUSTICE SYSTEM

The inadequate constitutional protection extended to women against discrimination on the basis of sex has seldom been perceived by the American judiciary as debilitating. Instead, it has been argued that women's lack of rights under common law resulted in lenient or preferential treatment under the Constitution. The 'chivalry factor' is the euphemism used to describe the alleged leniency rather than justice that women experience in the courts.[55] It is particularly evident in the criminal justice process where women are seldom viewed as adult persons, but rather as dependent persons who cannot take care of themselves and who must be protected. This largely unconscious paternalism pervades the American legal system and knows no class boundaries.[56] For example, women are sentenced to longer jail terms than men who have committed the same crime on the grounds that their basically docile, malleable natures will profit from behavior modification programs inside prisons. Conversely the chivalry factor results in less harsh treatment of female than of male felons prior to sentencing.[57] Nonwhite females receive somewhat harsher treatment in terms of pretrial confinement, dismissals, acquittals and percentage of convictions. If questions of juvenile morality arise paternalism automatically results in a legal double standard with the reverse impact of the chivalry factor, whereby the sexual misbehavior of girls is viewed more seriously and punished more severely than the similar misbehavior in boys.[58]

There is no doubt that adult female criminal offenders have enjoyed certain benefits of the chivalry factor in the American legal system. They are arrested, prosecuted, and institutionalised less often than men. Paternalism can mean freedom to such women. The price these and other women pay for the supposed benefits of paternalism is a perpetuation of a state of public consciousness which holds that women are less able than men and therefore in need of protective treatment. This in turn results in extensive personal, psychological, social, economic and political damage to women offenders, whether or not they are aware of the longer sentences they receive or the crippling features of the rehabilitation programs to which they are routinely subjected.

Paternalistic criminal justice, however well intentioned, also violates the democratic notion of self-determination and equality. The alleged advantages accruing to all classes of American women because of their lack of constitutional status and hence ambiguous legal position have to be weighed against the obvious disadvantages of treatment based on archaic views of the innately inferior characteristics of females. If paternalism is literally or figuratively equated with freedom for all classes of women, it must be remembered that if the 'free' woman is assigned to a pedestal by the courts she will ultimately find the space uncomfortably confining.

Judicial paternalism is only one form of unequal treatment for women in the courtroom. The increasing number of cases in the United States focusing on well known women in civil and criminal litigations has alerted us to another kind of male bias, especially in cases involving radical or violent political behavior on the part of female defendants. This bias is compounded when these women are represented by female attorneys (see pages 192–5). For example, whether Patricia Hearst is ultimately found guilty or innocent of the many charges brought against her for actions committed after she was kidnapped in February, 1974, the legal questions will remain: was she ever judged as a 'person' in her own right or was she inevitably the victim of sex, class and cultural discrimination? From the very beginning public sentiment in California was hostile toward her on account of both her wealthy family and her association with the radical/hippy Symbionese Liberation Army (SLA). When she was convicted of armed bank robbery in the spring of 1976, Americans all over the country were satisfied that justice had prevailed because her trial symbolised all of the following, according to one reporter on the scene.

> The rich cannot buy their way out of things. A stern lesson has been administered to terrorists. The victim is seen to have been asking for it all along. Flashy out-of-town lawyers and fast-talking shrinks have been beaten back by just plain folks. The government, like the big bad wolf, disguises its appetite for radicals beneath the lacy cap of egalitarianism, and in their pleasure at the fate of the rich snitch, the people rush to get into bed with Grandma.[59]

Outside of 'ratting on her radical friends' and 'asking for it', these simplistic, reassuring reasons from groups on the Left and Right do not touch what many feminists believe to be the underlying causes of conviction in *U.S.A. v. Patricia Campbell Hearst*, namely, the sex-stereotyped perceptions of the judge, jury, and even her own male attorneys. Judge Oliver Carter and the women and men of the jury appeared to view her in one of two ways – either as an ungrateful daughter or 'uppity' woman who had lived unmarried with her boyfriend in a Berkeley apartment – or both. Her passively docile answers during the trial, especially the often repeated response to government prosecutor James Browning, 'I just don't know what happened to me', were lost upon ears that also heard her cite the Fifth Amendment against self-incrimination when asked about events unrelated to the bank robbery. Browning doggedly portrayed her as willful and independent. The jury probably would have reacted positively to her only if convinced she really embodied the virtues of Miss Teenage America. Her defense based on theories of 'coercive persuasion', brainwashing similar to that experienced by Korean prisoners of war, and 'personality destruction via terror' proved totally ineffective. That she was not a virgin, might have smoked grass as a teenager (she was only nineteen when kidnapped), felt ambivalent about getting married, and used abusive and foul language against her parents and other authority figures counted more than any complex state of 'demoralised acquiescence', or involuntary actions based on diminished capacity due to duress.[60]

Considering that Hearst was held captive in a closet off and on for fifty-seven days during which time she was sexually assaulted by both SLA leader Donald 'Cinque' DeFreeze and William Wolfe, it becomes all the more amazing that sexist and cultural assumptions about her previous behavior were held against her. Even if the members of the jury did not believe that she had been raped, why could they not empathise with other physical hardships she endured for most of those eight weeks? The prosecution never even seriously disputed that she initially had been allowed to eat, bathe, and use the bathroom only when her captors permitted.[61] Yet the jury doubted that this self-proclaimed terrorist group, which had already taken credit for the murder of Oakland educator Marcus Foster, could be capable of subjecting her to mental anguish and physical abuse? One juror later said the SLA 'appeared to treat her in some reasonable fashion' (assuming the treatment of any kidnap victim can be deemed reasonable). Still another said that the jury finally 'didn't think she had been in the closet that long ... we felt she had been in the closet only two weeks'.[62] More important, why was this shattering experience not argued in simple, human terms – a frightened young woman, who in all likelihood did not know her own mind before or after her kidnapping and intimidation by fanatic terrorists? Surely, not simply because Patricia Hearst was a 'rich bitch'.

Judge Carter's series of evidentiary rulings enormously decreased chances that defense attorneys F. Lee Bailey and Albert Johnson may have had to break through the sex-stereotyped views of the jury. The appeal of her conviction was based on the now deceased judge's rulings 'allowing the jury to receive evidence offered by the government and against allowing the jury to receive evidence offered by the defense'. Bailey and Johnson have also charged the late Judge Carter with a number of 'judicial errors', including admitting evidence which was illegally seized and which was not admitted in the trial of her former companions Bill and Emily Harris; permitting testimony by two prosecution psychiatrists on the key issues of duress and 'voluntariness', while excluding testimony on the same subject by two defense psychiatrists, one of whom was a woman (observers later reported that the elderly judge felt uncomfortable about female expert witnesses); allowing a tape recording of a jail conversation in which she said she was 'pissed off' to be admitted; and forcing her to take the Fifth Amendment by permitting questions unrelated to the particular crime with which she was charged.[63]

We shall never know why Judge Carter made these rulings. Taken together they reflect some common, contradictory male images of women. Independence is a moral defect when exhibited by women, yet 'demoralised acquiescence' (she did not physically resist her captors) is apparently a condition only male prisoners of war can credibly claim. Diminished capacity and duress are often assumed in cases involving kidnapping, but not when the defendant is a famous (or infamous), willful, wealthy female. Although guilt or innocence cannot always be determined by cause and effect relationships, in disallowing consideration of cause, Judge Carter appears to have 'dictated the verdict of guilty', as her attorneys have contended.

A feminist analysis of Hearst's first trial does not stop with suspicions about the sexist inclinations of the judge and women and men of the jury. It also questions the basic tenor of her defense. F. Lee Bailey, the chief counsel, was widely quoted in the San Francisco press as saying his prime interest was in freeing his clients – not in obtaining justice for them. Moreover, his brainwashing, 'coercive persuasion' approach was didactically male, and curiously unmoving given the dramatic and emotional circumstances of the case. It is not surprising, therefore, that he never succeeded in explaining her dependency on, yet fear of, her SLA kidnappers or in presenting a convincing case for how her apparently brazen actions and language were the product of a mind brainwashed into vacuousness. Neither did Bailey ever satisfactorily document that the SLA employed any but the most primitive brainwashing techniques, nor why she might have gratefully welcomed the SLA's ostentatious acceptance of her as a self-proclaimed revolutionary.

Hearst was neither a man nor a victim of a concentration camp, but an impressionable young woman who exhibited symptoms of personality destruction, docility, and infantile regression upon her arrest, according to one of the male psychiatrists (who was allowed to testify for the defense) and the one female psychiatrist (who was not). Even her well-publicised revolutionary name 'Tanya' did not last for more than a few weeks of the nineteen months she 'survived' with various members of the SLA. During her underground exodus across the country Bill and Emily Harris renamed her 'Pearl', a clear indication of at least their opinion of her lack of revolutionary zeal.[64] It is possible to explain Hearst's passive, regressive condition in standard psychological terms and military metaphors, as both her lawyers and psychiatrists for the defense did. That she 'didn't do anything' to resist the initial physical and mental abuse, then appeared to 'identify with the aggressor' by joining her captors in several criminal acts, and finally passed up opportunities to escape when she had every possibility – these facts do not need to be rationalised by exotic mind-control techniques of modern warfare or the latest psychotherapeutic theories.[65] All are characteristics exhibited by a certain group of women for centuries, namely those who are victims of what used to be called 'white slavery'. Women who have been captured and sold into sexual slavery[66] do not resist, do ingratiate themselves with their masters, and seldom try to escape, regardless of the opportunity. Once they have been sexually humiliated, cut off from traditional normative patterns, and then rewarded for compliance, these women have universally demonstrated one goal: *personal survival by any means necessary.*

Before and after her first trial it was evident to many feminists that this age-old, documented phenomenon of what happens to 'captive women' was the only defense that could be made to explain her seemingly contradictory actions. Hearst was obviously guilty of robbing a bank with a gun in her hand. Pictures proved that. Since her wealth and fame would not allow for dismissal on the normal grounds of duress that a less well-to-do defendant might have been permitted, and since the FBI wanted the heretofore elusive and 'dangerous radical' prosecuted, no normal, male adversary defense was possible. The only logical defense would have been a feminist one based on what had happened to her as a human being socialised for nineteen years to be an American female. Such a strategy might not have overcome the sexism of the judge and jury, but certainly segments of the press and public might have come to a better understanding of what actually happened to Patricia Hearst during the first two months of captivity and the remaining seventeen months of hiding and flight.

In November 1976, six months after her first trial ended, Hearst was set free on one million dollars bail pending appeal of the seven-year Federal sentence she had received. She has also since pleaded *nolo contendere* to one count of armed robbery and one count of assault with a deadly weapon in a plea bargaining agreement whereby the prosecution dropped eight other robbery and assault charges for which she could have been sentenced to life imprisonment. In May, 1977, approximately a year after her first conviction, Superior Court Judge E. Talbot Callister placed her on probation for five years saying: 'I don't think there is a heart in America not full of compassion for the parents. I have never met Mr. and Mrs. Hearst, but I am sure they are good people, full of love and compassion for their daughter.' Once again Hearst had been judged not as an individual, but as a female, this time the child of doting parents. On 2 November 1977, Hearst's conviction was upheld by the 9th US Circuit Court of Appeals. On 3 February 1978, Patricia Hearst appealed her case to the US Supreme Court.[67] This appeal was denied on 24 April. It will be curious to see what sex-based stereotypes emerge in the wake of subsequent appeals or during a retrial. Hearst *was not initially convicted because she defied traditionally ascribed gender behavior.* On the contrary, she quite readily and understandably *fell into the sexual slavery syndrome which is the female adaptation to patriarchy in its most blatant form.* Ironically the American legal system proved incapable of dealing in this instance with what it so often exhibits: sexism carried to its logical extreme.

A feminist interpretation of the first Hearst trial does not mean that there is a general consensus within the current women's movement in the United States on this or other cases involving controversial female defendants charged with criminal offenses of a political nature. If anything, the trials and sentencing of former Weatherwomen like Jane Alpert, Pat Swinton, and Susan Saxe have divided movement women more than they have united them.[68] However, the same is not true of criminal cases that are by definition more personal than political. Such cases have demonstrated that legal defenses based on conditioned female behavior and motivation may be effective. They underscore the differences which continue to exist between the socialisation of men and women in the United States, and the need to understand these differences during litigation. A few minority women charged with murder, claiming they had been raped or were defending their children, for example, have been acquitted, although usually only after appealing to higher courts, as in the cases of Inez Garcia (charged with murdering one of the men who participated in her rape) and Yvonne Yarrow (charged with murdering a man she suspected of being a child molester who entered her house drunk). On the other hand, the first jury to hear the case of Joann Little found her not guilty of murder after she killed a jailer in self-defense when he tried to rape her. All three women received widespread support from organised women's groups in the United States. Like most criminal trials, not simply those involving rape and murder, the laws, as well as social attitudes about women and evidentiary procedures, *all* make it more difficult for a female defendant to receive a fair trial.[69] Unless concerted efforts are made to convince the legal profession in particular and society in general of the sexist nature of many of the crimes and charges against women, justice will continue to elude half of the population.

There have been some effective attempts in thirty states, most notably California and Iowa, to educate police and other civil and legal authorities on the personally traumatic issue of rape. But the other twenty states have shown little inclination to follow this lead. As a result Representative Elizabeth Holtzman (Democrat, New York) and ninety-seven other members of the House have introduced the Privacy Protection for Rape Victims of 1977, which would bar evidence of sexual reputation and virtually all cross-examination on the victim's sexual relations with persons other than the defendant and even the latter could only be introduced if the trial judge determines in a private hearing that it is not unduly prejudicial to the woman. The Supreme Court also held in June, 1977, that the death penalty may not be used as punishment for rape. Women's legal rights groups had entered *amicae* briefs in this case arguing against the death penalty because it was an outgrowth of the view that women were the property of men rather than a crime against women. They also hailed the decision because the capital punishment for rape was seldom applied except in cases involving black men, making it an inadequate (and racist) protection of women against rape.[70]

The situation is much less encouraging in cases involving battered women and prostitutes. Largely ignored as a legal and social problem, wifebeating in particular cuts across all class lines and is apparently on the rise, or at least being reported in greater numbers than ever before, in the United States, England and most western countries. (Latest estimates indicate twenty-eight million or half of all American wives are beaten by their husbands.) Yet, like rape, it is seldom handled in a sex-neutral way by the police or courts.[71] One recent exception occurred when fifty-nine battered wives filed a class action suit against New York City policemen and Family Court personnel charging they had been unlawfully denied assistance after reporting assaults by their husbands. Unexpectedly, in June, 1977, the State Supreme Court agreed to hear this case. In the meantime the New York legislature passed a bill giving the victim of family violence the choice of seeking reconciliation in the Family Court or punishment for the assailant in the Criminal Courts.[72] Similar attempts to alleviate the legal and personal problems of prostitutes have not yet met with much success. There is now an antifeminist movement to legalise,[73] rather than to decriminalise prostitution. At the very least, pimps and johns should be prosecuted on the same basis as prostitutes.[74] Ingrained in the traditional patriarchal family and marriage contract, protected by a conspiracy of silence among men, reinforced by the degrading aspects of certain public welfare systems, and perpetuated by legal and economic discrimination, the use and abuse of women are often taken for granted or ignored.

PART TWO

JUDGES AND GENDERS: A NEW LOOK AT FAMILY LAW

3 *Britain:* From Head Servant to Junior Partner

A century after the courts had decided that it was unlawful in England to use force to keep a slave in the house, lawyers were still maintaining that it was permissible to use force to keep a wife in the house. An Englishman's home was his castle, and her prison. When in the celebrated Clitheroe case the judges finally held – and then only on appeal – that a writ of habeas corpus should issue against a husband who with his solicitor's aid had kidnapped and confined his runaway wife,[1] the court was condemned by *The Times* for weakening the institution of marriage (1891). What this case reveals, however, is that the judiciary and legislature were in fact strengthening marriage by slowly modernising and rationalising aspects of the middle-class union and bringing family law into line with the new kinds of family home and family property that were developing.

It is convenient to distinguish two main periods of reform of family law in the direction of greater equality between spouses. The first took place in the latter part of the last century, the second commenced in the late 1960s and is still under way.

In contrast with the position later in many newly independent states, where the franchise and civil rights were to be gained before family law was reformed, in Britain major reforms of family law preceded the obtaining of political rights by women.[2] However, none of the legal ameliorations for married women in nineteenth-century England were brought about through the spontaneous goodwill or sense of justice of the male Members of Parliament. Every campaign was bitterly conducted, and the objectives of each were conceded in a reluctant and piecemeal manner rather than with enthusiasm. The difficulties encountered by the female reformers show that there is no such thing as a self-evident injustice – the beneficiaries of inequality will always justify it, while its victims will have to struggle to get its very existence acknowledged. On the contrary, it is the dominant values of the time, or rather, the values of the dominant group of the time, that are spoken of as though they are self-evident. Injustice only becomes self-evident retrospectively, that is, after it has been removed.

The task of the feminist campaigners was facilitated by profound changes that were taking place in the character of the family and the nature of property. In formal terms, the family remained the same, its legal basis continuing to be the Christian monogamous marriage. Similarly, the major legal classifications of property were still based on distinctions between land and things separate from land. However, industrialisation under conditions of capitalism transformed the social situation of the family and created entirely new forms of wealth. As O. R. McGregor has put it, the nineteenth century saw a transformation of entrepreneurial activity brought about by the creation of a national capital market through the Stock Exchange and a national labour market through the Poor Laws; Parliament also recognised limited liability companies as an incentive for the investment of risk capital, and set up the Board of Trade to regulate companies. And so it came about that state intervention created the conditions necessary for laissez-faire.[3] He might have gone further and suggested that these processes also paved the way for reforming the law relating to the family.

As soon as land ceased to be the main form of property and chief index of wealth and status, new forms of family law and rules of inheritance could be developed. In the eighteenth century the device of the trust settlement was used to protect a daughter's inheritance from being squandered by a profligate husband.[4] In the nineteenth century, after much campaigning of feminist groups, married women were authorised by statute to hold property separately from their husbands. The Married Women's Property Act, 1882, is often held out as a milestone in the march of women to equality, but in reality it did little more than save wealthy women from the irksome restraints of holding property through trustees. In fact, men continued to control the property of women, even if only in the capacity of advisors rather than husbands or trustees, since women were precluded from acquiring the skills thought to be needed for the proper administration of their property, such skills being locked within the male professions. Since few married women were able to earn sufficiently to acquire their own property, the effects of the Act were necessarily limited. And although the man who drafted the basis of the Act, Dr Richard Pankhurst, supported sexual equality in every sphere, the Members of Parliament who let the measure go through unopposed did so generally because they saw it as an alternative to granting women greater public rights. The law went some way towards protecting wives from being abused inside the home; it did not create opportunities for them to be useful outside the home. A curb on spending by husbands was not the same as a licence to earn independently by wives. Thus the destiny of woman as wife rather than as independent person was enhanced rather than reduced by the Act.

Feudal law had merged the legal person of the wife with that of the husband, a legal arrangement appropriate to land-based wealth, where the family lands, house and name remained intact from generation to generation through eldest sons. It was the growth of limited liability companies in the nineteenth century that created new forms of economic power divorced from ownership of land, and that relegated the home from the public domain to the domestic sphere. This was the converse of the process noted by Karl Renner, in terms of which property increasingly lost its private and family character and became public in function; he gave the example of the railway station and the laundry, which were still described by law as privately owned but which in social practice had become public utilities.[5] These two simultaneous developments – the home becoming private and the land becoming public – were not inconsistent. Increasingly the home was being separated from the land on which it stood and from productive activity. Formerly only the soil of foreign territories had been subjected to speculative capital ventures, but now the surface area of Britain itself was appropriated to the market. Land was bought and sold not merely for the produce that grew on it, but for the minerals that lay beneath it, the railways and canals that could be cut through it, and the housing that could be built upon it. At the same time, manufacture ceased to be a household activity. The factory system destroyed family industry, and the home lost its character as the centre of work and became instead a place of rest and reproduction. The home was domesticated, as was the role of women in it. Women's work in the home became an end in itself, extolled for its own sake and incorporated by men into the myth of femininity.

The merging of husband and wife into a single legal personality had been an appropriate legal form for a feudal-type society in which the home and the land around it had formed the centre of production. Holy wedlock had given a sacramental character to these unions, which had necessarily been for life – divorce would have disrupted production, undermined security of land tenure, brought families into conflict and created acute problems over the succession of land. The conflict between the old values and the new life patterns, which were generating new concepts of individual endeavour and personal happiness, formed the basis of a particularly poignant late-nineteenth-century literature. Is a marriage ceremony a religious thing, asked one of Thomas Hardy's heroines, or is it only a sordid contract, based on material convenience in householding, rating and taxing, and the inheritance of land and money by children, making it necessary that the male parent be known?[6] Her failure to resolve that question led to her destruction, as it did to the lives of many of her generation.

The domestication of the home drastically reduced women's public influence and converted relatively independent wives, whose contribution to production had given them a strong position within the family, into totally dependent and frequently unhappy housewives. Yet despite the near-complete public subordination of the middle-class housewife, the judges, as we have seen, extolled the position of the Englishwoman as being without compare. Judge Willes declared that the honour and respect in which women were held was one of the glories of British civilisation. Similarly, Lord Ardmillan stressed that because the elevation of women in domestic and social position was one of the blessed fruits of Christianity, it was especially necessary to keep women out of mixed anatomy classes.

These semi-mystical sentiments served not only to obscure the true position of the great majority of women in Britain, but also to suggest a false status for Englishwomen when compared with that of women abroad. Experience in the Empire possibly helps explain why British women were alleged to be in so favoured a position. In many colonies the major objective of British policy was said to be to teach the indigenous inhabitants the dignity of labour. By this was meant labour in the employ of British settlers or administrators, since no amount of labour by indigenous inhabitants on their own land was regarded as dignified. The destruction of the self-sufficient traditional family was a prerequisite for employment, and it was to further this end that the menfolk of Britain, so reluctant to grant rights to their own wives, became so solicitous about the rights of women in colonised societies. In his work on the legal status of African women, Jack Simons remarks that colonists in southern Africa complained that the tribesman had too much land, leisure and sex.[7] Instead of earning his living by the sweat of his brow in proper employment, the tribesman allegedly battened in ease on the labour of his wives. African women were said by colonists to be hardly better off than slaves, and polygamy was described as being less a form of marriage than a licensed system of lust, which enabled a privileged class of cattle-owners to live in sensual indolence at the expense of their womenfolk. Simons points out that this colonialist belief had little substance. In reality the tribesmen had attained a high standard of political and legal organisation, they observed a strict moral code, and governed themselves with dignity and self-restraint. 'The pity showered on the women', he writes, 'was largely misplaced. They did not constitute a separate class, were not oppressed, and were not segregated behind a tribal kind of purdah. They shared the rank of their fathers and husbands, and held an honoured, if junior position in their domestic households.' Nevertheless, he observes, the banner of Christianity, progress and female emancipation provided a moral pretext for invading African territory and forcing peasants off the land. Since irony is intrinsic to mythical belief, it is not all that surprising that the colonial gender beliefs were later turned around to reinforce metropolitan gender beliefs. Lord Curzon, one of the leaders of the anti-suffrage movement, declared from his experience as a former Viceroy of India that the hundreds of millions of subjects in the Empire would cease to have respect for the Imperial Government if they got to know that it had been put into office by the votes of women.

In Britain itself, the institution of separate property for wives was not regarded as destroying complementarity in marriage or replacing it with equality. James Fitzjames Stephen declared in an extended reply to the egalitarian ideas of John Stuart Mill – he called his polemic *Liberty, Equality, Fraternity* – that he did not in any way object to women owning property separately from their husbands, which through the medium of the family trust they had done for generations already. But when it came to status within and without the home, he had no doubt that any attempt to place men and women on an equal footing would lead to social catastrophe. Stephen represented a powerful ultra-conservative trend within the legal profession, and in his view there was simply no denying the fact that

> physical differences between the two sexes affected every part of the human body, from the hair of the head to the sole of the feet, from the size and density of the bones to the texture of the brain and the character of the nervous system. Men are stronger than women in every shape; they have greater muscular and nervous force, greater intellectual force and vigour of character.[8]

This classic exposition of sexism was joined in his book by many other equally anti-feminist statements, all presented with a courtliness and elegance which belied the notion that bigotry belonged to the uncouth or the untutored. He declared that he hesitated to discuss the subject: 'there is something – I hardly know what to call it; indecent is too strong a word, but I may say unpleasant in the direction of indecorum – in prolonged and minute discussions about the relations between men and women, and the characteristics of women as such.' Furthermore, he contended, inequality of the sexes was one of those propositions that it was difficult to prove, because they were so plain. But it was in women's interests that the contract of marriage be avowedly understood as being between stronger and weaker parties rather than as between equals. If, for the sake of argument, it was supposed that: marriage became a mere partnership in which women were expected to earn their living just like men, men's manners towards women became identical to their manners towards men, and the cheerful concessions to acknowledged weaknesses, the obligation to do for women a thousand things that it would be insulting to offer to do for a man were exploded, what, he asked, would be the result? Women would become men's slaves and drudges and be made to feel their inherent weakness to the utmost. 'Submission and protection are correlative. Withdraw the one and the other is lost, and force will assert itself a hundred times more harshly through the law of contract than ever it did through the law of status.' If there was a dispute in the family, the wife ought to give way, and for her to regard submission to the orders of her husband as a wrong, was a mark not of courage but of a base, unworthy and mutinous disposition. Women should remember that they lost the qualities which made them attractive to men earlier than men lost those which made them attractive to women. 'Furthermore, when a woman married she practically renounced the possibility of undertaking any profession but one, and the possibility of carrying on that one profession in the society of any man but one.' Thus to Stephen the recognition of inequality was fundamental to the happiness of both men and women, so that the claims made for equality, particularly in regard to sex, deserved to be stigmatised as the 'most ignoble and mischievous of all the popular feelings of the age'.

Stephen's book created a stir when it was published, and a number of pamphlets and articles were written by feminists and their supporters in reply. It would be convenient to see the controversy as a quaint battle belonging to the Victorian era, but the truth is that Stephen's views were until very recently well-represented in the higher reaches of the British judiciary. In 1925 a member of the House of Lords referred scathingly in a judgment to borough councillors who had become such ardent feminists as to bring about, at the expense of the ratepayers whose money they administered, sex equality in the labour market.[9] More directly on the point of the family, as late as 1957 the Master of the Rolls (whose position as the head of the Court of Appeal made him probably the single most influential judge in England) explicitly deplored the tendency to move in the direction of viewing marriage as a partnership between husband and wife.[10] In an introduction to a book dealing with the development of family law over the previous century, he stated that he had read that in Russia the social circle of a man's wife depended on her own status rather than that of her husband, so that the social circle of each might be largely independent of the other. For his part he hoped that 'the English race would in this as it had done in many other aspects of life, resist the logical conclusion. ... The fires of human emotion must continue to burn in human breasts.' Queen Victoria had declared that God had created man and woman different, and he agreed with the authors of the book when they quoted her dictum with approval.

Within a decade his successors on the Bench were emphatically endorsing the very trend that he and Stephen had denounced so strongly. The second era of reform of family law was on its way. Judges insisted in statements both on and off the Bench, that marriage should be regarded as precisely that which had previously been viewed as so abominable, namely a partnership between equals. The dangerous fantasies of John Stuart Mill and the wicked practices of the Soviet Union were now not only being embodied in legislation passed by Parliament, but also spoken of with approval, even enthusiasm, by leading judges.[11] This rapid change in approach requires explanation, and it is suggested that the usual reference in legal literature to changing values is quite inadequate. It might be that the near overlap in time of conservative statements by outgoing judges and liberal statements by newcomers to the Bench, gives a dramatic contrast that pays undue regard to the continuity and gradualness of reform. However, the swiftness and sweep of recent alterations in family law suggest something more pervasive than differences of attitude between individual judges. There are in fact four distinct areas in which major reform has taken place, and each is based on acceptance of the concept of the family as a partnership rather than as an enterprise subject to patriarchal control.

The first area of reform consists of measures designed to protect the wife in the home from eviction and from violence at the hands of her husband.[12] The existence of wife-battering on a massive scale in England has been forced to public attention by Women's Aid groups which have to some extent overcome the resistance by male police and legislators to the idea of interfering in family disputes, i.e. to challenging the power of husbands to abuse their wives.

The second area of change relates to grounds for divorce, in respect of which the concept of matrimonial fault has been replaced by the notion of irretrievable breakdown of marriage.[13] Cruelty, adultery and desertion still survive in modified form as facts evidencing breakdown of the marriage, but they are supplemented by divorce by consent after two years' separation, and divorce without consent after five years' separation. The sacramental character of marriage has thus been largely replaced by the notion of marriage as a shared undertaking dissoluble at the instance of either party.

Thirdly, financial provision for wives on divorce has been substantially improved. Formerly, they could only hold on to what was theirs by purchase and inheritance according to the ordinary rules of property law. The Married Women's Property Act of 1882 had represented an advance in that it acknowledged that husbands and wives were separate individuals in the eyes of the law, but because husbands generally had greater earning and therefore greater purchasing power, the creation of separate property regimes usually left wives with little or no property at the end of their marriages.[14] The only claim that they had on their husbands was for periodical maintenance payments out of future income. Some judges attempted to stretch the concept of the implied trust to give the wife a legal claim on a share of the matrimonial home, but they did not get far, and eventually it was legislation that introduced the changes.[15] The situation now is that on divorce all the assets of husband and wife are pooled together and then distributed according to what is regarded by the judge as fair and just rather than according to who technically owns what. A rule of thumb adopted by the court is to award one-third of the joint assets and one-third of the joint income to the wife, together with such maintenance as needs to be paid for any children.[16] This represents a considerable improvement in the position of the non-earning spouse, usually the wife, who will not be forced as previously to continue with a broken marriage because the alternative was economic destitution. An anomaly that remains, though, is that the wife normally gets only one-third of the joint assets rather than one-half; in the leading case on the subject, this inequality was justified on the basis that the husband would have the special expenses of employing a housekeeper, something the wife would not be required to do.[17]

Finally, the law dealing with the division of the matrimonial property on death was brought in line with that on divorce. This represented a return to the concept that a husband was not free to dispose of his property as he wished by will, and a restoration in altered form of the notion that a portion of the estate went as of right to the widow. The principle of freedom of testation, in terms of which the owner of property could 'use and abuse' his property as he wished after death as in life, was consistent with laissez-faire ideas,

and may be regarded as the ultimate in entrepreneurial indi-
vidualism. In 1938 a small inroad was made into this principle when
surviving spouses and other disinherited dependants facing destitution were permitted to claim through the courts that they be paid
maintenance out of the deceased's estate. This has now been widened
into a major breach by the recent extension of the class of people who
could claim, including so-called mistresses, and by a provision which
entitles the surviving spouse to claim a reasonable portion of the
estate, and not just what she needs to live on, irrespective of what the
will says.[18] Although the inclusion of lovers in the class of potential
claimants led this statute to be labelled a 'mistresses charter', it was
really wives who gained the most under it, since they now can expect
roughly one-third of the estate to come their way even if they have
been completely excluded from the will. The widow's portion thus
returns, not as a fixed proportion of the estate as in feudal times,
but as an amount at the discretion of the court.

These changes came about after considerable public discussion
and extensive investigations by law reform agencies. They coincided
with the enactment of statutes granting greater tolerance to abortion[19] and homosexuality[20] and the adoption of measures designed
to make contraception freely available. Family law came out of the
shadows at University, and publishers lost little time in realising the
new marketing possibilities.

The transformations of family law in this second period of reform,
then, reflected fundamental changes in policy which went beyond the
emergence simply of this enlightened or that liberal judge on the
Bench. The current approach to the family clearly reflects new
attitudes, but the problem that remains is why these new attitudes
should have emerged and gained general currency at precisely this
stage. Part of the explanation, of course, comes from the re-
emergence of the women's movement as a powerful force in the
period under consideration. Many of the reforms can be seen as a
response to Women's Liberation, not by conceding to its more
radical demands to transform or abolish the family, but by offering a
consolation to women for being in the family. None of these changes
represent an abandonment of the notion that the wife is primarily a
housekeeper and child-raiser, but cumulatively they offer her a
greater reward for acting in these capacities. To the extent that the
more equitable approach lessens the economic subordination of
wives to their husbands, the advances appear to have been welcomed
by feminists. But, while strengthening the wife's position in the
home, they do little to help her get out of the home. Her maternity

leave entitlements have been improved,[21] but she has no right enforceable either against the community, her employer or the father of her children, to have pre-school substitute child-care provided. Coupled with a tax and social security system that generally treats women as the dependants of men with whom they are living but never regards men as the dependants of women, this means that if the law regards marriage as a partnership, it is in no doubt as to who is the senior and who the junior partner. Thus campaigns by women's organisations have undoubtedly contributed both directly and indirectly to changes both in the content of family law and its status as a subject to be taken seriously. But that still leaves unresolved the question of why these long-standing claims should have been met just at this stage, and why other demands for equality are still being ignored by the legislature and the courts.

The suggested explanation is that the source of the changed ideas is to be found in the changed character of the family itself.[22] Material changes in family life preceded changes in attitudes and changes in the law. Although at the formal level we are still dealing with the monogamous nuclear family of Stephen's day, the character of that family has altered considerably. The women's movement did not create the new family but it did precipitate the paying of attention to these changes, and encouraged the search for new concepts and formulations to describe something that had already happened. Family law was not quite as progressive, then, as claimed by the reformers who saw it as being ahead of social developments and facilitative of further change; rather, it gave belated recognition to a new form of middle-class household that had already emerged.

If the most noticeable change in the middle-class household from the period of feudalism to nineteenth-century industrial society was the separation of the home from production and the creation of the 'idle' wife, the main development in such households in this century has been the virtual elimination of domestic servants and the creation of the dual-earning couple. The disappearance of domestic service can be related to many social and political developments, such as the growth of public housing and of social security; it is not so much that the number of governesses, cooks, cleaners and groundsmen has declined, as that people in these occupations have found new employers, namely the state and local authorities, with the result that they live at home, work during office hours and negotiate their wages through trade unions. At first sight it might seem paradoxical that the middle-class wife who has to do her own housework is more independent of her husband than were her forebears who had servants to do all the chores, but the chains leading to the drawing room were even tighter than those leading to the kitchen sink. The task of supervising a large body of domestic staff tied the middle-class wife more securely to her home than does the actual responsibility for cooking and cleaning in a period when modern labour-saving devices are used. Management of labour in the home had formerly been the wife's stipulated career; in Stephen's words, it had been her one profession, and only when wives were freed from careers in the home were they able to embark upon careers outside it.

Another change in the character of the modern middle-class home has been the decline in conspicuous consumption and conspicuous idleness. This has gone hand in hand with the reduction in the number of servants, but it has also been associated with such different factors as changes in patterns of marketing, the growth of political pressures directed at the rich, and increases in the rate of income tax, the latter encouraging expenditure directed towards capital gains rather than displays of wealth. Mass production of goods for a mass market has given rise to new kinds of consumption and a new ethos of instant personal gratification, with the result that the upper classes are distinguished by the sophisticated intimacy of their consumption rather than by its gross conspicuousness. Furthermore, political action by the dispossessed has rendered the flaunting of idleness disreputable rather than grand; whereas formerly such display was calculated to induce awe and submission, today it is likely to produce anger and a visit from the tax inspector. It may even be argued that political and industrial action by the workers has had the indirect and unexpected consequence of helping to liberate middle-class wives, inasmuch as it has helped to destroy the mansions in which the latter were trapped.

Thus the concepts of matrimonial partnership and of marriage being a contract from which each party could withdraw, really were founded on the emergence of the modern servantless middle-class home. The law might still impose on the husband a duty to support and on the wife a duty to serve, but it no longer presupposes that her major function will be to supervise minions at home while he is in charge of subordinates at work.

4 *United States:* Control by Husbands, Control by State

'I feel, as never before,' Elizabeth Cady Stanton wrote to Susan B. Anthony in 1853, 'that this whole question of women's rights turns on the pivot of the marriage relation, and, mark my word, sooner or later it will be the topic for discussion.'[1] To the degree that marital problems remain at the heart of family law, Stanton was correct. As we have already noted the Married Women's Property Acts did little to alleviate the myriad legal disabilities faced by nineteenth-century wives. In 1837 law professor Timothy Walker had described the legal relationships between husbands and wives in the United States as a 'disgrace to any civilized nation'.[2] In particular, contractual and proprietary rights of wives remained limited because, as another legal scholar noted in 1925, 'the interpretation of [Married Women's Acts] fell into the hands of judges who as young lawyers had been educated in the legal supremacy of the husband'.[3] As late as 1965 a law school case book laconically stated: 'Today the more obvious legal disabilities of married women have been eliminated, notwithstanding a determined rear-guard action by the Courts, who demonstrated a real hostility to the Married Women's Acts. Some strongholds of disability remain unconquered, however. ...'[4] Of these 'remaining strongholds', marriage and divorce laws, reproductive freedom, child custody, various pension benefits, and protection against physical abuse are most important.

Marriage: the Contract that Isn't

Unlike most contracts, the legal marriage contract in the United States is unwritten and its terms are not defined. Technically speaking, neither party knows exactly what provision they are agreeing to because they are not allowed to specify through negotiation what their legal relationship will or will not be, as they would before signing a standard contract. A marriage 'contract', therefore, is a legal fiction as far as traditional contractual rights are concerned because the civil roles of both parties have already been determined by law, custom, or religion. Yet marriage is commonly referred to as a contract by society in general and the courts in particular even though neither spouse defines the marital role of the other. This is done by state law, although in recent years there has been increased federal regulation of certain aspects of marriage largely through complex interpretations of the constitutional right of privacy and due process.[5] Thus the Supreme Court has intervened in several instances when states appeared to be infringing upon the rights of individuals involved in intimate marital relationships, familial concerns, and personal, sexual, or medical decisions, e.g. the right of married couples to use contraceptives [*Griswold v. Connecticut*, 381 U.S. 479 (1965)] and of women to abortion [*Roe v. Wade*, 410 U.S. 113 (1973)]. Fundamentally, however, state laws continue to determine the roles and rights of married people.

Such a description of American marriage might lead one to believe that, despite the fact that it was not a legally contractual relationship, state laws assigned equally arbitrary privileges and obligations to men and women. This is not the case because the origins of the status of husband and wife go back to common law which clearly gave higher status to men. Although Blackstone's proclamation about the civil death of married women has been undermined over the years, the inferior role ascribed to women under common law still affects family law decisions, especially at the state level. In 1970, for example, the Ohio Supreme Court held that a wife was 'at most a superior servant to her husband ... only chattel with no personality, no property, and no legally recognised feelings or rights'. As recently as 1974 the Georgia legislature approved a statute that defined the husband as 'head of the family' with the 'wife ... subject to him; her legal existence ... merged in the husband, except so far as the law recognises her separately, either for her own protection, or for her benefit, or for the preservation of the public order'.[6] Presently one out of eight heads of households in the United States is female.

Such arbitrary and archaic rulings have led to the suggestion that perhaps marriage should be converted either into a true contract relationship where men and women would negotiate the terms as equals or into a partnership status where the law would mandate the same rights and responsibilities for each person.[7] Given the current unequal socialisation of women in American society it is unlikely that most women could negotiate a fair contract for themselves at this time, especially when under parental or peer pressure to marry. However, it remains a tempting alternative for those women who now feel confident of their ability to negotiate reasonable contracts (usually in the form of antenuptial agreements regarding both support and property settlements in the event of divorce). Few states currently honor even these limited postnuptial or antenuptial agreements, let alone contracts in lieu of marriage, although a number of models for the latter have been drafted. Obviously contracts in lieu of marriage would allow for legal relationships between two or more people of the same or different sex not presently possible under state-regulated marriage.[8] Moreover, most American courts simply will not recognise or enforce at the present time any kind of marriage contract between men and women that either alters the essential elements of the marital relationship, namely, 'the husband's duty to support the wife and the wife's duty to serve the husband', or is made to facilitate divorce.[9] The few exceptions to this generalisation have all occurred since 1970 and hopefully represent the beginning of a new legal trend.

A partnership relationship, therefore, within traditional marriage seems to offer a more immediate if less comprehensive way to eliminate the remaining inequalities between husbands and wives. This would mean replacing patriarchal status with partnership status. The likelihood of this value change taking place on a wide scale is also not too great at the present time, but is possible on a private basis between heterosexual couples. Its legality remains questionable 'because the law still prescribes sex-differentiated marital roles and male domination'.[10] Even while recognising the narrow judicial parameters within which reform of the patriarchal institution of marriage can take place, it is worth looking at those legally debilitating 'remaining strongholds' of family law in which some improvement has taken place.

Two Steps Forward; One Step Backward?

There are at least ten major areas of legal concern to married (and divorced) women, in addition to a number of minor ones. Those of most importance are: (1) the right of personal support during marriage; (2) alimony; (3) child custody and child support; (4) property and credit rights during and after marriage; (5) access to abortion and all forms of contraception at nominal cost; (6) social security, and other pension benefits; (7) an adequate and nonsexist welfare system; (8) pregnancy and other disability insurance; (9) maternity leave policies and benefits; and (10) protection against child and wife abuse. These legal matters assume significant proportions in the lives of almost all women in the United States because 98.7 percent of them have been or are married by the age of forty-five. Married women with children work an average of twenty-five years at full- or part-time jobs; those without, an average of thirty-five years. Married women now constitute 57.7 percent of the female labor force in the United States and almost one half of them have husbands earning less than $10,000 a year.[11] Of varying degrees of importance to women who plan to cohabit with men are such things as the assumption of the husband's surname, differing qualifying ages of consent for male and females; the widespread refusal of states to recognise common-law marriage; and all matters arising from the patriarchal assumption that the husband is automatically head of the household, such as his right to establish the marital domicile, his presumed sole responsibility for family support (which assumes the economic incapacity of the wife), and the unrecognised and unpaid status of domestic work and child-care services of wives.[12]

Among those things valued most highly by many women is the option to remain in their homes, supported by their husbands. What society does not tell them is that their presumed right of support is *legally unenforceable* while they remain married. According to the courts, marital support does not have to be commensurate with either the wife's efforts or the value of her husband's earnings or assets. It is more accurately a right to be supported by a husband in the fashion and manner he chooses. The most bizarre case in this area took place in 1953 when the Nebraska Supreme Court refused to order a husband to provide adequate grocery or clothing money or to supply indoor plumbing for the couple's residence even though he owned a farm valued at $90,000 and had additional assets of $117,500. The Court refused to interfere with an ongoing marital relationship on the question of what constitutes 'reasonable' support, although lower courts regularly make such determinations when a marriage has ended in divorce.

All marriages do end – either in divorce or because of death. Traditionally, divorce statutes prescribed dissolution of marriage proceedings that assumed one party was responsible or 'at fault' and where a double standard involving extramarital sexual relations prevailed. Since 1969, however, major reforms in divorce laws have occurred in one out of three states. All have made divorce easier to obtain and more sex neutral than ever before. Several national uniform marriage and divorce laws have been drafted by such groups as the National Conference of Commissioners on Uniform State Laws and the American Bar Association. By 1973, for example, this reform process had led to eleven states adopting 'no fault' divorce statutes that place no blame on either spouse but simply declare 'irretrievable breakdown' as the major basis for dissolution of the marriage (California, Missouri, Iowa, Colorado, Florida, Michigan, Oregon, Kentucky, Nebraska, Arizona, and Washington). Six other states (Alabama, Connecticut, Georgia, Hawaii, Indiana, and New Hampshire) have simply added 'no fault' to previously existing grounds for divorce, while a dozen others have made 'irreconcilable differences' or 'incompatibility' reasons for divorce in addition to their traditionally fault-based ones.[13] Regardless of how a marriage ends, the emotional and economic hardships accompanying dissolution are exacerbated by diverse state laws. This lack of uniformity and the resulting confusion and hardship it causes those seeking divorces would be in part ameliorated by passage of the Equal Rights Amendment. 'No fault' divorce is not a perfect solution by any means because in practice there is some evidence indicating that it reduces the amount of support allocated to needy women since technically no one is at fault. This is obviously a sexist implementation of what was intended to be a progressive, sex-neutral reform.

Marriage usually places women at a financial disadvantage. Most simply do not obtain enough work experience or education before marriage to maximise their wage-earning capacity during or afterwards. In forty-two states, divorce courts seldom rule that women have equity in property acquired during marriage. This is especially true in rural midwestern areas where female labor is indispensable to family farm operations, but virtually unrecognised in terms of property ownership. During childrearing years, a homemaker loses work experience, and often her self-confidence as well. Many women work while their husbands pursue extended educations without ever receiving comparable training themselves or considering repayment of the 'debt' they are owed. Nor are women paid for their years of work in the home. (Chase Manhattan Bank has placed a value of $13,391 per year on housework.) Finally, women often take custody of children upon divorce. Thus, they have few ways to acquire money unless their husbands give it to them. When a woman's marriage dissolves, she has lost her 'job' as surely as a man who has been fired from his. Unfortunately, alimony remains the major way of compensating women for financial disabilities aggravated or caused by marriage. Divorce insurance and 'displaced homemakers' legislation are potential, but as yet unrealised, alternatives.

The only nationwide study of alimony reported in 1965 that alimony awards were part of the final judgment in only two percent of divorce cases and were awarded temporarily in ten percent of cases to allow the wife an opportunity to find employment. Some states (Indiana, Pennsylvania and Texas among others) do not provide for permanent alimony at all. The International Women's

Year (IWY) Commission reports that even in those cases where alimony is awarded, only forty-six percent of these former wives collect; ten years after divorce, seventy-nine percent of husbands originally responsible for alimony are no longer making payments. A majority of states have no laws giving preference to one parent in divorce or separation proceedings involving children. Nevertheless, judges tend to prefer awarding mothers custody of young children and girls, and fathers custody of older boys. Most states do place child support responsibility on men. In 1976, the IWY Commission reported that only forty-four percent of divorced mothers are awarded child support, and that less than half of these women collect regularly. Court-awarded payments are usually less than enough to provide half of a child's support.

There are only two ways in the United States for married couples to own property: common law ownership and community property ownership. Both systems contain serious economic disadvantages for women, although at first glance community property states appear to offer more legal and monetary benefits to wives. For example, if a woman fortuitously resides in one of the eight 'community property' states (Arizona, California, Idaho, Louisiana, Nevada, New Mexico, Texas and Washington), she will inherit one-half of property acquired during her marriage, independent of any will left by her husband. This is an absolute interest, and she may in turn will such property to whomever she chooses. Wives dying before their husbands in these states may will half of community property to whomever they wish. In Louisiana and California, even a divorced wife is entitled to half the marriage's property. The major disadvantage to wives in these eight community property states is that until recently husbands traditionally had exclusive managerial control over the couple's real property (including her wages) during the marriage. While in theory the community property system is based on a partnership relationship, it does not work out that way. By 1973, five of the eight community property states had increased the right of wives to manage the common property and to control their own earnings. Currently all community property states except Louisiana, where a commission is now studying the issue, have made these changes. However, many of these new statutes remain ambiguous or subject to very limited interpretations.[14] It must also be remembered that all property owned by either spouse before marriage or acquired by gift or inheritance remains apart and not subject to equal division. This includes any rents, issues, proceeds, or profits either may have brought to the marriage or acquired afterwards as separate property.

As for the women who live in the other forty-two states, their property rights are based on English common law. This means that each party owns what he or she has actually purchased and retains full legal rights to his or her separate property. Uncompensated work in the home does not entitle a wife to any interest in property acquired during marriage or any rights to her husband's income. The apparent inequity and harshness of the common law system is modified somewhat by state statutes allowing widows to acquire one-third to one-half of their husbands' property at death. This dower right is not an absolute interest, however, and a woman may not be able to will such property to whom she chooses. In some common law states, a widow is not entitled to any share of her husband's estate unless he chooses to will it to her. Although women are almost never compensated for years spent as homemakers while they are alive, in the community property states their contribution is at least nominally recognised at their husbands' deaths. Women who die before their husbands in non-community property states literally die penniless, with no property whatsoever to leave to children, parents or others they might wish to care for – unless they have been able to acquire or inherit separate property of their own during their lives. According to interpretations of the various Married Women's Property Acts, husbands in common law states do not control or manage any separate property or earnings their wives may have acquired during the marriage. For those women who are totally dependent on their men for support (a rapidly vanishing breed in time of run-away inflation), their main hope in the event of divorce is alimony, statistically an unstable source of income.

In actuality neither system of property ownership – common law or community property – produces anything like economic or personal equality between spouses in any of the fifty states.

Labor Pains for Women

Other legal areas of increasing interest to married American women, because so many of them now work, revolve around pregnancy disability insurance. Regarded as one of the most important issues involving women's rights since the Supreme Court legalised abortion in 1973, a most discouraging decision was handed down on December 7, 1976. It represented a clear victory for male supremacy and the brand of capitalism on which it is based in the United States. In *General Electric Co. v. Gilbert*, 321 U.S. 125 (1976), six of nine

Justices ruled that employers need not compensate women for maternity related disabilities as they compensate employees for other disabilities. The insurance plan in question provided workers with sixty percent of their salaries on the eighth day of total disability (or immediately if hospitalised) continuing up to twenty-six weeks. Sports injuries, attempted suicides, venereal disease, elective cosmetic surgery, disabilities incurred while committing a crime, prostate disease, circumcision, hair transplants and vasectomy *are all covered* by the GE plan. Absences associated with pregnancy, miscarriage, childbirth, and pregnancy complicated by diseases both related and unrelated to childbearing *are excluded* from coverage.

The women suing General Electric argued that its insurance plan constituted illegal sex discrimination under Title VII of the Civil Rights Act of 1964 (see pages 210–11 below). They also cited a 1972 Equal Employment Opportunity Commission (EEOC) guideline for Title VII which stated that

> disabilities caused or contributed to by pregnancy, miscarriage, abortions, childbirth and recovery therefrom are, for all job-related purposes, temporary disabilities and should be treated as such under any health or temporary disability insurance or sick leave plan. ... [Benefits] shall be applied to disability due to pregnancy or childbirth on the same terms and conditions as they are applied to other temporary disabilities.[15]

In rejecting this guideline and the opinions of six federal courts of appeal, which had found the General Electric plan discriminatory, the Supreme Court resorted to its own 1974 decision in *Geduldig v. Aiello*, 417 U.S. 484 (1974) involving a similar California disability plan. Seeing no reason to distinguish *Geduldig*, two-thirds of the Justices simply reiterated that there was no violation of the equal protection clause of the Fourteenth Amendment because neither insurance plan excluded anyone from coverage on the basis of gender, but rather merely removed one physical condition for coverage. Because of its heavy reliance on *Geduldig*, the majority opinion in essence held that the concept of discrimination based on sex was identical under Title VII and the equal protection clause – refusing to distinguish between the two. Moreover, the decision questioned the validity of the 1972 guideline on two grounds: (1) that the 1972 one contradicted a 1966 EEOC guideline and (2) that

> Congress in enacting Title VII, did not confer upon the EEOC authority to promulgate rules or regulations.... This does not mean that EEOC guidelines are not entitled to consideration in determining legislative intent. ... But it does mean that courts properly may accord less weight to such guidelines.

Thus *Gilbert* summarily dismissed the 'great deference' that lower courts had previously given EEOC guidelines when interpreting Title VII.

Even more significant was the concluding paragraph of the majority opinion in which it was stated: 'When Congress makes it unlawful for an employer to "discriminate ... on the basis of ... sex ...", without further explanation of its meaning, we should not really infer that it meant something different from what the concept of discrimination has traditionally meant.' At this point the opinion referred to several earlier Supreme Court cases defining what discrimination meant. None of those cited dealt with sex discrimination and one dated from 1922 as though no societal changes had occurred since that time to question what was meant by the traditional definition.

It is difficult to convey the enormity of the negative implications of *Gilbert* for married working women in the United States. The cost of bearing a child ranges between $500 and $1,500 if a woman's medical insurance does not cover it. After childbirth there are other economic dilemmas to be faced outside of the major long-term one. (As of 1977 the Population Reference Bureau reported that to raise an American child required from $44,000 to $64,000 depending on the income of the average low or middleclass family. This estimate figure jumps to $107,000 for middle-income families if the wife sacrifices a part-time job to raise the child.)[16] Immediately, however, the working mother faces inadequate or expensive childcare services. As of February, 1975, less than two percent of all children (326,000) were in day care centers largely because of the high cost or absence of organised day care facilities. 'Desirable' day care costs between $300 and $500 a year and is already beyond the means of low-income families.[17] What childcare is available is not within the reach of approximately twelve million working women whose husbands earn less than $10,000 a year. General Electric was not concerned with the economics of pregnancy and childrearing for their employees; neither were the other large companies who submitted *amicae* briefs in this case. Instead, they were more impressed by the $1.4 billion a year it would require to pay disability benefits to pregnant workers, to say nothing of what it would cost to provide adequate federal day care.

Congressional reaction to *Gilbert* has been encouraging, however. Legislation has been introduced into both Houses of Congress to protect the rights of pregnant workers by expanding the definition of sex discrimination in Section 701 of Title VII. The new subsection would read:

The terms 'because of sex' or 'on the basis of sex' include, but are not limited to, because of or on the basis of pregnancy, childbirth, or related medical conditions, and women affected by pregnancy, childbirth, or related medical conditions shall be treated the same for all employment-related purposes, including receipt of benefits under fringe benefit programs, as other persons not so affected but similar in their ability or inability to work, and nothing in Section 703 (h) of this title shall be interpreted to permit otherwise.[18]

Such legislation has the support of all major feminist and professional women's groups, the Congressional Black Caucus and the AFL–CIO Executive Council, which has gone on record against *Gilbert* saying although 'the Court may have ignored it, the facts of life are that discrimination against pregnant people is discrimination against women alone'.[19] This constitutional issue is not yet closed because the Supreme Court has agreed to hear at least two more cases involving maternity leave policies and benefits.[20]

Family Law for the Unmarried

Given recent societal trends one can no longer assume that what is called family law applies only to people who are married or divorced. Increasingly changes in family law have been directed at individual adults and their children who happen to cohabit, whether or not the relationship has been legally sanctioned. Although we have devoted much attention to formal marriage and divorce with their lingering discriminatory features still endorsed by private law, informal marriages and *de facto* relationships, both heterosexual and homosexual,[21] are beginning to be recognised in various ways by public law. While legal fictions about traditional marriage remain strong, there are a few indications of a gradual blurring of the distinction between the married and unmarried conditions. These trends are more apparent than real at the moment, but they remain potential harbingers of the future, especially in the areas of public assistance, child custody, children's rights, taxation, and social security and other pension programs.

It is ironic that the shift in family law currently in progress has developed in the last decade following the Supreme Court decision in *Loving v. Virginia*, 388 U.S. 1 (1967), which invalidated antimiscegenation laws as violations of the equal protection clause, and held that the 'freedom to marry' was a 'basic civil right of man'. This right to marry was proclaimed at the very moment when some states were reducing their control over formal marriages to minimal licensing and registration procedures and were creating greater access to divorce. Thus, the binding contractual nature of marriage discussed above is not only a legal fiction, but increasingly an anachronism as well. A recent article has provocatively suggested that

> the ideologising of the freedom to marry seems to have appeared on the scene, just when legal marriage is ceasing to have much significance. As marriage impediments and formalities fall away, those exercising the 'right to marry' may find that life on the other side of the door they have tried so hard to open is not much different from life on the outside. In passing through the door, however, they may encounter an unlooked-for intimacy with the State. Long before it gets to the point where their photographs and fingerprints are taken and a package of contraceptives is pressed into their hands as they cross the threshold, many couples may decide that the 'freedom to marry' is not worth pursuing.[22]

Government involvement with the family is not disappearing; it is simply taking new forms that concentrate on the *de facto* aspects of cohabitation, namely, economic and child-related matters. The legal regulation of who can marry and the rigid enforcement of marriage contracts embodying sex-steroyped status have yielded to the bureaucratic regulation of formal and informal families through federal, state, and local agencies designed to dispense money, food, medicine, advice, comfort, nursing care, education, and childcare. All of these are services once provided in part by churches, volunteer community welfare groups, or the family itself. Thus, as one form of legal control of family matters seems to be passing from the scene, another one is taking its place. Such future de-legalisation of marriage and family relationships as might take place would not represent a decline in government control or even more legal neutrality, but ultimately control of a more insidious and pervasive nature than ever contemplated by traditional regulations.

Early family law was property oriented and reflected, as most laws do, the values of the ruling middle class. Subcultural groups at both ends of the socio-economic scale have not regularly complied with common marriage and divorce proceedings either because they could 'afford' not to or because they could not 'afford' to. The new developments in family law are different, but not inherently any less reflective of mainstream culture. For example, census figures indicate that approximately a half-million people in the United States are informally cohabiting. The number of unmarried couples recorded as living together increased 700 percent from 1960 to 1970, while there was only a ten percent increase in that same decade of married couples. These figures on informal living arrangements are probably low because of underreporting. While the number of those practicing alternative family styles may or may not have reached 'critical mass' proportions,[23] the fact remains that more and more middle class Americans find themselves involved in serial monogamy or successive polygamy through easier divorce procedures and a high remarriage rate. Until recently it could be said 'that Americans like marriage so much ... that they do it over and over again'.

But these same Americans now face a political economy that can no longer provide or guarantee economic growth. Instead they have been alternately living through the ravages of inflation or recession or both in the form of 'stagflation'. Hence, property and inheritance considerations are not as important even to members of the middle class as income support, credit, and social welfare policies. Recent changes in family law and marriage and divorce patterns demonstrate these altered needs and concerns. Until the last few years, for example, high divorce rates in the United States were balanced by remarriages. As of 1974, however, statistics showed a record high increase of 109 percent in divorces over 1962 and the first significant decline in marriages since the end of the Second World War.[24] While these figures are not yet conclusive evidence of a permanent demographic change, they are more responsible for the new family law than the more publicised, unconventional activities of subcultural groups.

There are four areas where this new family law now significantly affects unmarried as well as married people – public assistance legislation, children's rights, taxes and pension systems. In particular, American public law has definitely begun to recognise the economic consequences of de facto dependency. Although private law continues to cling to legal fictions about informal relationships, even it is beginning to change. This change has been especially evident in community property states like California and Washington, where the economic rights of a de facto or 'meretricious spouse' have been recognised by the courts. In non-community property states separate property rights have already diminished the practical differences between married and unmarried persons for the reasons discussed above. Public assistance law represents a less clear-cut case because traditionally this type of law has been imposed by the rich on the poor. Even here, however, there has been an increased emphasis on actual need and dependency rather than on the sexual morality of the recipients. What make all social welfare programs so significant in terms of family law is the enormous amount of money involved. On the federal level alone there has been an increase since 1950 from $10.5 billion to almost $170 billion per year, an increase from one-fourth to one-half of the federal budget. If state and local programs are included, the figure rises to $250 billion. This represents an increase from four to fifteen percent of the national income between 1950 and 1974 that is spent for social welfare purposes.[25]

Some of the worst features of early welfare legislation have been eliminated through Supreme Court rulings denying states the right to discriminate against informal families.[26] Yet welfare policy in the United States, dating back to the Great Depression, remains based on a misreading of 'not only the nature of the American economy, but also the social structure of poor families'.[27] Probably the most recent disturbing side effects of massive public assistance programs came with the passage of the Social Services Amendments Law of 1975. Opposed by civil liberties groups, this law set up a federal system for enforcing support orders of state courts, which makes nonsupport of welfare mothers a federal crime and requires such women to co-operate in civil or criminal prosecution of a nonsupporting father *as a condition of receiving public aid*. Again, this is a reflection of both the moral standards of the dominant culture and an attempt to place economic responsibility on family members rather than on taxpayers. What is usually not recognised in this misguided attempt to clean up the welfare system is how deeply such legislation touches the private lives of individuals despite 'freed up' formal marriage and divorce or informal 'living together' and 'splitting' situations. It is possible that regulation of traditional marriage in the past by state law was less an invasion of privacy than state enforcement of public assistance programs will be in the future. As Stanton said in 1853: 'The right idea of marriage is at the foundation of all reforms.'[28]

Children's rights have also become an important issue in the United States largely because of the emergence of a second women's movement in the late 1960s. Since one out of every six American children under eighteen is now being raised by a single parent, family law often involves the unmarried. In addition, it raises the question of where the parent's right to raise a child conflicts with the rights of the child as a person. State intervention with, or termination of, parental rights remains one of the most controversial and amorphous aspects of contemporary family law. Another issue focusing on children concerns their 'legitimacy' if born outside of formal marriage. The trend since 1968 in the United States (and the world) has been to consider dependency not legitimacy or gender when determining custody and rights of children to parental support and inheritance. Currently one out of ten births in the country is technically illegitimate, but this does not mean that such children are without *de facto* families. Less concern over legitimacy has been accompanied by increasing concern over problems of child neglect and child abuse.

Tax law affecting married couples, as opposed to single people, is in a state of flux. Most laws still tend to favor or subsidise the 'traditional' American family where only the husband works. As noted earlier, this family is no longer typical, but old tax laws continue to favor one-income families. Tax benefits for one-income married couples are significant enough to discourage some women from working. Married couples with two incomes, for example, are not allowed to declare the standard individual deduction of $2,200 each. Instead they are limited to declaring $3,000 if they file jointly. Their combined earnings also automatically place them in a higher tax bracket. Single people pay a more progressive tax rate than one-income couples, but less than two-income couples. Congress has been unable for the last five years to reform these differential tax rates for married and single taxpayers.[29] Similar inequalities exist in public and private pension programs.

All pensions paid to single and married women, including those under the federal Social Security system, discriminate against them, especially if they are older. Private pension plans are almost always inadequate for women because of their low paying jobs; they provide limited coverage for women as dependents and terminate fringe benefits upon the husband's death. Most women have no choice, therefore, but to rely upon Social Security which now (but not originally) contains automatic survival benefits and coverage for part-time work. Social Security benefits do not yet accrue equally for working wives and working husbands. Currently, a wife, regardless of whether she has or has not been employed, is eligible for benefits equal to one-half her husband's benefits when she reaches retirement age. If a working wife is eligible for benefits based on her own earnings, she may receive the amount which is higher – the benefit based on her own earnings or a benefit based on her husband's, but not both. If she chooses the latter she receives the same amount as if she had never been employed and had not paid Social Security taxes. If her husband dies she forfeits his benefits. If she remarries she loses again if the second husband had a lower income than the first. Such inequities have prompted some older couples to 'live together' unmarried in order to maintain an adequate retirement income. Divorced women also continue to be denied certain benefits available to married women even if they were married for over twenty years and have dependent children.[30] Housework, of course, is not covered by Social Security because no monetary value is placed on it.

Family law remains deficient in many areas for American women who routinely outlive their husbands or who, in the case of divorced women, receive nothing for their years of work inside or outside of the home. Single, divorced, or widowed women are generally penalised by lower paying jobs and hence lower public and private pensions. Taxation and pension policies remain flawed by discrimination based on sex, age, and marital status. Credit discrimination should diminish when the Equal Credit Opportunity Act (ECOA) goes into effect in 1977.[31] Child custody and children's rights appear to be increasingly handled on the basis of common sense, rather than from the point of view of legitimacy or sex-stereotyping. As family law for the married and unmarried changes, its directions and pace can only be approximated at this time. To the degree that it increasingly focuses on women and children as individuals, rather than on traditionally prescribed roles within the conjugal, nuclear unit, family law could precipitate a veritable revolution in American public policy.

The Right to Control One's Body

By far the most liberating aspects of female existence in the twentieth century have been improved means of contraception and access to hygienic abortions. Until a woman is able to control her own reproductive functions, it is literally impossible for her to plan her life or career with any certainty. There are other prerequisites for full female emancipation, such as a level of urbanisation, industrialisation, and technology high enough to free women from traditional domestic, as well as subsistence-level economic, duties and from general immobility in a mobile society.[32] Only since the Second World War have a majority of middle class American women experienced these liberating material conditions. Without freedom from unwanted and unplanned pregnancies the other prerequisites for complete emancipation lose much of their significance.

Two Supreme Court decisions in 1965 and 1972, permitting dissemination of information about contraceptive devices,[33] paved the way for the Court's decisions legalising abortions, among them: *Roe v. Wade*, 410 U.S. 113 (1973), *Doe v. Bolton*, 410 U.S. 179 (1973), *Planned Parenthood v. Danforth*, 428 U.S. 52 (1976) and *Maloney v. Lady Jane*, May 23, 1977. While these and other abortion cases leave many questions unanswered, they continue to uphold the principle that abortions during the first trimester are matters of private conscience to be decided by women, even minors, and their physicians. This does not mean, however, that state legislatures where 'right-to-life' forces are strong will not proceed to pass restrictive legislation that will require lengthy court battles to overturn. Women in such states will be denied their constitutional right to free choice and control over their own bodies indefinitely until this type of litigation runs its course. Even with these favourable rulings, it is estimated that from 250,000 to 750,000 women – the majority of them poor, young, and living in small towns and rural areas – still lack access to abortions because only fifteen percent of public hospitals provide abortion services.[34]

In light of recent pro-abortion decisions, 'right-to-life' groups have adopted a new strategy. Five states (New Jersey, Arkansas, Louisiana, Missouri, and Indiana) have passed resolutions calling for a constitutional convention to consider an anti-abortion amendment and eleven others are considering similar resolutions. This method of amending the federal Constitution never has been employed before. Naturally this raises a number of questions because there are no legal precedents or guidelines for conducting such a convention. It could conceivably consider other issues in addition to abortion, and the American Bar Association has warned that 'a grave constitutional crisis' could ensue if guidelines were determined in a 'time of divisive controversy and confusion'.[35]

In the meantime anti-abortion forces have succeeded in pressuring Congress to modify the Labor–Health Education and Welfare (HEW) appropriations bill by adding the Hyde Amendment banning Medicaid reimbursement for abortion, except where the life of the mother would be endangered. Suits were immediately filed on behalf of the constitutional rights of poor women who would be adversely affected by a ban on federally funded abortions. On October 22, 1976, New York Judge John F. Dooling issued a preliminary injunction in *Califano v. McRae* that nullified the Hyde Amendment in all fifty states until all such court challenges to it were decided. On November 8 the Supreme Court refused to block Dooling's decision.

Then on June 20, 1977, the Court handed down two opinions substantially undermining the effectiveness of its earlier pro-abortion decisions. In *Maher v. Roe*, 45 *Law Week* 4787, the Justices in a 6–3 decision held that exclusion of Medicaid reimbursement for nontherapeutic abortions did not violate protection under the Fourteenth Amendment for indigent women because the Court has never ruled that financial need alone identifies a suspect class. Moreover, they held that the state's action was 'rationally related' to a 'constitutionally permissible' purpose. In *Beal v. Doe*, 45 *Law Week* 4781, the Courts specifically denied that either the Constitution or any federal statute, such as Title XIX[36] of the Social Security Act required states to use public funds to offer elective abortions to the poor for free. Dividing 7–2, the majority of Justices declared that while states may not make abortion illegal, they may 'make a value judgment favoring childbirth over abortion, and ... implement that judgment by the allocation of public funds'. Dissenting in *Beal* Justice Marshall asserted that the majority opinion would in reality 'impose a moral viewpoint that no State may constitutionally enforce' and 'have the practical effect of preventing nearly all poor women from obtaining safe and legal abortions'. Noting that public officials were already 'under extraordinary pressure from well financed and carefully orchestrated lobby campaigns to approve more such restrictions,' Marshall concluded: 'the effect will be to relegate millions of people to lives of poverty and despair. When elected leaders cower before public pressure, this Court, more than ever, must not shirk its duty to enforce the Constitution for the benefit of the poor and powerless.'

On June 29, 1977, the Court ordered the lifting of Judge Dooling's preliminary injunction and reconsideration of *Califano v. McRae* in light of *Maher* and *Beal*. While Dooling's court continued to litigate the constitutionality of the 1976 version of Hyde Amendment, Congress remained deadlocked in the summer and fall of 1977 over the exact wording of that amendment, which was still appended to the Labor–HEW appropriations bill. The Senate wanted to 'liberalise' it to read that federal funds could be used to perform abortions in case of reported rape or incest and when there would be severe and long-lasting physical damage to the mother. The House preferred the more restrictive wording of the original amendment, which allowed for termination of only life-threatening pregnancies. In the meantime salaries for the 200,000 Labor–HEW employees were being voted by Congress on a month-by-month basis because $60.2 billion was tied up in the stalemate over the appropriations bill. This financial crisis finally forced a compromise on wording between the House and Senate on December 7, 1977.[37] Even this new language of the Hyde Amendment meant that most poor women would not be eligible for federally funded abortions.

In addition to justifying such class legislation at the Congressional level, *Maher* and *Beal* have predictably encouraged state legislatures to initiate or continue prohibitions on the use of Medicaid funds for legal abortions. Since many public health plans allow middle class women to obtain abortions from tax monies, this decision becomes all the harder to justify in terms of social justice. However *Beal* did not come as a complete surprise. HEW Secretary Joseph A. Califano, Jr. was an early supporter of the Hyde Amendment and the Justice Department had already advised the Supreme Court that 'the government has no constitutional obligation to relieve all the burdens of poverty'. President Carter echoed these sentiments when he defended the *Maher* and *Beal* decisions as 'adequate' and 'reasonably fair' by saying:

> Well, as you know, there are many things in life that are not fair, that wealthy people can afford and poor people can't. But I don't believe that the Federal Government should take action to try to make these opportunities exactly equal, particularly when there is a moral factor involved.[38]

Both the President and Califano have endorsed a child adoption plan under the Public Assistance Amendments of 1977 that would eventually cost more than $500 million a year, compared to the $61 million that the government paid in 1976 funding approximately one-third of the million legal abortions performed in the United States. For those who personally oppose abortions this large amount of public funding to adopt unwanted children is apparently preferable to the lower cost of allowing poor women the freedom to choose to have an abortion. (The average cost of an abortion in 1976 was $280 or $42 more than the average monthly family welfare payment.) It is clear that low-income women cannot now follow the callous advice of General Electric when it told its female workers that 'if a woman has not saved enough to get pregnant, she should get an abortion'.[39] The adoption subsidy plan of the Carter administration has come under criticism because it would not only draw upon Medicaid funds to pay childbirth expenses, but also because in some states it would amount to twice what welfare mothers are now paid to support a single child. To complicate this emotional issue of abortion v. adoption further, an HEW study group on alternatives to abortion disbanded in November, 1977, after concluding that the only real alternatives were 'suicide, motherhood, and some would add, madness',[40] The Hyde Amendment and *Maher* and *Beal* decisions have placed public policy in the absurd position of saying that while abortion is legal, it is immoral, but only the poor can be saved from this immorality, whether or not they want to be.

The most significant constitutional aspect of all these abortion rulings lies in the Supreme Court's definition of the 'viability of the fetus' as that stage of development 'when the life of the unborn child may be continued indefinitely outside the womb by natural or artificial life support systems'. Although doctors in both cases wanted the Court to define viability in terms of gestational time based on the three medically determined stages of pregnancy, the Justices refused. Instead, in *Danforth* they referred specifically to *Roe*, indicating that the 'stage subsequent to viability' was 'purposefully left flexible for professional determination, and dependent upon developing medical skill and technical ability'. After this indefinite period of viability is reached, states can legally prohibit abortions. At first glance the ambiguousness of the definition appears to open the door for future state interference with a woman's right to have an abortion after the first trimester. And indeed it does. Despite its ambiguities, the *Roe* decision with its definition of viability has been attacked by antiabortionists as 'the willful imposition of pure judicial preference'. Even some legal scholars in favor of a woman's right to abortion have criticised *Roe* as simply being bad constitutional law because it represents an implicit return to substantive due process or 'Lochnerism'.[41] (See pp. 112–16.)

On the other hand, Laurence H. Tribe has persuasively argued that the very absence of precise time limits on viability may be *Roe's* most significant contribution to less dogmatic interpretations of the Constitution in the future. He states that this is one of the few examples of what he has called 'structural due process' or 'structural justice' whereby the Court can structure 'the process of change in constitutional principles without dictating endproducts'. In other words, this definition of viability, far from reflecting arbitrary judicial preference, allows for considerable flexibility. It permits each generation, depending upon advances in medical technology, to determine when the 'fetus may become viable' and it may well mean 'at points ever closer to conception itself'.[42]

The constitutional significance of such a flexible definition may not be immediately apparent to non-lawyers on either side of the abortion issue until it is examined in the historical context of the struggle for women's rights. As we have noted throughout this work, the attempt to obtain equality of treatment for women in the late nineteenth and early twentieth centuries, as well as now, inevitably means that at various levels the courts have been asked to question standard sex-stereotyped assumptions. Over time the Supreme Court in particular has been reluctant to abandon traditional gender distinctions. When asked 'to identify areas of moral flux and normative transition' and 'to facilitate ... the evolution of moral and thus legal consciousness', generations of Justices have been slow to respond to demands of either the first or second women's movements. Tribe believes there is a less direct way for the Court to act as an instrument for social change in the present without dogmatically restricting the options of future generations as has often happened with past doctrinaire decisions. It can do this by providing the *structure* for the evolution of social values. Following 'structural due process', Supreme Court decisions would become a vehicle for continuing dialogue between state regulations and those whose liberty is limited by such laws.[43]

While there is the danger of individualising each case with this approach, the risk is outweighed by the reduction of the probability of imposing a rigid societal concept (in this case a time-bound definition of fetus viability) which will become obsolete in light of changing opinion or technology. In all likelihood, 'structural justice' is not necessarily what either the pro-abortion or 'right-to-life' forces would prefer from the Justices. It is, nonetheless, a more realistic estimation of what it is possible to expect from this particular Supreme Court under Chief Justice Warren E. Burger in light of *Maher* and *Beal*. Such decisions suggest that the more conservative Justices, including Burger, would like to isolate the Court as much as possible from further societal change, especially where females are concerned. (See pages 214–23.)

Citing increased workloads of the Justices, the Burger Court, for example, has employed a variety of devices to restrict access to federal courthouses. It has raised procedural difficulties for plaintiffs, eliminated some fees awarded to lawyers, and demanded that civil rights advocates prove a discriminatory intent in cases of racial or sex segregation. The Burger Court has also insisted that more constitutional claims be heard by state rather than federal courts.[44] Most important, the Chief Justice has already displayed his inability to rise above stereotypical classifications of women based on ascribed gender differentiation. In oral argument before the Court in 1971 he insisted 'that women are manually much more adept than men' and therefore the reason the Department of Justice did not hire male secretaries was because females 'are better and you hire women assembly people [in factories] because they are better. ...'[45]

PART THREE

THE LEGAL PROFESSION

5 *Britain:* Barristers and Gentlemen

A major reason for the obdurate resistance by judges and lawyers to the entry of women into the professions was simply their determination to exclude competitors seeking to participate in a lucrative monopoly activity. The feminists themselves had no doubt that this was a prime consideration, though only two of the many judgments referred to earlier alluded directly to this point. In one case a Scottish judge relatively sympathetic to Sophia Jex-Blake's claim went out of his way to emphasise that the exclusion of women from medical practice was not, as alleged, due to economic jealousy, but a leading South African judge openly stated that the choice was between denying women the right to economic independence and increasing the ranks of an already overcrowded profession.

In general, however, the exclusion of females was justified on the basis of maintaining professional standards. Maleness was converted into one of the attributes of professionalism (just as the capacity to be professional, that is, intellectually detached and emotionally uninvolved, became one of the attributes of the middle-class male). The professions, like clubs and elite schools, were not simply institutions from which women happened to be absent. Their maleness became part of their character, so that the admission of women was seen as not merely adding to their number or introducing some novelty, but as threatening the very identity of the institutions themselves.

Whereas the medical profession expressly set out to take healing away from women – many female folk-healers being condemned on the testimony of professional male doctors as witches – the legal profession established a monopoly of litigation and conveyancing that only incidentally excluded females. The procedures designed to protect the income and status of the professional lawyers from the competition of unregistered scribes and other unqualified persons were not specifically anti-female, but their consequences were such as to make it impossible for women to practise law. Once this exclusion of women had been established, however, maleness became part of the ethos of the profession, and male-exclusiveness was elevated to the level of a principle. A legal profession centralised around the courts in London, as opposed to community lawyers dispersed through the population, favoured the exclusion of women. The monopoly established by the profession over litigation and later over transfers of land, defined the function and the style of the profession from the first, and tied it in firmly with landed and commercial interests, creating what to this day has become the model of lawyers' work. In the neighbourhoods there were of course wise-women as well as wise-men who were consulted and asked to arbitrate informally on local disputes, but since they did not work for a fee in association with the courts they were not regarded as lawyers.

Incidentally, it is interesting to note that the professions were almost invariably described as 'overcrowded'. It is in the nature of professions dependent on fees from private clients to be permanently 'overcrowded', just as it is in the nature of publicly-funded professions to be perpetually 'short-staffed'. It would seem that public funding through such agencies as the National Health Service and the Legal Aid Fund has played a major role in weakening the opposition of males to the entry into the professions of females. Public funding, however, makes specialisation and progress through a career structure the crucial determinants of income and status, and it is suggested that males have shifted their control away from the point of entry towards the routes of advancement. To say this is not to suggest that men conspire as a secret brotherhood to exclude women – though male condescension may well be nearly universal and male hostility fairly common – or even that individual male bigotry is the dominant bar to female advancement. Institutions tend to have machinery for their self-perpetuation, and all professions are structurally organised so as to maintain male domination and female subordination. This is most noticeable in areas such as health, education, and the social services, where men are in a small minority as far as all occupations are concerned, but grossly over-represented in the highest echelons. The social services have been built up by women and are largely staffed by women, but nine out of ten top posts are held by men.[1] And anyone who doubts the special role of professionalism in maintaining male privilege need merely to look at what professionalism has meant in relation to the kitchen. Women do the cooking in almost every home – men are at pains to perpetuate their inferiority here – but women are almost entirely excluded from the well-paid and prestigious activity of professional chef.

Women have been struggling for at least a century to find a place in the legal profession. Just over a hundred years ago ninety-two women signed a petition requesting permission to attend lectures in Lincoln's Inn, a preliminary step to being called to the Bar. The Benchers (leaders) of the Inn regretted that this was 'not expedient'.[2]

Although there appear to have been examples in the distant past of women acting as attorneys in England, the first application in modern times for a woman to be enrolled as a solicitor seems to have been made in 1876, which was seven years after Arabella Mansfield had become the first woman to be admitted to legal practice in the United States. The English application was rejected by the Law Society and when six years later a male solicitor proposed to offer employment to female clerks, the *Solicitors' Journal* treated the suggestion as a huge joke.[3] In fact it was the typewriter rather than the law degree that opened the way for women to enter legal offices. Initially, all important documents were hand-written by male clerks, and typing was regarded as a form of copying appropriate for inferior materials only, fit to be done by women at low rates of pay. The subordinate status of women typists continued even after they became responsible for the preparation of important documents. Lawyers in fact long resisted the entry of both typewriters and women into their offices, but eventually gave way to economic pressures that favoured the replacing of male clerks by machines and by women. In his study of the black-coated worker, David Lockwood points out that in the century 1851 to 1951 clerical workers increased from one in a hundred of the general labour force to one in ten, and that the proportion of women clerks during this period rose from less than one in a thousand to nearly two out of three.[4] Clerical work thus became largely feminised, which acted to the advantage rather than the disadvantage of male clerks in that they tended to be the ones who offered themselves or were preferred for promotion. The characteristic office situation was thus of the supervisor or manager being an older man and his assistants being younger women, the men exercising discipline through personal contact, 'whether the ensuing relationship [was] paternalistic, petty tyrannical or sexually exploitive'. The lawyers' office, it should be mentioned, tended to take on a three-tiered structure, with men occupying virtually all of the top or professional sector, as well as most of the middle or managing layer, while women filled almost all of the bottom or clerical zone.

There were, however, some women who from the 1880s onwards practised neither as clerks nor as qualified lawyers, but as legal workers dealing directly with the public or else giving assistance to solicitors and barristers. The admission of women to the Universities in the last quarter of the century led to a number of women receiving law degrees, a state of affairs which was not objected to by the profession as long as it led nowhere. But, as has been seen, when in 1903 Bertha Cave brought a test application on behalf of herself and other recent graduates, including Christabel Pankhurst, seeking admission to the Bar, both the Bar and the judges insisted that the profession be confined to men only. It is interesting to speculate what the result on the suffrage movement would have been had women been admitted to legal practice at that time; if many leading rebels and revolutionaries have been lawyers, few leading lawyers have been rebels, and it is highly likely that even the spirited Christabel Pankhurst would have been totally contained by the Bar. As it was, 'the hot strife at the Bar', which allegedly was too much for women, appealed to her temperament, and in her capacity as a defendant she manifested such forensic brilliance that it was the male witnesses, magistrates and lawyers who found the combat too intense, not her. The courtroom became an arena in which she was far more effective as a feminist law-breaker than she would have been as a female barrister, and the occasion when she humiliated Lloyd George in the witness box – a Government Minister, solicitor and orator of note – stands out as one of the notable pieces of cross-examination of her era.

Not all the women rejected by the Bar followed her example of embarking on full-time political activity. Ivy Williams, who eighteen years later was to be the first woman to be called to the Bar in England, declared in 1903 that women holding University law degrees could set up practice outside of the profession without being trameled by the lawyers' trade union rules. The *Law Journal* countered what it called 'these threats which have been added to the weapons with which women are assailing the legal fortress', by reporting the comforting news that women had not been triumphant rivals in countries where the profession had been opened to them, quoting as evidence a letter from a member of the American Bar.[5] The Bar and the Law Society were not merely unhelpful to women, they resolutely set their organisations against women, fighting tenaciously both inside and out of Parliament to maintain their male-exclusive character. To the extent that they bothered to argue the matter at all, male lawyers insisted on evaluating possible female lawyers against the stereotype woman rather than the stereotype lawyer – either they suborned male judges and juries with feminine wiles, or else they became 'un-sexed'.[6] Even after women won the vote at the end of World War I, the professions hoped to uphold a legal barrier to women entering practice, but once women had the franchise, Members of Parliament were not willing to risk their seats in order to support a male monopoly in which they no longer participated. The Sex Disqualification Removal Act of 1919 expressly authorised what the profession had expressly resisted, namely the right of women to set up as barristers and solicitors.

By 1921 there were twenty women barristers listed, and by 1929 the number had grown to seventy-seven.[7] By 1955 the total had actually declined to sixty-four (3.2 per cent) and ten years later it had grown only to ninety-nine (4.6 per cent). By 1970 the increase had been rather more rapid and the total stood at 147 (5.7 per cent) while by 1976 it had reached 313 (8.1 per cent). In that year only four out of 370 practising Queen's Counsel (senior barristers) were female. As one female barrister recently put it:

> The successful jealously guard their right to remain overworked, and junior tenants who have only just got on to the bottom rung of the ladder are frequently the least sympathetic to the plight of those waiting below. . . . Females become a luxury the profession cannot afford.[8]

The fact is that nearly half of all sets of Chambers have never had a female member.[9]

A similar picture of male predominance can be seen with regard to solicitors, that branch of the profession that deals directly with the public, calling in barristers only to give advice in complex legal matters or to appear in serious litigation. In 1921 there were seventeen women solicitors on the roll, and for many years women lawyers tended to be barristers rather than solicitors.[10] Even now the proportion of female barristers is higher than the proportion of female solicitors. There has, however, been a steady increase in recent years in the number of women qualifying as solicitors, from sixty-two out of 1009 (6.1 per cent) in 1965, to 283 out of 1849 (15.3 per cent) in 1974. In that year only 2296 out of 36,150 solicitors on the roll were female (i.e. 6.4 per cent) while the proportion of those in practice was even lower (1299 out of 28,741, i.e. 4.5 per cent). There are thus still twenty male solicitors in practice for every female.

The rate of advance of women in the paid judiciary has not surprisingly been even slower. No woman has ever sat in the Judicial Committee of the House of Lords or as a judge in the Court of Appeal, and it is only in recent years that women have been appointed to the High Court.

The full table for judicial and other senior appointments going to barristers is as shown on p. 175 (figures are for 1976).[11]

While the position now represents an advance on that ten years ago when there was only a single woman on the High Court bench, one in the County Court and one Queen's Counsel, male barristers still seem to find it easier to get on to the bench than do females. One estimate is that whereas a half of all male barristers of ten years' call or

	Men	Women
Law Lords and Court of Appeal	25	0
High Court Judges	70	2
Circuit Judges	265	5
Masters and Registrars (barristers only)	21	1
Stipendiary Magistrates	50	2
Recorders	359	7
Practising QCs	368	4
Benchers (leaders) of the Inns of Court – 1975	377	2

more have been appointed to the bench, less than a quarter of female barristers of equal seniority have been so elevated.[12] The only sector of the judiciary in which there is any appreciable female representation is amongst the lay magistrates, the great unpaid, who hear ninety per cent of criminal cases.[13] A third of these magistrates are female, which suggests that women are regarded as possessing the qualities of detachment and discernment thought to be necessary to the judicial function only when they act without a fee.

The solitary area of judicial activity where gender equality has been achieved has been in relation to the jury. As late as 1964 only eleven per cent of persons on the jury lists were female,[14] but since the recent opening up of the jury lists to make them roughly coincide with the Parliamentary voters' lists, the proportions of male to female are almost exactly even. Judging from reports in the press of major trials, however, a small preponderance of male jurors seems still to be achieved in most cases. Unlike in the United States where jury selection can take days or even weeks, juries in England are usually empanelled in a matter of minutes, and challenges for cause are virtually unknown, with the result that little attention has been paid to the question of gender on the jury.

The position, then, is that the legal profession and the judiciary continue to be overwhelmingly dominated by men, not only in quantitative terms, but in relation to positions of authority and access to fees. Representation of women has not even reached a token level in the higher judiciary, and such political appointments as go to lawyers with each new government (Lord Chancellor, Attorney-General and so on) have never been offered to a woman.

Similarly, women are rarely if ever appointed to sit on any of the many tribunals requiring the presence of lawyers. A tally published in 1973 showed that not a single one of the forty-four 'Chairmen' of Industrial Tribunals was female, while only seven out of nearly 400 ordinary members were women.[15] The figures for the Tribunal concerned with Industrial Injuries were none out of twenty-seven (chair) and two out of more than 260 (ordinary); for Pensions Appeal none out of sixteen (chair) and six out of thirty-four (ordinary); and for Rent seventeen out of 250 (chair) and ninety out of nearly 500 (ordinary). In the case of National Insurance Tribunals, only two per cent of the 'Chairmen' were female, as contrasted with twenty-seven per cent of the ordinary members, while in the case of Supplementary Benefit Tribunals the figures were eighteen and twenty-two per cent respectively. As will be seen later, the Industrial Tribunals have a particularly important role to play in the implementation of recent anti-discrimination statutes, and it is interesting to note that in a period when the number of Tribunals has grown extensively the gender disproportion has been corrected to some extent, so that by the end of 1976 there were 494 women to 1769 men, i.e. twenty-eight per cent of the total.[16]

It has recently been suggested by an anonymous barrister in a legal periodical that the real reason why women make no progress in the English legal profession is that firms cannot afford 'to nurse their practices while they nurse their brats', and that accordingly women should set up their own firms of barristers and solicitors so as to share the cost of a rotating maternity on an equal basis.[17] This faintly mocking approach expresses what is probably the major justification offered by male lawyers for the weak position of women in the profession today, namely, that as actual or potential child-bearers, women are more likely than men to withdraw from practice. The biological fact of maternity is said to give rise to the social fact of unavailability, and it is argued that a highly competitive profession cannot be expected to bear the expense and inconvenience of absentee members. Women barristers, however, have contended that even though many of their male colleagues are sympathetic to the idea of equal opportunity, many others are actively hostile to women's advancement in the profession. Some sets of Chambers operate a quota system, while the many that have never had a female member are accordingly hardly in a position to state from experience that women perform less effectively than men. As for absentee barristers, many sets of Chambers have been happy to nurse the practices of male Members of Parliament while the latter nurse their constituencies.

One self-styled Angry Young Woman has pointed out that the legal profession is not a celibate one, and that becoming a parent has never prevented a man from developing his career; why must it be assumed that it would have that effect on a woman?[18] In her view equal opportunity should include the right to combine a career with a family, something men had taken for granted for ages.

It may be noted in passing that the Bar appears to have been far less supportive to females than to males seeking to combine legal and political careers. Lawyers have long been the largest single occupational group in Parliament as a whole, accounting in recent years for about one-fifth of all members of the House of Commons. A survey done in 1967 indicated, however, that out of fifty-one female M.P.s who had declared specific occupations since the first woman was elected in 1918, only two had been barristers, while none had been solicitors.[19] One of these two was of course Margaret Thatcher, and her achievement in becoming leader of the Conservative Party might possibly increase the number of women lawyers who are permitted to combine professional and political careers. As it is, there have been many more women teachers, political organisers, trade unionists and journalists in Parliament than women lawyers.

If maternity has replaced delicacy as the major justification for keeping women out of the professions, paternity apparently works the other way – men should be given opportunities because they have children to support, while women should be denied opportunities because they have children to rear. Without getting into the wider question of whether such divided parenthood is necessary or equitable, it is possible to point out that the maternity argument, if valid for law, should be valid for all full-time occupations. Yet women have managed to predominate numerically if not in terms of authority in many professions, such as nursing, teaching and social work. What distinguishes them from law is not the character of the work involved, but the way the profession has been organised; there is no intrinsic reason why women should be able, despite maternity, to attend to the educational, medical and social needs of the community, and yet be rendered unfit through motherhood to attend to its legal needs. It is suggested that the extent of male dominance in the legal profession is to be attributed to the social constitution of the profession rather than to the biological constitution of women.

Furthermore, a fuller examination of the structure of legal work shows that, notwithstanding the alleged deleterious effects of maternity on women's work outside the home, there are as many women employed in the general provision of legal services as there are men. However, whereas men occupy the lucrative and prestige-carrying sectors of legal work, women are employed to do the secretarial and reception work. The report of the Prices and Incomes

Board for 1969 showed that there were 98,000 persons working in all capacities in solicitors' offices, of whom just over 50,000 were female clerical staff. The proportion of females to males in barristers' offices is probably not quite as high; managing clerks are nearly all male, whereas typists, telephonists and receptionists are virtually all female. Thus one may estimate that roughly half of about 110,000 persons involved in the legal profession as a whole are female, but of this number only two per cent are in the fee-earning sector, as contrasted with fifty per cent of the men. And lest it be thought that there is some unusual skill that justifies the great discrepancy in income and status between professionals and secretaries, it should be remembered that half of legal income comes from conveyancing, which is basically clerical work and which in the United States is in fact done by insurance clerks rather than lawyers. The bulk of matrimonial work, another important source of income, is also basically standardised as practised today, and a number of litigants are now finding it possible to learn in a few minutes how to do for themselves by post the sort of form-filling that was formerly alleged to require years of study and experience.

Male domination in the law has thus expressed itself in a number of different ways. Undoubtedly the legal profession in the past did its utmost to exclude women, not simply by making females unwelcome, but by using Parliament and the courts to impose a formal sex bar. It was hardly to be expected, then, that when the formal disabilities were removed, women would find a comfortable place for themselves in legal practice. It has been claimed that women have had to work much harder and endure many more secret humiliations, just to reach the position from which male lawyers start. The very lists of female 'firsts' – the first woman to handle a brief in the House of Lords, the first woman to conduct a murder trial, and so on – are reminders of continuing male domination rather than signs of female advance.[20] Half a century after women were permitted to enter the profession it should hardly require proof that they are no more nor less capable as lawyers than men.

At the level of equal opportunity inside the profession, there would appear to be strong evidence of discrimination in favour of men, certainly enough to merit investigation by the Equal Opportunities Commission. Despite the poor prospects that await them in the profession, approximately a third of law students today are female, yet far fewer than a third of entrants to the profession are female. One of the main reasons for what is called this 'wastage' (notably higher in law than in either medicine, teaching or social work) is that women have greater difficulties then men in getting the necessary professional training after graduation. The House of Lords Select Committee on Discrimination reported in 1973 that women often had difficulty in becoming articled to solicitors and encountered even greater problems in obtaining interesting work once they were qualified, while those who wished to become barristers often found their sex a disadvantage when seeking places as pupils or tenants in Chambers.[21] As far as the Bar is concerned, it should be pointed out that tenancies are extremely difficult for anyone to come by, male or female. Under the mantle of maintaining professional control, the Bar imposes severe restraints of trade on intending barristers, the crucial limitations being that no one may practise as a barrister except from a recognised set of Chambers. Since a tenancy in Chambers is a prerequisite for practice, a qualified person does not even have what must be regarded as the minimum right in a competitive society, namely the right to be unsuccessful. The extraordinary position has thus arisen that solicitors complain of a shortage of barristers while highly talented and fully qualified persons queue in vain for a chance to exercise their talents. The existing barristers thus regulate their succession not only indirectly by controlling education, but directly through their monopoly of tenancies. Merit plays some part in the selection of new barristers, but the greatest merit of all is still to be well-connected. If all would-be barristers suffer from unequal opportunity, some have more inequality than others, and so a conservative profession remains conservative, and a male profession remains male.

The regulation of entry and advancement is just one of the ways in which male control of the profession is expressed. The atmosphere of legal practice is strongly coloured by attitudes indicative of male arrogance. These attitudes are sometimes revealed in flagrant fashion, as when senior counsel in two recent sex assault cases respectively argued that all men wished to spank women's bottoms, and that when a woman said no to a man she frequently really meant yes. More often, however, male condescension is expressed through archaic courtesy and banter and by a refusal to take women's ideas and actions seriously. This phenomenon may be a generalised feature of our society, but it is emphasised by the club-like character and mannered quality of the legal profession and by the absence of women in positions of power within it. By all accounts the manners that maketh the legal man can in certain circumstances be most oppressive to the legal woman.

British lawyers have over the generations cultivated a characteristic mode of speech, bearing and appearance, which manifests itself today in a distinctive legal style. This style is based on well-elocuted speech, carefully considered language and a detached manner, all of which are wrapped around with an aura of integrity, which, incidentally, policemen and offenders seem equally to find irksome. These qualities are represented by supporters of the profession as being the hallmarks of erudition, objectivity, intellectual strength and moral trustworthiness, and by critics as being evidence of pomposity, complacency, desiccation and lack of contact with the real world.

Many of the older female barristers pride themselves on having achieved what the Bar Council has termed the 'male disposition' necessary for success at the Bar,[22] but some of their younger colleagues are challenging this conformism, and insisting that women have a special contribution to make.

> If there is one thing [I] believe strongly [one of them writes in an article on women at the Bar] it is that women barristers can make a separate contribution, and that the Bar will be the loser if women are forced to behave just like men. The 'Masculine approach' of the Bar is characterised all too often by a combination of arrogance and insensitivity; and the sort of qualities which women can bring to their work (and which need not exclude the power to reason) are a greater awareness of people's feelings, a sense of humility and a genuine desire to help their clients rather than to impress them. They might in the process persuade the men to be a little less conscious of their own importance and a little more responsive to the needs of the people they claim to serve.[23]

The identification of lawyers with upper-middle-class manners is one of the reasons why arrogance and aridity are attributed to lawyers as a group, but professionalism itself may be an important factor. If the knowledge and skills possessed by the professionals were manifestly superior to those of the non-professionals, there would be no need for professionalism, since professionals would stand out by virtue of their greater expertise and nothing more, and not be embarrassed to have the same appearance as the members of the community they served. But professionals in fact deal mostly with routine matters, and their special knowledge is frequently merely information supplied to them by ancillary workers, so that to justify their special status and income they need to impart a stamp of distinction to their work. This professional style is learnt by initiates largely through imitation; accents, impulses and modes of dress that jar against the accepted standards are rapidly eliminated. A second feature of professionalism is that it involves the grouping together of people who compete fiercely with each other for income and prestige but stand firmly united against encroachment on their territory from the outside world. It is this dualism of interests that produces the combative camaraderie so characteristic of lawyers. Gender enters the picture because as a rule it is the males rather than the females of the middle and upper-middle classes who are brought up to possess the virtues seen to be helpful to members of the professions. They are trained in particular to suppress their feelings and to accept formalised codes of conduct, to be intellectually aggressive and emotionally restrained. For men of this class, a career is seen by our society as a necessity not an option, whereas for women it is at most seen as a complement to full-time motherhood. Women's education is accordingly not directed so single-mindedly towards producing the intellectual gladiators thought to be necessary for the competitive professions, so that women may more easily than men escape the pressures to be eternally striving for individual success. Like all newcomers not born with what may be called a silver wig on their heads, women in the past have been compelled when entering the legal profession to adapt their styles and personalities to the mould of the institution into which they were moving.

Changes in work-style are closely bound up with changes in office organisation and changes in relationships with clients. Clearly, if members of a legal office work as a team that shares tasks and eliminates status lines, the resulting relationships and manners both with regard to one another and with regard to clients will be very different from those currently found in most firms. Changes in work-style do not take place in a vacuum but in the setting of an office and in relation to clients. Many feminists, when arguing that male domination in the legal profession extends beyond merely denying opportunity to qualified female professionals, point to the fact that there is hardly a legal office in the country that is not structured around female subservience. The figures already quoted show that half of all persons concerned with legal work are female, but that only one in thirty of these are involved in the professional sector, that is, for every woman barrister or solicitor in a legal office there are twenty-nine women typists and receptionists. The ratio for men, on the other hand, is one to one. Any real move towards sex equality would have to take this maldistribution into account. The work that the clerical staff does is vital to the functioning of any office, but it is poorly paid, carries low status, and offers little prospect of advancement. Male domination and female sub-ordination are epitomised by the characteristic office situation in which a male principal issues instructions to a female clerk. The reverse situation of a female boss giving dictation to a male shorthand typist is so extraordinary a phenomenon outside of Royal and senior government circles as to be news; perhaps it is precisely because the patterned subservience of female office workers is so omnipresent that it is rarely if ever questioned, the principle being that small inequities establish scandals, while great inequities create norms. Thus the gender hierarchy and the professional hierarchy tend to coincide, and reproduce themselves from generation to generation. Outsiders coming into a legal office are immediately made aware of who is in command in the office. The professional person issues instructions, can be seen by appointment only and usually has an office tucked away from public access; such a person is almost always male, normally speaks in an authoritative manner, and clearly is someone of importance. If lawyers went on house-calls like general practitioners used to do, they would immediately lose three-quarters of their aura, since clerical workers are not merely the functionaries who keep the office going, but a fixed entourage who enhance the status of their principals. Lawyers feed on deference; they defer to the judiciary, exact deference from their clerks, and expect deference from their clients. Lawyers are supposed to be servants of their clients, but in reality they use the power granted them by their professional position to control their clients. This they do quite conscientiously, in the sense that they regard it to be in the best interests of the client for him or her to accommodate to the legal system as it operates, rather than to put pressure on the legal system to adapt to his or her particular needs. People in our society have become so accustomed to having their lives controlled by experts – medical experts, religious experts, social work experts and legal experts – that often they are content to leave all responsibility for decisions to their lawyers. Possibly in the world of high commerce, the lawyer meets with his client on a basis of equality or even inferiority, but in the ordinary range of cases, the lawyer is in control and the client is subservient.

A small number of radical lawyers, both male and female, have started to challenge the traditional way in which lawyers deal with their clients, and some feminist lawyers have been particularly active in this regard. This is not because they as women in some mystical way are more tender or motherly than men, but because their own experience in struggling for equality and against having their lives arbitrarily controlled by others, predisposes them in this direction. What is in issue, then, is not the substitution of so-called feminine charm for male aloofness, but the development of a more direct, friendly, spontaneous and egalitarian relationship with clients. Men are as capable as women of manifesting this new style, but they usually have more to overcome if they wish to achieve it. In addition, the existence of a women's movement directed towards the advancement of all women has made a number of professional women sensitive to the lives of the secretaries and clerks with whom they work, and has encouraged friendships and association at work that blur traditional status lines. The elimination of subservience in the office is half way towards the elimination of deference from the client, since it helps to reduce professional elitism, which, like peace, may be regarded as indivisible.

It is significant that male domination on the reformist fringe of the profession is far less pronounced than it is at the centre of the profession itself. The Legal Action Group, which was formed recently to make the legal profession more responsive to community needs, receives much of its thrust from women lawyers, and most of its male personnel have been exposed to and influenced by the ideas of the women's movement. Similarly, women are far more actively represented in Neighbourhood Law Centres than they are in private firms, and they contribute substantially in these centres to breaking down barriers between lawyers and clients. It is the very informality and lack of professional style of these centres that has led to their being criticised by private practitioners as allegedly offering an inferior service. Rigid status lines inside these centres would be inconsistent with the informal ambience that they attempt to create, but it would seem that none of these centres has gone so far as to eliminate the distinction between professional (male and female) legal workers on the one hand and clerical (female) legal workers on the other, the latter receiving lower salaries and having relatively little direct influence over decisions involving clients. The issue has been raised by women working in law centres in London, who point out in a discussion paper that although there were more women than men in such centres, only a few of them were professional legal staff.[24] The paper observes that even though the percentage of women at the professional level was in fact much greater in law centres than in private practice, male professionals still predominated, and this had its influence on policy, as for example where the law centres accepted the existence of a bar against doing matrimonial and family work. A number of problems had arisen that specially affected women working at the centres but were of concern to men as well. In the enthusiasm to get the centres going, little attention had been paid to terms of employment and to the difficult question of whether the wage structure should be on a par with that of private firms and/or the public service. If professionals in the law centres accepted low salaries, this would result in the centres being staffed by solicitors who were predominantly dedicated women without pressing financial obligations, and young men doing a couple of years in an interesting and useful field before moving to the greener and more lucrative pastures of private practice. The paper states that the problems facing non-legal staff were even greater than those facing the professionals. This was the area where most women in law centres were to be found, since bookkeepers and community workers might be of either sex, but receptionists tended to be women and nearly all those with secretarial skills were women. To the outside world these people were clerks, receptionists and typists, whatever the internal attitudes might be. However, within the centres they could achieve much, particularly with educative support from the solicitors, and this raised the question of whether it was right to continue to define non-professional staff in ordinary commercial terms. In some law centres it was accepted that their contribution was much greater than their nomenclature suggested, and this was reflected in their salaries and by the dropping of specific titles.

By its concrete approach to the legal office, this paper highlights the extent to which the ordinary legal office is based upon female subservience. It demonstrates the extent to which the question of male domination in the law can be pushed far beyond the single issue of whether qualified male lawyers have greater opportunity in the legal profession than do qualified female lawyers. What it establishes is that there is a structural connection between sex differentiation, economic inequality and psychological domination in our society, and that the elimination of sex discrimination requires far more than merely curbing the bigotry of individual males.

The final question that may be asked is the degree to which male domination has operated to influence the very manner in which legal concepts are expressed. This is an enormously problematic area, but it is worth at least posing the question of whether patriarchy is reflected in the emphasis that the law puts on such concepts as ownership rather than use and rights rather than responsibilities. It is also possible to contend that similar influences have led to the willingness of the law to recognise individuals, partnerships and companies as legal entities, while it refuses similar recognition to families.

The past fifty years have shown that the removal of disabilities is not the same as the creation of opportunities. The struggle now presents itself primarily as one for equal opportunity with regard to entry into and advancement within the profession and it is possible that the Equal Opportunities Commission, indirectly rather than directly, will make a contribution towards reducing the discrimination faced by individual women who seek to develop legal careers. What is less likely is official activity that goes beyond the elimination of individual discrimination to produce affirmative action supporting women in the profession; affirmative action would require positive steps to counteract the mechanisms whereby an institution reproduces itself in its own likeness, and would entail the imposition of sanctions for failure to work out effective programmes to redress past discrimination.[25] This necessarily involves operating primarily on a quota system: the offending person or employer is required over a period of years to organise hiring, firing and promotion activities in such a way as to produce an end result more consistent with ratios in the population at large. Precisely how this is achieved and who the individual beneficiaries are, is left to the person or organisation concerned.[26]

Today, male leadership in public life and male control of the professions is more or less taken for granted by most men and many women, but except in the case of the church and the armed forces, male-exclusiveness is regarded as rather archaic. The major tendency is to accept the practice of male domination and the principle of equal opportunity.

The concept of equal opportunity has the potential to encourage substantial inroads into male dominance, but as the more radical sections of the women's movement have pointed out, it by no means absorbs the full possibilities of what can be achieved by the elimination of sexism. Sexism not only holds back the entry into and advance of women within the legal profession, it leads to offensive and patronising behaviour, helps to structure office organisation around female subservience, and, indirectly, promotes undue competitiveness, aloofness and pedantry. In the past, the real or imagined ability of women to react to issues more concretely and spontaneously than do men, has been seen as a disadvantage from which would-be women lawyers needed to be rescued; now it may be projected as a virtue that male lawyers should seek to acquire. The legal world is overwhelmingly male in all its critical areas of operation, from the courts, to the legal profession, to law teaching and even legal publishing. What we male lawyers need to be aware of is that it is not enough for us to help eliminate the barriers to women entering the profession on equal terms with ourselves, or even to support special measures to overcome the shameful discrimination of the past. We must also re-examine our own conduct and our own styles of work and investigate the extent to which we can learn from the women's movement how to make our activity more useful to the client and the community.

6 *United States:* Portia's Plight

Women and the American Legal Profession

Although justice is portrayed as a woman, the legal profession in the United States remains predominately male. Portia is almost as much an oddity today as she was when Shakespeare first caricatured her as a female advocate in the *Merchant of Venice*. In 1975 figures indicated that there were over 400,000 practicing attorneys in the United States and the American Bar Association estimated that anywhere from five to seven percent of the total were women.[1] As late as 1976 women lawyers concerned about their low status within the profession maintained that they represented at most four percent or approximately 16,000 of all attorneys. Nonetheless, recent figures show a distinct improvement since 1910, when women constituted only one percent of the legal profession. In 1948 they were 1.8 percent and from 1963 to 1970 they remained stable at 2.8 percent. By 1973 they had progressed to 3.5 percent, by 1975 to 6 percent, and they now hover around 9 percent. The 1970 census reported that of all federal and state judges in the country, 869 or 7.5 percent of 11,380 were women.[2] Only 1.1 percent of these are federal judges.

The increase in licensed attorneys, however, has not at all kept up with the increase in the number of women attending universities and colleges or those working in the general labor force. In both instances women make up almost forty percent of students in higher education and of the adult working population. In 1966, for example, only 4.3 percent of those entering law school were women; in 1970, 8.5 percent; in 1972, sixteen percent; in 1974, twenty percent; and, in 1975, twenty-three percent.[3] Thus, the number of women attending accredited law schools jumped dramatically from 2600 in 1966 to 26,000 in 1975. But the rate of increase has gradually declined with each entering class since 1973. 'As long as these figures prevail,' former president of the New York Women's Bar Association Doris L. Sassower wrote in 1976, 'talk of women having power is just that – talk. ... Women's essentially powerless role in society is cause and consequence of laws that have enforced that condition'.[4]

One often reads that thirty-six percent of all lawyers are women in the Soviet Union, thirty-three percent in East Germany and nineteen percent in Poland. Higher figures can be cited for women doctors, dentists, engineers, and even judges (over thirty percent in both the

Soviet Union and East Germany) in these and other countries.[5] What is usually forgotten, however, is that although these foreign women are statistically more prominent, they are usually found in the less prestigious professions. The practice of medicine and law in the Soviet Union simply does not carry with it the same status or socio-economic power that it does in the United States. Consequently, the highest paid and influential professions in most countries, regardless of ideological orientation, remain almost exclusively the preserve of men. In the United States this happens to be still true of medicine and law, while it is not in some areas of the world, especially in those suffering from any degree of labor shortage. As Cynthia Epstein has noted, 'sex typing of occupations occurs in all cultures. Some occupations become known as "male", others as "female", and some are not assigned to either sex. Each society rationalises the appropriateness of these attributions, but societies vary greatly in whether a male or female sex status is paired with a specific occupational status.'[6]

The law in the United States represents the epitome of the stereotypic masculine or agentic characteristics of rational thinking, competitiveness, aggressiveness, strength, and seriousness. Conversely feminine or affiliative characteristics are routinely described as those of emotional responses, weakness, delicacy, gentleness, and frivolity. Yet the most cursory sampling of the vast literature about women (written largely by men) reveals a number of contradictory attributes. This schizoid male image of women as somehow morally superior yet intellectually inferior, as the embodiment of both all that is good and asexual symbolised by the Virgin Mary and all that is evil, including insatiable sexuality, symbolised by Eve, has forced women through the ages to live with contradiction, with an internal discord and confusion about their true nature. It has also made them the object of both man's love and hate. In addition to these contradictory attributes, the standard ones associated with affiliative human qualities are compassion, passivity, irrationality, receptivity, childlikeness, sensitivity, creativity (in those disciplines which require disassociation of thought and feeling), intuitiveness, dependence, emotionalism, manipulativeness, meticulousness (especially for detailed work), timidity, motherliness, and a variety of instincts including sensuousness, common sense, earthiness, and oneness with nature.[7]

While other specific attributes could be added to this list of feminine characteristics, it is clear that they generally are associated with the absence of initiative, of ego-drives, ambition, aggression, exploitativeness (except through sexual manipulation) and domination – all so-called masculine characteristics. Obviously since most women and men exhibit a combination of both kinds of agentic and affiliative attributes, it is ridiculous to claim sex-determined superiority for one group or the other. Most are conditioned responses. All we can say with certainty is that those male qualities associated with violence and patriarchal societies have prevailed in modern societies with disastrous results. Perhaps it is time to start to reassess and propagate the value of the conditioned characteristics of the other half of humanity. At least it is time that women, particularly those who decide to become lawyers, undertake such a re-evaluation for themselves.

They can begin by questioning such assertions as 'the law is born of conflict and its practice, almost by definition, must be aggressive and warlike in nature' and that women do not have the capacity of a legal mind, i.e. 'women feel while men think.' Female attorneys also have to meet the charges that they 'are not industrious and have no stick-to-it-iveness [and] would waste the court's time with endless arguments, off the point . . .', in addition to the inability of some men to 'imagine a woman sitting still for hours with only Blackstone for company'.[10] They must confront other unfounded allegations as well: women lack ability, dedication and emotional stability; they feel an obligation to home and family, which they invariably fulfill; women can't be shining lights at the bar because they are too kind; in criminal law women can't handle discussions of sex; women are not good corporation lawyers because they are not cold and ruthless; women lack a high grade of intellect; women in firms will alienate clients; and finally, women are poor employment risks. These *a priori* judgments upon which discrimination against women in the legal profession is based are so widely and unconsciously accepted that they are seldom questioned. The thankless task of feminist lawyers is to challenge them again and again in and out of court.

Sex typing in all professions tends to create a self-perpetuating defeatist attitude among those who are conditioned to believe they are 'outsiders'. Consequently, some women who dare to 'break in' to such masculine professions as law or the hard sciences suffer from a negative self-fulfilling prophecy syndrome or exhibit symptoms of what is known as 'fear of success'. This means that women often practice self-exclusion or self-effacement and so are less visible in a male dominated profession. Often they will specialise in what are considered traditional female areas of the law. As of 1965, for example, sixty percent of a sample of women lawyers surveyed in one study engaged in trusts and estates; another fifty percent in domestic relations; and thirty-one percent in taxes. This was far higher than the proportions of men engaged in these activities and this imbalance in professional specialisation remains down to the present.[11]

Many female attorneys can be found handling real estate, matrimonial, and child custody cases – all concentrations commonly considered, at best, paralegal and, at worst, nonlegal. The Legal Aid Society remains the domain of women lawyers in part because as much as forty percent of its cases concern the family-desertion, abandonment, and juvenile problems. Ironically, legal aid work also involves women lawyers in problems of child abuse, rape, murder, wife beating, incest, and bestiality.[12] These are the types of cases, of course, that female attorneys, according to the stereotypic view of their nature, would be least capable of handling. One could ask, however, whether a man should or could be expected to exhibit any more understanding or compassion in such cases of violence and perversity than a woman. Yet on those rare occasions where women are appointed to the bench or win elections and become judges, they are most likely to be found in family courts because those who appoint or elect them (and often they themselves) think that women are temperamentally more suited to handle family reference matters.

As a result of this combination of self-exclusion and discrimination by their male colleagues, female lawyers constituted less than five percent of all faculty members at accredited law schools in 1970. This nearly doubled to eight percent in 1972, but the increase took place mainly at the lowest levels of hiring and largely in response to federal antidiscrimination laws – not necessarily in response to a basic change in values among male professors. Men still dominate among the highest ranks and in the top law schools of the United States. As a direct result of this academic discrimination women who teach law earn less than men, and women who practice law can also expect to experience at least an average differential of $1,500 between their income during the first year of practice and that of the men with whom they graduated. Well over half of women lawyers surveyed in 1965 felt that they had been discriminated against when seeking employment within the profession.[13] As of October 1970 the *American Bar News* noted that nine out of ten large law firms categorically refused to interview women lawyers. Top law schools like Harvard and Yale did not admit women until after World War II and the percentage of women at the most prestigious institutions still remains low, thus further limiting their chances of selection for the best legal jobs upon graduation. Finally, a

New York Times survey article reported in March 1975, that in law school classes 'professors still make jokes about women, male judges still treat women – even women judges – differently than they treat men, and women still feel less than welcome, if welcome at all, in the legal profession'.[14]

Such figures and attitudes can be found within other male dominated professions in the United States. But in the case of the legal profession there is special cause for concern because of the strong suspicion that the sex of an attorney may adversely affect judicial action and therefore the outcome of any criminal or civil suit in which a client is represented by a woman. As of 1975, despite the negative implications of such a situation, if in fact it does exist, there had been no scholarly research or professional investigation of the interactions between female advocates and judicial functionaries.[15] In fact, neither the American Bar Association nor any other major state bar association in the United States has yet officially protested offensive treatment of women lawyers by judges in particular or the discrimination against women in the legal profession in general. This refusal to examine male biases that may be negatively affecting female lawyers and their clients all over the country is regarded by feminists as one of the most discouraging aspects of the American legal profession as it enters the last quarter of the twentieth century.[16]

Behind this legal blindness is age-old prejudice and the 'old boys' system within the profession. Known as male bonding, this form of sex discrimination takes many forms. First, women are not counseled to become lawyers in their early education; too few are accepted at the top law schools; then, if they do insist on studying law they are often directed into the so-called female fields of specialisation; when it comes time for job recommendations and interviews they find the male network closing ranks even more and peer acceptance painful, at best, as the following personal testimony indicates.

Ms. Attorney or the 'Trials' of Women Lawyers

Nonetheless, women lawyers in the United States, where the feminist and radical sector of the legal profession is relatively well-organised, have been assertive in explaining how humiliating everyday casual male condescension can be. Examining the special problems facing women lawyers, two young radical lawyers from Los Angeles claim that even the few well-intentioned males fail to get beyond agreeing in general with the concept of women's liberation, and so fail to

reach the reality of the problems confronting women lawyers.[17]
These problems, they state, need to be presented concretely rather
than abstractly, starting from the moment the woman lawyer enters
the court buildings. Older women lawyers are treated by the male
functionaries with a combination of disinterest, because they are not
the model of 'female sexuality', and/or resentment, because as
lawyers they have achieved a higher professional status. Young
women lawyers, on the other hand, are either overlooked entirely,
since they are clearly not some of the important people in the
building, or else looked up and down with some kind of subtle or
outright 'come-on'. Once inside the court, they are excluded from the
fraternal repartee so important for eliciting information or arranging
plea bargains or settlements, since as young women they are clearly
not regarded as part of the fraternity; joking becomes flirting, and
negotiations a kind of prostitution.

The dilemma which these two young women lawyers note is
whether in the interests of their clients they should play along with
men they find obnoxious. 'We are expected to be laughing, smiling,
light-headed and flirtatious. When we don't fulfill these expectations,
we are openly accused of being hostile. ... Often we have been told
by other attorneys how glad they are to see more women becoming
lawyers, only to learn in their next sentence that it is because women
are "more fun" and "better to look at".' Judges, they further
observe, have a peculiar condescension reserved for women who
appear before them; males can get away with bluster and histrionics,
but for women to appear foolish only reinforces the female
stereotype. Court appearances are particularly galling for women
because they cannot use the normal methods of dealing with
insulting situations – they cannot wear clothes that make them feel
relaxed, or walk away in disgust, or laugh at or cut down the person
insulting them, since to do so might jeopardise their client's welfare.
They share the fears which all young lawyers have of not doing well
enough for the client, but these fears can be dealt with by detailed
legal research, good investigation and continued experience. It is the
things they experience as women that they have little control over.

Many women lawyers have tried to deal with these problems of
gender by taking on so-called male characteristics. The stereotyped
male lawyer is seen as deep-voiced, arrogant, able to project
knowledge and certainty even when he is really ignorant about
something, self-important, and too busy to explain to people facing
jail or ruin the bewildering legal terms judges and lawyers throw
around. The two women commenting on discrimination in their

profession realise that by assuming such characteristics, they could receive more of the deference given by the system to professional people, but they oppose all these qualities. They wish to share their knowledge with their clients rather than exercise power over them, not because they are overly emotional, but because they appreciate the emotions involved in litigation; they wish to create a new kind of lawyer, not because they are too sensitive or irrational to succeed in a male profession, but because they are committed to the involvement of lawyers in the community.

As a direct result of pressure from persons such as the two women attorneys from Los Angeles, a number of legal collectives have been established in which attempts have been made to break down all hierarchical divisions based on function, dress, status, workload, and income.[18] Far from becoming redundant, female clerical workers were trained to handle as much of the interviewing of clients and preparation of cases as professional rules allow, while qualified practitioners have learnt to receive clients, take telephone calls, prepare and file documents, type letters and keep books. It can hardly be said that these legal centers have become typical even of radical American legal organisations today, but they have, by virtue of the contrast they offer, underscored the existing subordination of women in average law offices, as well as in the courtrooms across the country.

Ironically the traditional subordination of women clerical workers in the legal profession often works against female attorneys in the form of internalised sexism. One of the few attempts[19] to survey attitudes toward women lawyers investigated not only the biases of judges and male colleagues, but also the role of bureaucratic functionaries within the legal system, namely court clerks. Most lawyers readily admit it is extremely important to be on good terms with the court clerk. If the clerks are 'rude to you or treat you abruptly,' said one respondent in this study, 'it is difficult to do anything'. Others described the problem in the following ways.

> I notice particularly when I go into a clerk's office in court, they immediately assume I'm there to look at a file or get some forms or file something. . . . Most of the clerks in the court and clerk's offices are women and they, I don't think they want to accept the fact that there are women attorneys. . . .

> Sometimes the clerks in the courts are just very snotty and I think it's because I'm a woman, especially if they're women clerks, you know, they just snap at you or just kind of treat – they don't give you any respect that, say, they give to the male attorneys. . . .

Sure you run into your problems, but they are not with the judges, but more with the people in his office.

It is entirely possible that female attorneys face more difficulties in penetrating the *informal* structure of the legal profession where there are more women workers, than they do in the official courtroom appearances where men dominate. If this is true, the 'trials' of women lawyers in overcoming gender discrimination are more complex than usually assumed. Until their increasing numbers reach a parity with men, the discrimination women lawyers experience at every level may simply become covert and therefore all the more difficult to expose and eradicate, since in most instances male attorneys, judges, and their female subordinates are not even aware it is taking place. As one respondent lamented:

> It's a very subtle thing. I have talked to other women who regularly try cases. None of us I think articulate it very well. You can feel it, but it's very difficult to articulate. I suspect that some of the same patronising tones, some of the same sloppiness of behavior occurs with any minority group in the courtroom, because I've seen the same thing, the same tones used with black lawyers as a trial lawyer. The same there–there dear, everything is going to be all right. Only that's the way I translate it. I don't know how they translate it, but I've seen it.

What Is To Be Done?

Despite all of these obvious difficulties, women in the legal profession are currently finding more career opportunities than women in academic and business fields. Lawyers continue to dominate government circles and a number of female attorneys have been appointed to middle-management positions in the Carter administration. One in six of the Presidential appointees at the cabinet, sub-cabinet, federal agency, and White House staff levels has been a woman and one-third of these have been lawyers.[20] Moreover, these appointees are in their thirties, approximately ten years younger than men usually named to such posts. Most come from public interest firms, government work or law schools – not from corporate law or private practice. Judgeships are also being offered to women in greater numbers than ever before. Although no woman has ever been appointed to the Supreme Court, it is worth noting that 'two of the breakthrough court appointments in this century, Justices Louis Brandeis and Thurgood Marshall, represented the public interest law of their times. The first woman appointee', according to Eli N. Evans of the Carnegie Corporation, 'will likely reflect contemporary public-interest law.'[21]

Female attorneys have the unprecedented opportunity to affect policy at the federal level if they come to these new positions of responsibility with their consciousnesses *not merely raised, but changed*. It is only when the number of women lawyers, whose values are qualitatively different from those of their male colleagues, reach 'critical mass' proportions that we will begin to see significant changes in the legal profession and in public policy. Clearly the law offers the clearest and most direct route to power to career-minded American women. But if they do not wield that power differently from men, then diminishing the sex imbalance will not effect societal change. As long as female attorneys continue to endorse unquestioningly the adversary system of jurisprudence it will remain as warlike and hierarchical as it ever was under complete male domination. 'Otherwise,' as Jerold Auerbach has noted, 'equal justice under the law will remain subservient to unequal justice under lawyers.'[22] Also, as long as older female attorneys at law conferences continue to insist that the 'biggest problem women attorneys have are other women', it will be difficult for younger women to encourage a feminist renaissance within the legal profession.

Whatever problems exist between women lawyers and their female clients or among professional women in general, male bias remains the most serious drawback to a more human, cooperative approach to the law and to high status function of women generally in society. Devising different ways for dealing with conflict remains a major stumbling block within the current women's movement as well as within the legal profession, and feminist attorneys of both sexes may hold the key to its solution. Some male lawyers, albeit not usually for feminist reasons, are beginning to talk about expanding small claims courts where legal representation is not required, of relying more on arbitration, mediation and conciliation, and of forming neighbor legal centers or tribunals staffed by non-lawyers.[23] When Chief Justice Burger talks about such reforms it is because he is afraid that

> if we do not devise substitutes for the courtroom processes, and do not do it rather quickly, we may well be on our way to a society overrun by hordes of lawyers hungry as locusts competing with each other, and brigades of judges in numbers never before contemplated.[24]

Such an approach could bode ill for the increasing numbers of women entering the legal profession if it resulted in channelling them exclusively into nonlegal or paralegal positions or discouraging them entirely from public interest law careers and judgeships. They must consciously place themselves in the vanguard of legal reform or they will find themselves bringing up the rear as so often has happened in past American reform movements.

Female attorneys already have been responsible for much expansion of women's legal rights at federal, state, and local levels. It seems clear that they will effect the most substantial changes in American society through reform of public policy, rather than through private practice or corporate law. Because laws in the form of constitutions, statutes and court cases are a part of public policy, this raises the question of whether American women should concentrate their efforts on changing private law through the litigation process or on changing public law through national and state legislation.

PART FOUR

TOWARDS EQUAL OPPOR-TUNITY . . . AND BEYOND

7 *Britain:* Citizens, Workers and Parents

For many decades the vote was at the centre of struggle for the emancipation of women in Britain: the franchise was regarded both as a symbol of general citizenship and as a means of eliminating specific areas of inequality. The securing of the vote in 1918 and the removal of sex disqualifications in relation to professional and public life in 1919, were seen as putting paid to sex inequality in Britain. For the next half century, the Woman Question, as it had once been called, was treated as officially solved. Parliament took no further steps to eliminate gender discrimination in any comprehensive way, and there was little litigation on the subject.

Such cases as did reach the courts indicated a general tendency on the part of the judges to regard discrimination against women – particularly in the area of employment – as both natural and reasonable. What was held to be unreasonable, to the point of being declared *ultra vires*, was a decision by a radical borough council to equalise pay between men and women;[1] what was held to be reasonable and lawful was the so-called marriage bar, in terms of which women teachers but not men were required to resign as soon as they got married.[2] More recently, however, there was one decision which indicated a greater willingness on the part of the judges to support claims against discrimination. This related to an application by a trainer to be registered with the Jockey Club, which insisted on registering her senior male employee instead; the court held that since the Club exercised a monopoly for the whole country, it could not refuse her a licence since this would deprive her of the opportunity to follow her vocation.[3] The discrimination *per se* was not unlawful, but it did make the exercise of the monopoly unreasonable.

Two factors led to the sudden proliferation of anti-discrimination statutes in the 1970s. The first was the re-emergence of the women's movement, and the second the pathbreaking accomplished by race relations legislation.[4] In the background were attempts by both males and females in Parliament to get a Bill adopted which would outlaw sex inequality;[5] particularly influential was the collection of evidence by a House of Lords Select Committee on Sex Discrimination. In fact, the women's movement had never died – various research and pressure groups had continued to direct attention to specific areas of inequality, and there was a consistent demand in the trade union movement for the enactment of equal pay legislation. But Women's Liberation in the late 1960s dramatised the issues in a way unknown since the fierce suffrage struggles at the beginning of the century, and legislation was once more thought of as a relatively safe and respectable means of dealing with the situation.

The first step was the enactment of the Equal Pay Act, 1970, which gave employers five years within which to ensure that equal pay was granted to all persons doing work of a like character. The second was the enactment of the Sex Discrimination Act, 1975, which was modelled largely on the Race Relations Acts of 1965 and 1968 but which incorporated changes later to be introduced into the race relations area as well. Taken together, the two statutes prohibit gender discrimination in employment with regard to entry, pay, conditions, promotion and firing, and provide that all disputes in these areas be referred to Industrial Tribunals. The Sex Discrimination Act goes on to outlaw discrimination in education, advertising and the provision of public facilities, and makes such discrimination actionable in the ordinary civil courts. The Act also creates an Equal Opportunities Commission with wide powers of investigation and publicity, and with authority to issue legally enforceable non-discrimination notices against persons guilty of persistent and widespread discrimination.

Both Acts came into force at the beginning of 1976, and the operation of both has been severely criticised.[6] The main shortcoming of the Equal Pay Act has been its failure to bridge the gap between earnings of men and women. The newly created Women's Rights Unit of the National Council for Civil Liberties, which found itself inundated with queries about the Acts, points out that despite improvements average wages for women are still only sixty per cent of those for men.[7] Although the Unit does feel that the legislation has given women workers a basis for organisation and a means for improving their conditions, it also points to the tendency of employers to stratify jobs on a gender basis, so that only men are engaged in the more skilled positions, and only women in the less skilled, a state of affairs not outlawed by the Acts. The Unit's report on the first year of operation of the statutes shows that many employers have been strongly reluctant to grant equal pay: one argued, unsuccessfully, that cleaning men's toilets was more arduous than cleaning women's toilets, while another contended, successfully, that machine-wrapping chocolates, a job done by men, required more skill and responsibility than machine-wrapping chocolate boxes, a task for women. Generally speaking, the Industrial Tribunals, which normally consist of a lawyer in the chair assisted by a trade unionist and employer's representative, have tended to apply the law conservatively, but the Employment Appeals Tribunal, headed by a High Court judge, which hears appeals, has laid down a number of judgments strongly favouring equality.[8]

The anti-discrimination legislation has also been criticised for the numbers of exemptions it tolerates – such as for the Church, the armed forces and Northern Ireland – and for procedural weaknesses, such as placing the onus of proof on the victim instead of requiring proof of non-discrimination on the part of employers. But the main attacks have been directed against the strategy of basing remedies on individual complaints – almost impossible to prove – rather than on structured discrimination, and against the unwillingness of those charged with enforcing the Acts to take vigorous action.[9] As one writer put it, what is needed is not so much equal opportunity, as opportunity for equality.[10] There is at present no basis in British law for requiring affirmative action on the part of employers and educational institutions to remedy past discrimination.[11] On the contrary, so-called positive discrimination is forbidden save for the field of training for industry, where it is permissible but not compulsory. As far as the implementation of the legislation is concerned, the main target of criticism has been the Equal Opportunities Commission, which has been condemned for failure to make its presence felt, unwillingness to risk offending discriminators, aloofness from women's organisations, and general lack of support for those who are tackling discrimination.[12] It is alleged that the Government was so careful to avoid antagonising anyone that it produced a Commission that was not so much evenly balanced as deadlocked, with a resulting paralysis of action and a failure even to use all its limited funds for research.

For all these criticisms, however, it is clear that the legislation has already had a considerable impact on public life and consciousness. The media are constantly reporting cases of litigation – some successful, some not – involving such diverse matters as equal pay, the right to play snooker or have a drink and the right to be appointed a golf professional. In principle, equal opportunity has ceased to be a vague slogan and has now become a legally enforceable right, hedged in though it may be with qualifications. Trade unions have been forced to examine the sexism within their own ranks, and the Trades Union Congress has conceded the impropriety of ratios which show that although there are only about three men for every woman trade unionist, there are thirty-two male full-time officials for every female one.[13] Some unions point to the fact that industrial action is a better remedy than applications to the Industrial Tribunals, but even if this is so, the legislation has helped create the climate in which actions for equality can be successful. The unions which are more advanced in this area are now setting the pace for the more backward ones, and women workers are increasingly becoming involved in campaigning for their rights both as workers and as women.

Recognition of the principle of gender equality in one area of public life throws into relief its denial in another. Thus much of social security legislation is at war with the principles of anti-discrimination legislation, basically through the concept running through welfare law that men are breadwinners and women housekeepers.[14] The Social Security Pensions Act, 1975, goes some way towards reducing the gross inequalities in the state pensions scheme, previously justified on the basis that because women lived longer than men their retirement pensions should be lower.[15] Blatant discrimination in the payment of unemployment and sickness benefits is also being eliminated, but the basic income maintenance schemes are still geared to the concept of male breadwinners being the head of the household. Thus the much-criticised 'cohabitation rule' entitles the Supplementary Benefits Commission to withdraw benefits from a woman reported to be sleeping regularly with a man, on the assumption that if they have a steady sexual relationship, he must be supporting her financially.

The question of special protective laws for women still arouses controversy, as it has done for more than a century. The NCCL Women's Rights Unit declares that the main question is whether repeal of the laws would improve women's lives or not, and in their view it would not.[16] The main point at issue is restriction on night work, and as long as women bear the brunt of parenthood, thus doing two jobs, and as long as they are relatively under-organised at work, it is not in their interests to be compelled to do night shifts. 'We are not in favour of equalising the laws', they wrote in a memorandum to the Equal Opportunities Commission, 'if it means a worsening of women's conditions – they already suffer enough disadvantages.'[17] They favour the use of exemptions to cover cases of women without family responsibilities, urge the extension to men of protections against special hazards, and generally call for the creation of a comprehensive system of social support for parents and genuine equality at work as a pre-condition for repeal of the laws. The Unit concedes that there are strong arguments the other way, in particular that differentiation in one area of the law leads to inequality in another, that women should have the right to choose and that conditions have changed since the protective laws were first enacted, but comes down decisively in favour of retention. In this they seem to be in line with the position of the Trades Union Congress and the great majority of feminist trade unionists, although the Confederation of British Industry speaking on behalf of employers, supports repeal. There does not appear to be strong pressure from any section of the women's movement in favour of repeal.

In fact, the legal issue which has most aroused the women's movement in recent years is abortion. Control of fertility is seen both as a necessary condition for economic independence and as a key to personal self-determination. Until 1967 pregnancies could be terminated only if continuation of the pregnancy posed a severe threat to the life or health of the woman. The Abortion Act of that year widened the criteria extensively, to include so-called social grounds, but still left the decision to doctors. The result has been that in areas where doctors are sympathetic, abortions can in effect be obtained on request without payment through the National Health Service, whereas in other areas women are compelled to resort to private practitioners or charities. Anti-abortion critics complain that the Act has led to widespread racketeering and a general loss of respect for the rights of unborn children, and have been campaigning vigorously for a narrowing of the criteria for terminating pregnancies. The issue is frequently debated in the streets, in the media and in Parliament, and remains one of the most controversial in British public and Parliamentary life.

Less controversial has been the question of legal support for women whose employment is interrupted by maternity. The Employment Protection Act, 1975, provides that dismissal on the grounds of pregnancy is normally unfair, and goes on to guarantee to women who have been in continuous employment for two years up to the eleventh week before the baby is due that they receive paid leave for six weeks, with a right to return to their jobs any time up to twenty-nine weeks after the confinement. This kind of provision has been supported as a possible beginning to a far more comprehensive scheme designed to enable women, and men as well, to combine their roles as parents and workers.[18] This could involve ultimately the requirement that employers and local authorities provide sufficient creche and nursery facilities to enable all parents to take up employment if they choose to do so, coupled with a duty on employers to introduce more flexible patterns of work. The question of the public rights of women cannot be separated from the rights of women in respect of the family. It has taken a century of intense struggle to secure full legal recognition of the fact that the social and personal contribution made by women in the family should not be used as a reason for denying them equal participation in the life of the country at large. But the concept of equal opportunity will remain largely fictional if the family continues to act as a trap preventing women from exercising that opportunity. Persons who choose not to live in families should not be penalised by the law either directly or indirectly for their choice. Neither should persons be penalised for living in families or for having children. Having at last accepted the notion that gender inequality is inconsistent with norms of public life, the law must now move to guarantee to all persons not only the rights to have a family, if they choose, and to participate without discrimination in the life of the society, but also the right to combine both these rights. Only then will gender inequality be finally eliminated.

8 *United States:* Recent Congressional Acts and Supreme Court Decisions

Equal Rights and the Rise of the Second Women's Movement

Except for the Nineteenth Amendment of 1919, there was no Congressional legislation that made gender a central issue until 1963. In the intervening years state statutes, common law precedents, and judicial interpretations defined the status of women primarily in terms of the rights of 'the sex', not in terms of the rights of individual persons under the Constitution. The phrase 'women as citizens' was almost always applied to their ascribed roles as mother, daughter, or wife. Only recently have the courts and Congress begun to recognise women as being independent people outside of the family. Both the 1963 Equal Pay Act and Title VII of the Civil Rights Act of 1964 were passed *before* the second women's movement had organised. In the early and mid-1960s most female activists concentrated their activities in civil rights and student or other antiwar groups dominated by black and white male leftists.

Consequently, the second women's movement cannot be credited with passage of either of these significant acts of Congress. In fact, the word 'sex' was added to the 1964 Civil Rights Act more by accident than design and there is every indication that Congress did not act with full knowledge of what it was doing. The word was introduced into the text of Title VII, which was originally intended to prohibit discrimination in employment on the basis of race, color, religion, and national origin, by the Southern Congressman Howard W. Smith in what appeared to be a last-minute attempt to defeat the bill. 'Now I am very serious about this amendment,' Representative Smith said when introducing it, 'I do not think it can do any harm to this legislation; maybe it can do some good.'[1] He later denied he added the word 'sex' to Title VII to delay or defeat the legislation. Smith nonetheless joked about it all through the brief debate that followed. But then, so too did the House liberals who opposed it with the blessing of the Women's Bureau of the Labor Department. February 8, 1964, went down in Congressional history as 'Ladies Day in the House'.[2]

In this cavalier fashion 'one of the most profoundly redistributive [public policy] decisions of our century' was made, according to political scientist Jo Freeman. Effective redistributive legislation is one of the least understood of the various kinds of public policies in a pluralist society. But it is always highly significant because it requires the redistribution of socio-economic resources among competing groups. Such policies are also 'incremental', meaning that their effects do not occur suddenly, but accumulate gradually over time.[3] This has indeed been true of Title VII prohibiting discrimination in employment on the basis of race, colour, religion, national origin or sex, *except* for *bona fide occupational qualifications* (BFOQ).[4]

Although the Equal Employment Opportunity Commission (EEOC) was specifically created to enforce Title VII, to put teeth into the act has taken over a decade, during which guidelines embodying the concept of affirmative action have been evolved, two Executive Orders (nos. 11246 in 1965 prohibiting racial, religious, and alienage employment discrimination by federal contractors and 11375 in 1967 adding sex to the list) have been promulgated and the 1972 amendments covering all employers with fifteen or more workers and allowing the EEOC to initiate suits have been passed. The Equal Employment Opportunity Reorganisation Act of 1977 would further amend Title VII, broadening EEOC jurisdiction to include the Equal Pay Act, Executive Order 11246 and the Age Discrimination Act. Yet the first EEOC Director Herman Edelsberg sought to ignore the sex provision of Title VII saying it was a 'fluke' and not the agency's first priority. Although subsequent directors have been more sympathetic, by the end of 1976 EEOC had a backlog of over 100,000 cases and had not made use of the additional clout given it by the 1972 amendments.[5] The second women's movement has been actively involved in enforcing these early acts, guidelines, and executive orders, although it had not yet coalesced when many of them were first passed or issued.

With the formation of the National Organisation for Women (NOW) in 1966 various women's groups began to bring political and legal pressure to bear at local, state, and federal levels in the late 1960s and early 1970s.[6] Since it remains virtually impossible to influence the Supreme Court directly with public demonstrations, the most significant past actions of the 'civil rights front' of the second women's movement have been focused on state legislatures, Congress, and executive branch enforcement agencies. Future activity will be similar. Immediate impact on the judicial review process is difficult to achieve, although feminist support for individual female defendants and specific state court decisions can be minimally effective in undermining some of the last strongholds of sexist justice.

A cursory examination of the most significant Supreme Court decisions on sex discrimination in the 1970s reveals first hope and then ambivalence, if not outright regression, under Chief Justice

Warren E. Burger. In 1971, for example, the Supreme Court invalidated *for the first time in its history* a state statute on the grounds of sex discrimination. The Justices ruled in *Reed v. Reed*, 404 U.S. 71 that when a woman and a man were otherwise equally qualified to administer an estate, the male could not be given arbitrary preference. (This Idaho state law had called for the automatic appointment of a male executor.) The statute was declared unconstitutional under an equal protection interpretation of due process, utilising the rational basis test. In delivering the unanimous opinion of the Court, Chief Justice Burger substantially narrowed the definition of what can be considered reasonable sex-based discrimination, saying a classification

'must be reasonable not arbitrary, and must rest upon some ground of difference having a fair and substantial relation to the object of the legislation, so that all persons similarly circumstanced shall be treated alike. ...' To give mandatory preference to members of one sex over another, merely to accomplish the elimination of hearings on the merits, is to make the very kind of arbitrary legislative choice forbidden by the Equal Protection Clause of the 14th Amendment ... the choice in this context may not lawfully be made solely on the basis of sex. ...

The *Reed* decision *did not* declare that sex was a suspect basis for classification under the Fourteenth Amendment. It merely held the Idaho law arbitrary, that is, 'unreasonable'. Two years later a minority of Justices came out in favor of establishing sex as a suspect classification in the case of *Frontiero v. Richardson*, 411 U.S. 677 (1973). Unfortunately this was not a unanimous decision. Although the Justices divided eight to one in *Frontiero*, in the holding of the case a majority did not agree to subject gender distinctions to close scrutiny under the Fourteenth Amendment. The plurality opinion of the four who did reads in part:

There can be no doubt that our Nation has had a long and unfortunate history of sex discrimination. Traditionally, such discrimination was rationalised by an attitude of 'romantic paternalism' which, in practical effect, put women not on a pedestal, but in a cage; our statute books gradually became laden with gross, stereotypical distinctions between the sexes and, indeed, throughout much of the 19th century the position of women in our society was, in many respects, comparable to that of blacks under the pre-Civil War slave codes. Neither slaves nor women could hold office, serve on juries, or bring suit in their own names and married women traditionally were denied the legal capacity to hold or convey property or to serve as legal guardians of their own children. Moreover, since sex, like race and national origin, is an immutable characteristic determined solely by the accident of birth, the imposition of special disabilities upon the members of a particular sex would seem to violate 'the basic concept of our system that legal burdens should bear some relationship to individual responsibility'. And what differentiates sex from non-suspect statutes as intelligence or physical disability, and aligns it with the recognised suspect criteria, is that the sex characteristic frequently bears no relation to ability to perform or contribute to society. As a result, statutory distinctions between the sexes often have the effect of invidiously relegating the entire class of females to inferior legal status without regard to the actual capabilities of its individual members.

The other five Justices refused to subscribe to this suspect classification argument. As a result of wide differences of opinion, the *Frontiero* decision has not yet set a constitutional precedent because the Burger Court has refused to honor it in subsequent opinions. In *Cleveland Board of Education v. LaFleur*, 414 U.S. 632 (1974) a law requiring mandatory unpaid maternity leave was held in violation of the due process, *not* the equal protection clause of the Fourteenth Amendment. Then in *Kahn v. Shevin*, 416 U.S. 351 (1974) the Court denied a widower's petition that he should be granted an annual $500 property tax exemption the same as widows. While Justice Douglas asserted in the majority opinion that 'Gender has never been rejected as an impermissible classification on all instances', Justices Brennan and Marshall dissented saying that 'a legislative classification that distinguishes potential beneficiaries solely by reference to their gender-based status as widows or widowers ... like classifications based on race, alienage, and national origins, must be subjected to close judicial scrutiny. ...' Likewise in *Schlesinger v. Ballard*, 419 U.S. 498 the Court sustained a sex-based classification that seemingly 'protected' women rather than offer them equality with men.

Shortly afterwards in *Weinberger v. Weisenfeld*, 420 U.S. 636 (1975) widowers were allowed to collect benefits on their wives' Social Security without having to prove dependency. Since a federal statute was involved this decision was based on an equal protection interpretation of the due process clause of the Fifth Amendment. As discussed earlier in this book, the Supreme Court also invalidated in 1975 all laws limiting jury service on the basis of sex in *Taylor v. Louisiana*, 419 U.S. 522 (1975). Finally, in March 1977, in the *Goldfarb* case the Supreme Court voided even more provisions of the Social Security Act which had made it harder for husbands and widowers of female wage-earners than for wives or widows of male wage-earners to collect survivors' and old-age insurance benefits. Feminists had opposed this provision on the ground that it gave the family of a female wage-earner less protection than it gave to a male wage-earner's family. Yet in that same month in the *Webster* case the Court refused to make retroactive equal treatment for retired men in calculating their average monthly wage. This represents one of the few times that the Court has upheld Congressional legislation designed to 'compensate for past employment discrimination against women'.[7]

Consistent doctrinal development is also difficult to perceive in other Supreme Court decisions involving sex discrimination, and the same muddled situation prevails at the state court level.[8] Distinctions on the basis of age seem to be disappearing. In *Stanton v. Stanton*, 421 U.S. 7 (1975) the Court struck down a state law requiring support payments for males until the age of twenty-one and for females until the age of eighteen. At the end of 1976 the Court ruled that it was not constitutional to allow eighteen-year-old women in Oklahoma to buy 3.2 percent beer while making men wait until they were twenty-one. Justice Brennan said that this was an example of 'invidious discrimination' and henceforth 'classifications by gender must serve important governmental objectives and must be substantially related to achievement of these objectives'. Logically this position should lead to disallowing different qualifying ages of consent for marriage under the equal protection clause.[9] When it comes to birth names, however, the Court left standing in 1976 a Kentucky law requiring a married woman to use her husband's name in applying for a driver's license, although she had never used his name for any other purpose. Early in 1977 a federal court in Ohio upheld the right of a married woman to vote in her own name. Thus, judicial confusion and diverse state practices continue on this issue.

Except for the *Frontiero* decision, *none of these gender decisions handed down by the Burger Court has declared sex a suspect classification under the equal protection clause of the Fourteenth Amendment.* Obviously, the divided and controversial 1973 *Frontiero* decision best represents the reluctance of the majority of the Justices to so rule. And in the meantime, as noted previously, the Court actually *held against sex as a suspect classification* when eliminating pregnancy from disability insurance programs in the *Geduldig* case. Other work-related decisions in recent years have demonstrated either ambivalence or resistance by the Court when faced with the issue of the 'proper role' of women in modern society. The *per curiam* decision of *Phillips v. Martin Marietta*, 400 U.S. 542 (1971), for example, overturned a decision of the Fifth Circuit U.S. Court of Appeals that had permitted 'one hiring policy for women and another for men – each having preschool-age children'. Nonetheless the Court indicated that a sex-based BFOQ regarding differential family obligations *might apply* if it could be shown at some time in the future that it was more important for mothers than for fathers to spend time with preschool children. Then a gender distinction could be made under the 1964 Civil Rights Act. Fortunately this interpretation of *Phillips* has not been validated in subsequent decisions.

Phillips was the first Title VII case based exclusively on sex discrimination to reach the Supreme Court. However, it cannot be considered a major landmark on the road to ending sex-based discrimination. Although a number of lower courts have ruled against exclusionary employment practices based on sexual stereotypes under both the Fourteenth Amendment and Title VII, to date the Court seems to be resisting this lower court trend.[10] On May 31, 1977, in a series of decisions involving the Teamsters Union it found that Title VII does not prohibit the use of 'bona fide' seniority systems that perpetuate effects of employment discrimination that occurred before the Civil Rights Act of 1964 went into effect on July 2, 1965.[11]

These decisions concerning racial discrimination similarly seemed to apply to cases of sex discrimination. They generally represented a setback for civil rights advocates because the unqualified retention of union seniority systems as long as 'there is no intent to discriminate' not only locks older blacks (and presumably older women and other minorities) into segregated or inferior jobs, but it also hinders the advancement on the job of young and inexperienced workers in time of high unemployment. Once again these are usually minorities and women. Dissenting in *Teamsters v. United States*, 45 Law Week 4506, Justices Marshall and Brennan pointed out that six courts of appeal have held 'without a single dissent' in more than thirty cases that Title VII does not 'immunize' traditional seniority systems. The battle to eradicate sexism and racism from the labor market is far from won if these latest Supreme Court decisions stand for long. They automatically place recently hired women and minorities who have been hired recently in a precarious position if lay-offs are forced by a sluggish economy. Affirmative action programs based on merit simply cannot work to alleviate past patterns of employment discrimination if there are proportionately fewer jobs available. The same is true of equal pay legislation whose impact has always been smaller than anticipated because it covers only wages, not other terms of employment.[12]

Generally the Justices have avoided ruling on the issue of compensatory legislation for women or minorities because this would automatically involve them in 'reverse discrimination' suits filed by white males. The Court did unanimously hold on June 25, 1976, that whites may sue under Title VII of the 1964 Civil Rights Act, but technically it has not decided a case on the ground of 'reverse discrimination'. The Court first faced such a decision in 1974 when a white male challenged a special-admissions programme at the University of Washington law school saying it violated his rights under the Fourteenth Amendment. Lower courts disagreed with each other and the Supreme Court in *DeFunis v. Odegaard*, 416 U.S. 312 (1974), declared the case moot because DeFunis had later been admitted to the law school and was about to graduate. In the fall of 1976 the Court agreed to hear another controversial case brought by a white male, Allan Bakke, against a special-admissions program at the medical school at the University of California, Davis. The California State Supreme Court, deemed one of the most liberal in the country, declared in September, 1976, that the quota system established for minorities at the Davis medical school was unconstitutional under the equal protection clause because no race 'may be afforded a higher degree of protection against unequal treatment than others'. It ordered Allan Bakke admitted. The university appealed this decision despite pleas from two civil rights legal groups representing blacks and Mexican-Americans who feared it would endanger minority admissions and affirmative action programmes across the country.[13] On November 15, 1976, the United States Supreme Court suspended the state ruling until it had disposed of the case.

In agreeing to hear *Bakke v. The Regents of the University of California* the Supreme Court has indicated its willingness to settle at long last the question of 'reverse discrimination' or what the university is calling the 'most fundamental equal protection question of the decade'.[14] In the interim HEW Secretary Califano has confounded the issue of racial and sexual quotas as a means of redressing past discrimination by first indicating in a March 18, 1977, interview that he endorsed preferential hiring and admission policies in higher education: 'How am I ... ever going to find first-class black lawyers, first-class black scientists, first-class women scientists if these people don't have the chance to get into the best schools in the country?' Later on March 31 he repudiated the idea of quotas for ameliorating patterns of discrimination, only to reverse himself again in June, saying: 'The country must rely on numerical goals in hiring and admissions.'[15] The forthcoming *Bakke* decision will be of enormous importance to women and minorities attempting through affirmative action to overcome two centuries of educational discrimination, but most civil rights legal analysts are pessimistic about its outcome.

Implementation of Title IX of the Educational Amendments of 1972 is also important. At the moment its sanctions are indirect, its numerous guidelines are vague, and there is a long list of exceptions to existing sex discrimination and sex segregation in schools at all levels. In addition, the United States Court of Appeals for the Seventh Circuit has upheld a lower court decision that *individuals* cannot sue for sex discrimination under Title IX in order to avoid a 'flood' of litigation as occurred under Title VII to create the current EEOC backlog. Title IX generally prohibits gender distinction in federally assisted educational programs and many of the regulations are specifically aimed at school athletic programs.[16] Probably its most immediate and impressive impact will be in equalising conditions and facilities for women athletes.[17]

Enforcement of much Title VII affirmative action through the courts has been thrown into a state of limbo because of the *Teamsters v. U.S.* and related decisions handed down in May, 1977. In ruling that unless a seniority plan intentionally discriminates among workers it is not illegal under the Civil Rights Act of 1964, the Burger Court placed more stringent requirements for proof of individual discrimination against complainants in cases after the act went into effect in July, 1965. Some civil rights lawyers are now speculating this will end effective class action litigation and group compensation for discrimination that have attracted much attention in recent years. It also casts a cloud over sweeping backpay settlements negotiated by EEOC with large companies, particularly the current one pending with Sears, Roebuck & Company, the nation's leading retail store. *Teamsters* is also viewed as an anti-affirmative-action harbinger for the *Bakke* case on 'reverse discrimination'.

Perhaps the most inadvertently negative view of the seniority decision came from David A. Copus, who until April, 1977, was an EEOC attorney in charge of litigation against employers. Now he works for a private law firm defending employers against the EEOC. 'I never lost a case arguing for the EEOC,' Copus unabashedly remarked upon hearing about *Teamsters*, 'and now I don't expect to lose one for the employers, thanks to this decision.' The single ray of hope in the immediate wake of the *Teamsters* decision came on July 12, 1977, when the EEOC issued a five-page memorandum indicating that it was taking a narrow view of the Court's ruling, namely, that it viewed the decision as applying only to seniority systems established before July 1965. The EEOC also promised to take a liberal stand on what constituted 'discriminatory intent'. Consequently whenever an employer or union maintained a seniority system 'locking in minorities or females' after being made aware of alternative employment systems, EEOC will initiate action despite *Teamsters*.[18]

It must always be remembered that even if equality before the law were achieved overnight for American women, sex discrimination would not end in the United States. The same is true of the hotly debated Equal Rights Amendment, necessary as that is in the long legislative and judicial process toward creating uniformity of legal treatment for women in all fifty states. Justice, it would seem, is not only blind; it is also interminably slow and sometimes regressive.

The Second Women's Movement and Alternatives to the ERA

The relationship of the second women's movement to all of these decisions and to Congressional legislation or Executive Orders that prompted judicial action is characterised by numerous ambiguities. Disillusioned by the male dominated civil rights movement, and by student and antiwar groups, women gradually formed their own organisations in the late 1960s. By the early 1970s this new women's movement was already beset by factionalism. NOW, the oldest and best known national organisation, could only claim 55,000 members at the beginning of 1977. In contrast with the first women's movement that was united, albeit too single-mindedly, in the face of defeats in court and lack of encouragement from Congress, the current movement has fragmented, in part over legal decisions and state and federal legislation that are not always easy to understand or organise around. Even the Equal Rights Amendment (ERA) did not until very recently command the support of the more radical or militant feminist groups.[19]

In an era of gradually expanding equal rights, despite *Gilbert*, *Teamsters*, and *Beal*, the women's movement is faced with an irony seemingly beyond its control: a political economy that is no longer capable of offering unlimited opportunity, let alone equality, to aspiring individuals and groups. Had the movement, recent affirmative action legislation, and antidiscrimination court decisions like *Frontiero* occurred early in the 1960s, women (and minorities of both sexes) would have seen dramatic gains, especially in the area of employment. At the historical moment, therefore, when middle class

American women have achieved all the prerequisites for total liberation or emancipation that modern technology can offer, the women's movement could easily flounder and drown in a sea of recession or depression. Also, socio-economic questions have arisen that make many women question mainstream values and activities before they have fully experienced them. Career-minded women are not being told, as in the past, that it is 'unladylike' or inappropriate for them to pursue their professions. They are accused instead of being elitist, reformist or male-oriented. These charges often place ambitious, skilled women in a guilt-ridden quandary. Other women have retreated to the comfort of ideological purity within socialist/feminist cadres and still others have isolated themselves in the false security provided by sex-segregated lifestyles. Such vanguard groups need to introduce to the vast majority of American women skills and alternative ideas necessary for creating more consciously controlled and less dependent lives for themselves and their children. The right to choose to live, love, and work as freely as possible, recognising the limitations of patriarchy; the right to work to remake societal values and institutions based on a newly emerging feminist ideology and culture – these constitute the enormous possibilities and difficulties facing the second women's movement in the last quarter of the twentieth century.

What has been both amazing and perplexing in the last fifteen years of advancement in female legal rights in the United States is how much was achieved before the second women's movement obtained widespread organisation and cultural significance and in spite of its current fragmented state. In fact, opposition to the implementation of the sex provision of Title VII within civil rights groups and the EEOC itself stimulated the first coherent national organisations among women.[20] Finally in March, 1972, after forty-nine years of sporadic effort, Congressional ratification of the ERA Amendment definitely documented the existence of a national *female network*.

Subsequently it has proven difficult to duplicate that effective coalition of women in enough individual states to achieve ratification of the ERA. Only one additional state has ratified the ERA since March, 1975. As of the fall of 1977, thirty-five of the necessary thirty-eight states had voted for ratification. The required three-quarters must be reached by March 22, 1979, or the ERA Amendment will die unless an extension of the deadline is approved by Congress. It has recently been defeated in North Carolina, South Carolina, Illinois, Oklahoma, Missouri, and Florida. Moreover, three of the thirty-five having ratified – Idaho, Nebraska, and Tennessee – voted to rescind. These rescissions represent a psychological rather than a political setback for ERAmerica, a coalition of more than 120 groups. In the nineteenth century Congress refused to honor votes to rescind the Fourteenth and Fifteenth Amendments by states that had previously ratified them. The same was true of the Nineteenth Amendment in 1920. In March 1977, the Justice Department gave President Carter's counsel a legal memorandum holding that states cannot withdraw their support of the ERA. Yet as March 1979 approaches, STOP-ERA forces under the direction of members of the Mormon Church, Daughters of the American Revolution, the John Birch Society, the National Council of Catholic Women, the Ku Klux Klan, and the American Nazi Party appear to gain strength. In addition to these established conservative groups, new ones have formed under the influence of antifeminist Phyllis Schlafly. They include: the National Right to Life Group, the Conservative Caucus of Falls Church, Virginia, the Eagle Forum, March for Life and Save Our Children, a group headed by Anita Bryant, a leading opponent of homosexual rights.[21]

Opposition to the ERA represents a curious amalgamation of right-wing political groups and fundamentalist denominations whose effectiveness lies in their emotional appeal and their single-minded dedication to this cause. Unlike the more loosely organised ERAmerica led by Sheila Greenwald and the fragmented women's movement, STOP-ERA has been well-organised in the southern and rural states now crucial in the ratification battle. At the grassroots level, therefore, the pro-ERA coalition has not been able to marshal as much popular support as its opponents, as indicated most clearly in some state International Women's Year Conferences throughout 1977. However, the national IWY conference held in November 1977, restored new energy and confidence in the PRO-ERA forces. Nonetheless, fear tactics employed by STOP-ERA forces, illogically based as they are, continue to be asserted. They largely consist of arguments about feminism being resonsible for the breakdown of the family (when demographic figures clearly show that change in family structure is an evolutionary process which cannot be attributed to any one cause); drafting women (when the United States no longer has a national draft), eliminating protective legislation (when Title VII has already settled this issue often by extending the same benefits to men), forcing women to share sleeping and bathroom facilities with men in public institutions (when this is already prohibited by the constitutional right of privacy enunciated by the Supreme Court in 1965), making alimony payments and support by husbands of wives more difficult (when these, as pages 151–3 demonstrated, are largely unenforceable rights at the moment and when, if anything, the ERA would result in more uniform and equitable marriage and divorce laws for both sexes). Finally, it is often implied by anti-ERA groups that the amendment would encourage communism, unisex, communal, or homosexual lifestyles. The latter is a good example of how STOP-ERA deliberately confuses the ERA with such unpopular or controversial social issues, including abortion.

The real fear the conservative opponents of ERA have is its potential for making the most progressively liberating laws affecting women's lives uniform in all of the states. It is basically a fear of freedom of choice for all women, regardless of class or race. The ERA is not designed to change values. Its purpose is to provide equality of opportunity through the Constitution and the American legal system for those women who want to realise full personal and professional expectations *now*. It is absolutely noncoercive when it comes to individual lifestyles and its enforcement powers are directed only against state and federal entities or public officials, not private persons.[22]

One way to anticipate the future impact of the ERA, if it is ratified, is to look at the application and interpretation of state equal rights amendments by state judiciaries. As of February, 1977, fifteen states had enacted constitutional provisions directly prohibiting discrimination based on sex; in eight the wording closely resembles that of the federal amendment, which reads: 'Equal rights under the law shall not be denied or abridged by the United States or by any State on account of sex.' In five of the fifteen states the language is more like that of the equal protection clause of the Fourteenth Amendment, rather than the federal ERA. The remaining two states – Utah and Wyoming – had added broad equal rights provisions to their constitutions around the turn of the century, but have not recently been actively implementing them.[23] To date, more cases have been brought under the Pennsylvania amendment than any other state. The results in all fifteen states have been encouraging because the courts have been interpreting these state equal rights amendments as strong mandates for sexual equality before the law. Generally speaking courts in ERA jurisdictions have exhibited a traditional bias against enlarging the scope of criminal liabilities under existing criminal statutes. They have been much more liberal in interpreting civil law, 'often extending statutory coverage by reading in sex-neutral language and standards when necessary to save important rights and obligations'.[24]

In the event the national ERA is not ratified, what alternatives are realistic possibilities for obtaining equality before the law for all American women? In considering these alternatives we are assuming that any legal system 'will continue to support and command an inferior status for women so long as it permits *any* differentiation in legal treatment on the basis of sex'.[25] What alternative or combination of alternatives would most effectively eradicate sex discrimination from the law? There are two basic answers to this question. The first is by piecemeal revisions and extension of existing state and federal laws. The hopeless inefficiency of this approach has been demonstrated again and again. Even when such statutes are most liberating they are subject to judicial interpretation that may not be, as the *Teamsters* and *Beal* decisions have so aptly demonstrated. Moreover, it cannot be argued with any seriousness that a coherent series of laws could be devised and coordinated at local, state and federal levels that would result in a uniform change in public policy. Piecemeal legislative reform began almost one hundred and fifty years ago with the Married Women's Property Acts. It could drag on for another one hundred and fifty and still not achieve full equality for women.

The second set of alternatives focuses on extending various constitutional clauses to women. 'The principle of equality [could] become firmly established in constitutional doctrine', according to the 1963 President's Commission on the Status of Women, through use of the Fourteenth and Fifth Amendments without the need for a new constitutional amendment. Obviously what is being argued here is that the due process, privileges and immunities, and equal protection clauses of these two amendments would be interpreted by state and federal courts to include and protect women from sex discrimination. Of all these clauses, equal protection is the most important because it alone would automatically make sex a suspect classification subject to strict judicial scrutiny. Since the *Frontiero* decision the Supreme Court has not demonstrated any inclination to make sex a suspect classification subject to strict judicial scrutiny under the equal protection clause of the Fourteenth Amendment. If anything, it has assiduously avoided the issue since 1973. In the absence of consistent doctrinal development on sex discrimination by the Burger Court to date, it would seem foolhardy to expect the Justices to begin suddenly to emerge from the safety of the 'gray zone' they have created. Even Tribe's concept of 'structural due process' or 'structural justice' is not one that a majority on the Burger Court has acknowledged as the doctrinal pattern it has established or wants to follow. At best, 'structural justice' is one among many hypotheses by legal experts about the future constitutional patterns these particular Justices might set.

Moreover, Raoul Berger, a respected legal historian, has recently opposed further manipulation of the Fourteenth Amendment by either liberal or conservative members of the Court. Therefore, the likelihood of dramatic Supreme Court application of any sections of the Constitution or its amendments is not too promising at the moment. That is why recent suggestions by feminist lawyers that the Thirteenth Amendment, which outlaws all forms of involuntary servitude, be reintroduced in sex discrimination cases are not too promising. For one thing, the involuntary servitude argument was used repeatedly and without success by Anthony and other feminists who took their cases to court in the last quarter of the nineteenth century. Not a single case based on this premise has reached the Supreme Court in the last half of the twentieth century. Even less likely to succeed in court is the assertion that the Nineteenth Amendment 'really had very little to do with the vote, but instead established the total equality of women with men'. This argument not only ignores the literal wording of the original amendment, but also suggests an interpretation of it that has no judicial precedent.[26]

We are left then with Congressional action in the form of application of either some existing aspect of the Constitution such as the commerce clause or the enforcement section of the Fourteenth Amendment which reads that 'Congress shall have the power to enforce, by appropriate legislation, the provisions of this article'. Again, nothing less than ratification of the Equal Rights Amendment that Congress passed in 1972 offers any comprehensive vehicle for ending sex discrimination. If ratified by 1979 it would still not take effect for two years, but would provide the foundation at long last upon which a coherent judicial pattern for women could be developed. The ERA is not a panacea. Sexist attitudes are so ingrained in American life and institutions that they will linger far beyond the year 2000. Regressive Supreme Court decisions like *Teamsters* and *Beal* have made ratification all the more necessary now that enforcement of Title VII has been brought into question. Only Congressional action in the form of a constitutional amendment cannot be obliterated through capricious judicial preference.

'Sex prejudice', poet and playwright Eve Merriam said in 1966, 'is the only prejudice now considered socially acceptable.'[27] This fact of American life will not disappear with ratification of the ERA, but the

Twenty-Seventh Amendment would be psychologically symbolic and permanent. It would also promote legal uniformity in the treatment of females in statutes and under the law in a way that no other act of Congress, nationwide action on individual issues by the women's movement, or Supreme Court decision could. Finally, the ERA would constitute a most fitting way for the United States to enter its third century, namely, by finally granting more than half of its population full rights, privileges and obligations under the federal Constitution.

POSTSCRIPT ON BAKKE: BREAKTHROUGH OR BACKLASH?

On June 28, 1978, the nine Justices of the Supreme Court handed down six separate statements, arriving at a complex 5-4 opinion in the controversial *Bakke* case. Four Justices, arguing on narrow statutory grounds, ordered the UC Davis medical school to admit Allan Bakke because it had violated Title VI of the Civil Rights Act, which they interpreted as forbidding all racial 'discrimination under any program or activity receiving Federal financial assistance'. Four other Justices, arguing on broad constitutional grounds, asserted that Congress had intended Title VI to be used to promote racial justice for minority groups and that race could legitimately be considered a factor in affirmative action programs attempting to remedy past discriminatory practices. Writing the majority opinion, Justice Powell cast the decisive fifth vote on each issue, thereby taking a constitutional stand that fell between both camps without reconciling their differences.

The American press widely hailed the decision as a victory for Bakke as an individual and for race as a component in affirmative action programs, although the Davis quota system was officially declared unlawful. However, the uncertainty inevitably generated by the narrow majority and division among the Justices prompted the strongest advocates of affirmative action to predict that progress against discrimination would level off as schools and employers waited to see how the Court would define 'permissible' affirmative action programs in the future.

Despite the stated willingness of the majority to consider race a factor in affirmative action, one of the most debilitating aspects of *Bakke* would be if the Court continued to hold that racial (and therefore gender) integration in admissions and hiring programs can only take place through the slow process of case-by-case, individual proof of discrimination, rather than on a general recognition of group discrimination. For the same reason, the decision also raises the spectre of white males systematically using the charge of 'reverse discrimination' based on constitutionally guaranteed individual rights to prevent women and minorities from obtaining redress for past discrimination.

Finally, in light of Congressional extension of the ERA deadline to June 30, 1982, *Bakke* assumes even more significance for American women because the only point on which the Justices appeared to agree was that discrimination based on sex was less important an issue on the scale of socioeconomic justice than discrimination based on race. Moreover, Justice Powell explicitly held that the Court has never viewed gender 'as inherently suspect or as comparable to racial or ethnic classifications for the purpose of equal-protection analysis'. Thus, *Bakke* represents but one more decision in which the Burger Court has backed off from *Frontiero*. Because of the Court's continuing hesitancy to apply the equal protection guarantees of the Fifth and Fourteenth Amendments to women and because of the backlash ramifications *Bakke* may have on remedial admission policies at educational institutions, as well as on the hiring practices of private businesses and public works programs, it is all the more important that proponents of equal rights for women take advantage of the extension of the ERA deadline to achieve ratification. The potentially negative connotations of the decision for women can only be counteracted with the passage of the ERA—once again proving that when litigation falters, women must always be prepared to resort to political action for legislative restitution of their still unrealized inalienable rights.

Conclusion

A study of sexism in the legal systems of Britain and the United States disposes of at least two pieces of conventional wisdom.

First, it explodes the notion that legal systems evolve according to inherent principles of logic and procedure. The great changes in gender status have come about not through the harmonious unfolding from within of legal concepts, but through vigorous attacks against the legal system from outside. Contrary to common assertion by lawyers, the law and the judges did not stand on the side of equality and individual rights, nor were they even neutral. By and large, they acted as a barrier to, rather than a guarantee of, equality between men and women. This was for the reason so obvious to outsiders and so invisible to lawyers, that the structures of the law were part of wider social structures rather than apart from them. The inequality in public life which the women complained about was as present inside the legal system as outside of it, while the stake which the male judges had in maintaining gender exclusiveness was in some ways more direct than any interest they might have had in maintaining race or class inequality.

It made no difference whether the judges were operating in the context of the British system which enshrines the supremacy of Parliament, or whether they functioned in terms of the American Constitution guaranteeing individual rights. From a formal point of view, the ways in which the male monopoly cases were presented in the two countries had nothing in common. British judges accepted their legal subordination to Parliament, and declared their role to be merely to act as impartial interpreters of particular words in particular statutes. Hence the 'persons' cases. American judges, on the other hand, saw themselves as the guardians of the Constitution, whose duty it was to apply in as just a fashion as possible the wide words of the Amendments to particular problems. Accordingly, the forms of action, the modes of procedure and the systems of logic in the two legal systems were totally different. Yet a perusal of the cases shows that the judges in the two countries almost invariably arrived at the same conclusions at almost precisely the same times, quite irrespective of the constitutional routes they followed. Thus they jointly upheld and justified the exclusion of women from the franchise right until the end of the second decade of this century, when legislation in Britain and a constitutional Amendment in the United States compelled them to change; similarly they both thereafter tended in areas outside of the franchise to preserve the roles of men as property-owning breadwinners and of women as dependent homemakers, until forced to a more egalitarian position by the challenge of the second women's movement in the late 1960s. One must conclude that the prevailing conception of womanhood proved to be a far more compelling determinant of judicial behaviour than the terms of the statute or the words of the Constitution. Moreover, such conceptions were not, in Holmes' famous statement, the inarticulate assumptions on which judgments rested: the judges expressly declared their support for the principle of treating women differently from men – they were enthusiasts for inequality.

The second claim that disintegrates when viewed through the perspective of gender relations is the assertion that historically the legal profession has acted as the guardian of the individual as against the public power. The legal profession both supported discriminatory laws and practices in society at large, and upheld discrimination in its own ranks. None of the supposed chivalry which men claimed underlay all their actions, was extended towards females endeavouring to join their ranks. To this day, the profession tends to manifest a grudging and uncomfortable tolerance rather than a facilitative welcome to women entrants.

Undoubtedly progress has been made towards gender equality, both inside and outside the legal system. But the record shows that each step forward has had to be strenuously campaigned for, and indicates that every future advance on the long journey to equality will have to be fought for with the same determination and skill.

Appendix 1   Landmark Decisions and Legislation

BRITAIN

1867 – Second Reform Act grants franchise to 'any man' who is a householder.

1869 – Manchester Voters case – *Chorlton v. Lings* declares that common law disability prevents women from voting.

1873 – Edinburgh Medical Students case – *Jex-Blake v. Senatus* – women's expulsion from University upheld.

1882 – Married Women's Property Act provides that spouses hold property separately and no longer jointly under husband's control.

1889 – London County Council cases – *Lady Sandhurst* case – exclusion of women elected to the county council upheld.

1891 – The Clitheroe cases – *The Queen v. Jackson* – court on appeal grants habeas corpus to free wife from forcible detention by husband.

1903 – Refusal by the Bar to enrol Bertha Cave upheld by the judges.

1908 – Scottish University Voters case – *Nairn v. Scottish Universities* – House of Lords upholds trend to exclude women from public functions and voting.

1914 – Women Solicitors case – *Beeb v. Law Society* – refusal by Law Society to enrol a woman upheld by the courts.

1918 – The Vote and the right to stand for Parliament granted to women.

1919 – Sex Disqualification Removal Act removes public disabilities imposed on women by the judiciary in terms of the common law.

1923 – The Lady Rhondda case – House of Lords refuses to seat Lady Rhondda.

1925 – The Marriage Bar case – *Price v. Rhondda UDC* – judges uphold a requirement that women and not men teachers resign on marriage as not unreasonable.

1929 – Canadian Senators case – *Edwards v. Attorney-General* – the Privy Council in London finally acknowledges that women fall within the term 'persons' and can therefore be nominated to the Senate in Canada.

1965 – Race Relations Act makes race discrimination unlawful, with conciliation machinery and civil remedies, in respect of public facilities.

1966 – The Jockey Club case – *Nagle v. Fielden* – judges require Club to register a woman trainer.

1967 – Abortion Act – widens criteria for legal abortions, still leaves decision to doctors.

1967 – Matrimonial Homes Act – gives wives some protection from being evicted from homes.

1968 – Race Relations Act extended to cover employment, accommodation and advertising.

1969 – Divorce Reform Act substitutes breakdown of marriage concept for matrimonial fault.

1970 – Matrimonial Proceedings and Property Act gives courts wide discretion to dispose of property equitably on divorce.

1970 – Equal Pay Act gives employers five years to grant equal pay for like work.

1975 – Inheritance (Provisions for Families and Dependants) Act gives courts wide discretion to ensure surviving spouses get a fair share of estate.

1975 – Sex Discrimination Act makes sex discrimination unlawful in work, education and advertising and creates Equal Opportunities Commission to sponsor moves to equality.

1975 – Social Security Pensions Act abolishes many areas of inequality in state pension schemes.

1975 – Employment Protection Act, Part II, provides for six weeks paid maternity leave for longer-term employees.

1976 – Domestic Violence and Matrimonial Proceedings Act provides for urgent remedies in court against wife-batterers.

UNITED STATES

1818 – *Connor v. Shepherd* – The Massachusetts Supreme Court undermined the right of dower by ruling that widows could not claim their dowers in unimproved lands.

1839 – Mississippi passed the first Married Women's Property Act.

1868 – Ratification of the Fourteenth Amendment to the U.S. Constitution.

1873 – *Bradwell v. Illinois* – The U.S. Supreme Court ruled that a state could preclude a married woman from practicing law.

1873 – *United States of America v. Susan B. Anthony* – A New York Circuit Court convicted Susan B. Anthony of the crime of voting as a female.

1875 – *Minor v. Happersett* – The U.S. Supreme Court declared that despite the privileges and immunities clause, a state could prohibit a woman from voting. While declaring that women were 'persons', the Court held that they constituted a 'special category of [nonvoting] citizens'.

1875 – *State v. Goodell* – The Wisconsin Supreme Court denied Lavina Goodell admission to the state bar.

1879 – *In re Goodell* – The Wisconsin Supreme Court reversed itself and granted Goodell a license to practice law.

1879 – Congress passed legislation permitting women to practice before the U.S. Supreme Court.

1887 – *Harland v. Territory* – The territorial Supreme Court of Washington barred women from jury duty.

1894 – *In re Lockwood* – The U.S. Supreme Court upheld a lower court decision denying Belva A. Lockwood the right to practice law in Virginia on the grounds that the word 'person' meant 'male'.

1908 – *Muller v. Oregon* – The U.S. Supreme Court approved protective legislation for women because of their biological and gender-based roles.

1920 – Ratification of the Nineteenth Amendment to the U.S. Constitution permitting all women over twenty-one to vote.

1923 – *Adkins v. Children's Hospital* – The U.S. Supreme Court struck down minimum wage laws for women.

1937 – *West Coast Hotel v. Parrish* – The U.S. Supreme Court upheld minimum wage laws for women and children.

1947 – *Fay v. New York* – The U.S. Supreme Court implied that women did not have a constitutional right to serve on juries because it was not 'customary'.

1948 – *Goesaert v. Cleary* – The U.S. Supreme Court upheld a state statute prohibiting women from tending bar except if the wives and daughters of bartenders.

1961 – *Hoyt v. Florida* – The U.S. Supreme Court ruled that women could be excluded from jury duty unless they officially registered to serve.

1963 – The Equal Pay Act forbade discrimination in wages on the basis of race, colour, religion, sex, or national origin for those engaged in the same work.

1964 – The Civil Rights Act through Title VII prohibited employment discrimination based on race, color, religion, sex, or national origin. This same act created the Equal Employment Opportunity Commission (EEOC).

1965 – Executive Order No. 11246 prohibited employment discrimination by federal contractors on the same grounds as Title VII, except sex was not included.

1965 – *Griswold v. Connecticut* – The U.S. Supreme Court struck down a state forbidding the use of contraceptives.

1967 – Executive Order No. 11375 added sex to the categories of people who could not be discriminated against by institutions with federal contracts over $10,000.

1971 – *Sail'er Inn, Inc. v. Kirby* – The California Supreme Court declared that women could tend bar equally with men.

1971 – *Phillips v. Martin Marietta Corporation* – The U.S. Supreme Court tentatively struck down the exclusion of women with preschool children from holding certain jobs.

1971 – *Reed v. Reed* – The U.S. Supreme Court for the first time invalidated state legislation that classified on the basis of sex by finally declaring that women were 'persons' and that males could not arbitrarily be given preference as executors of estates.

1972 – Additional amendments extended Title VII to include all employers with fifteen or more workers and gave the EEOC greater power by allowing it to initiate suits.

1972 – Title IX of the Educational Amendments made it illegal to discriminate on the grounds of sex in all public undergraduate institutions and in most private and public graduate and vocational schools receiving federal monies.

1972 – Congress sent the Equal Rights Amendment to the states for ratification.

1973 – *Roe v. Wade* – For the first time the U.S. Supreme Court legalised abortions.

1973 – *Frontiero v. Richardson* – The U.S. Supreme Court struck down armed service regulations that had denied women the same dependents' benefits as men. However, only a plurality of the Justices declared sex to be a suspect classification requiring close scrutiny.

1974 – *Cleveland Board of Education v. LaFleur* – The U.S. Supreme Court held that a law requiring mandatory unpaid maternity leaves was in violation of the due process of pregnant women.

1974 – *Geduldig v. Aiello* – The U.S. Supreme Court upheld a California disability insurance program denying benefits for pregnancy related disabilities.

1975 – *Taylor v. Louisiana* – The U.S. Supreme Court invalidated all remaining state laws restricting jury duty on the basis of gender.

1976 – *General Electric Co. v. Gilbert* – Relying heavily on *Geduldig*, the U.S. Supreme Court ruled that employers need not compensate women for maternity related disabilities under employee insurance plans.

1976 – *Planned Parenthood v. Danforth* – The Supreme Court continued to deny state challenges to first trimester abortions as proclaimed in *Roe*.

1977 – *Teamsters v. United States* – In a series of related decisions the U.S. Supreme Court undermined all affirmative action programs and class action-suits by upholding seniority plans in effect before July, 1965.

1977 – *Beal v. Ann Doe* – The U.S. Supreme Court ruled that states were not required to use public funds to perform abortions, thereby making it more difficult for poor women to benefit from *Roe* and other pro-abortion decisions.

1977 – The Equal Employment Opportunity Reorganization Act further amended Title VII and broadened EEOC jurisdiction to include the Equal Pay Act, Executive Order 11246 and the Age Discrimination Act.

1977 – The Equal Credit Opportunity Act (ECOA), originally passed in 1975 as an amendment to the 1970 Consumer Credit Protection Act, finally became effective and should eliminate remaining credit discrimination against women if enforced upon states that have not already passed affirmative action legislation extending equal credit to women.

1977 – The EEOC announced that it would narrowly interpret *Teamsters* in order not to undermine existing affirmative action programs.

1977 – Legislation pending in Congress to expand the definition of sex discrimination under Title VII in order to protect the rights of pregnant workers negatively affected by *Gilbert*.

1977 – Legislation pending in Congress to provide better protection for victims of rape, aid for displaced homemakers, and retirement benefits for divorced or widowed spouses married at least twenty years.

1978 – *Bakke v. The Regents of the University of California* – U.S. Supreme Court ordered Allan Bakke admitted to medical school, but also held that race "may" be a factor in affirmative action programs at educational institutions.

1978 – Ratification of the Equal Rights Amendment (ERA) pending. The current time limitation on this Twenty-Seventh Amendment to the U.S. Constitution has been extended to June 30, 1982.

Appendix 2 How Many Women?

BRITAIN

The proportion of women admitted as solicitors has increased steadily from 6 per cent in 1965, and jumped from 12.6 to 15.3 per cent in 1974.

	Total admitted	Women	Per cent
1965	1009	62	6.1
1966	1123	69	6.1
1967	1107	84	7.6
1968	997	89	8.9
1969	1365	100	7.3
1970	1877	165	8.8
1971	1682	166	9.9
1972	1713	198	11.6
1973	1764	222	12.6
1974	1849	283	15.3

In 1975 (October) 522 of the 2658 students whose names appeared in the list of Part II candidates who passed wholly or in part were women (19.6 per cent). But women have a long way to catch up:

1974
Total solicitors on roll	36,150
Women	2,296
Percentage	6.4

Total practising certificates	28,741
Women	1,299
Percentage	4.5

Source: Law Society's records department

Women represent a larger proportion of practising barristers than of practising solicitors:

	1974	1976
In practice at Bar	3,368	4,076
Women	252	336
Percentage	7.5	8.2

Source: Senate of the Inns of Court

In the year 1974–75, women's score for judicial appointments was:

High Court judges	1 out of 3 appointed
Circuit judges	0 out of 20
Recorders	2 out of 53
Metropolitan stipendiary magistrates	0 out of 2

Source: Senate of the Inns of Court *Annual statement 1974—75.*

UNITED STATES

Throughout U.S. history women have made up a very small proportion of the lawyer population. The percentage varied slightly between 1948 and 1970, from 1.8 percent to 2.8 percent respectively; since then it has started to rise:

	Directory listings of lawyers	No. of women lawyers listed	Percent of women lawyers listed
1963	268,782	7,143	2.7
1966	289,404	8,068	2.8
1970	324,818	9,103	2.8
1973	375,375*	13,025*	3.5
1975	400,000*	24,000*	6.0
1977	455,556*	41,000*	9.0

*These are approximate figures
Source: The 1971 Lawyer Statistical Report, American Bar Foundation (1972); U.S. Department of Labor (1977).

The number of law students enrolled in Law Schools has risen steadily over the same period, but so has the proportion of women students:

	Total enrollment	Women students	Percent of women enrolled
1963	49,552	1,883	3.8
1966	62,556	2,678	4.3
1970	82,499	7,031	8.5
1973	106,102	16,760	15.8
1975	116,991	26,737	22.9
1976	117,451	29,982	25.5

Source: Women Lawyers Journal 63 (Spring 1977)

The Women's Bureau, Department of Labor, reported in its 1970 census that of the 11,380 state and federal judges in the US, 869 were women, or 7.6 per cent. However, by 1977 only 1.1 per cent of federal judges were women. No woman has ever served on the US Supreme Court. Although there are presently* ninety-seven authorised judgeships in the federal Circuit Courts of Appeal, only two women have ever been appointed and only one is currently serving; of the 399 authorised federal district judgeships, a total of eight have been appointed but only three now actively serve; two are on the US Tax Court; and finally, two women have been appointed to the US Customs Court but both are now retired. By the end of 1977 there were seven female state supreme court justices and thirteen women sitting on the benches of state intermediate appellate courts. Only twelve women have ever sat on the federal bench in its almost 200-year history.

Source: Research and Information Service of the National Center for State Courts, 1977.

Bibliography

Abel-Smith, Brian and Stevens, Robert, *Lawyers and the Courts: A Sociological Study of the English Legal System 1750—1965*, London, Heinemann, 1967.

Alexander, Shana, *State-by-State Guide to Women's Legal Rights*, Los Angeles, Wollstonecraft Incorporated, 1975.

Anthony, Susan, Speeches from the dock, excerpted in *Guild Notes*, October 1974, from Dorsen and Friedman, *Disorder in Court*, U.S., 1973.

Arnold, Thurman, *The Symbols of Government*, New York, 1962.

Auerbach, Jerold, *Unequal Justice: Lawyers and Social Change in Modern America*, New York, Oxford University Press, 1976.

Babcock, Barbara Allen, Freedman, Ann E., Norton, Eleanor Holmes, and Ross, Susan C., *Sex Discrimination and the Law: Causes and Remedies*, Boston, Little, Brown and Company, 1975.

Baldwin, John, 'The Social Composition of the Magistracy', *British Journal of Criminology*, Vol. 16, No. 2, 1976, pp. 171–4.

Barnes, Janette, 'Women and Entrance to the Legal Profession', *Journal of Legal Education*, 1970.

Bell, Quentin, *Virginia Woolf*, Vol. I *Virginia Stephen*, London, Hogarth Press, 1972.

Berger, Raoul, *Government by Judiciary: The Transformation of the Fourteenth Amendment*, Cambridge, Harvard University Press, 1977.

Birks, Michael, *Gentlemen of the Law*, London, 1960.

Bittenbender, Ada, 'Women Lawyers' in Meyer (ed.) *Women's Work in America*, New York, 1891.

Blackstone, Tessa, 'The Limits of Legislating for Equality for Women', *New Community Journal of the Community Relations Commission*, special edition, Vol. V, no. 1–2, Summer 1976.

Blease W. Lyons, *The Emancipation of English Women*, London, 1913.

Bocock, Robert, *Ritual in Industrial Society*, London, Allen and Unwin, 1974.

Boggan, E. Carrington, Haft, Marilyn G., Lister, Charles, and Rupp, John P., *The Rights of Gay People: A Basic ACLU Guide to a Gay Person's Rights*, New York, Avon, 1975.

Brittain, Vera, *Women's Work in Modern England*, London, 1928.

Brookes, Pamela, *Women at Westminster*, British American books, n.d. circa 1967.

Brown, Barbara A., Emerson, Thomas, I., Falk, Gail, and Freeman, Ann E., 'The Equal Rights Amendment: A Constitutional Basis for Equal Rights for Women', *Yale Law Journal*, 1971.

Burns, Haywood, *Black People and the Tyranny of American Law*, The Annals of the American Academy of Political and Social Science, May 1973.

Campbell, Colin, 'Legal Thought and Juristic Values', *British Journal of Law & Society*, 1, 1974.

Cary, Eve, and Peratis, Kathleen Willert, *Woman and the Law*, Skokie, Illinois, National Textbook Company, 1977.

Center for Women's Policy Studies, *Rape and Its Victims: A Report for Citizens, Health Facilities, and Criminal Justice Agencies*, published by the Law Enforcement Assistance Administration (LEAA), Box 24036, Washington, D.C., 20024.

Chapman, Jane R. and Gates, Margaret, eds., *Women into Wives: The Legal and Economic Impact of Marriage*, New York, Sage Books, 1977.

Cheeld, Diana, 'The Rise of an Angry Young Woman', *Law Guardian Gazette*, 28 July 1976, p. 635.

Clevedon, Catherine Lyle, *The Woman Suffrage Movement in Canada*, Toronto, 1950.

Coote, Anna and Gill, Tess, *Battered Women and the New Law*, London, National Council for Civil Liberties and Interaction, 1977.

Coussins, Jean, *Equality Report*, London, National Council for Civil Liberties, 1977.

Cretney, Steven Michael, *Principles of Family Law*, 2nd edition, London, Sweet and Maxwell, 1976.

Cross, Rupert, *Precedent in English Law*, Oxford, Clarendon Press, 2nd ed., 1969.

Crozier, Blanche, 'Constitutionality of Discrimination Based on Sex', *Boston Law Review*, 1935.

Davidson, Kenneth, Ginsburg, Ruth Bader, and Kay, Herma Hill, *Text, Cases and Materials on Sex-Based Discrimination*, St. Paul, West Publishing Co., 1974.

Deacon, Alan and Hill, Michael, *The Problem of 'Surplus Women' in the Nineteenth Century: Secular and Religious Alternatives*, 5 Student Christian Movement Press, London, 1972.

DeCrow, Karen, *Sexist Justice*, New York, Vintage, 1975.

Defeis, Elizabeth F., *Women and the Law: A Video Course in Color*, Seton Hall University School of Law, Newark, N.J. 07102.

Eekelaar, John, *Family Security and Family Breakdown*, London, Penguin Education: Law and Society, 1971.

Ehrenreich, Barbara and English, Deidre, *Witches, Midwives & Nurses – A History of Women Healers*, Glass Mountain Pamphlets, Oyster Bay, New York; reprinted 1973, Detroit, U.S.A.

Eisler, Riane Tennenhaus, *Dissolution: No-Fault Divorce, Marriage, and the Future of Women*, New York, McGraw-Hill Book Company, 1977.

Ely, John Hart, 'The Wages of Crying Wolf: A Comment on Roe v. Wade', *Yale Law Review*, 1973.

Epstein, Cynthia Fuchs, *Woman's Place: Options and Limits in Professional Careers*, Berkeley, University of California Press, 1971.

Finer Report on One Parent Families, Vol. I, London, H.M.S.O., 1974.

Flexner, Eleanor, *Century of Struggle: The Woman's Rights Movement in the United States*, Cambridge, Harvard University Press, 1959.

Freeman, Jo, 'Women and Public Policy', paper delivered at the 1975 conference, *Pioneers for Century III: Women and Power*, in Cincinnati, Ohio.

Fulford, Roger, *Votes for Women*, London, 1957.

Gilsinan, James F., Obernyer, Lynn, and Gilsinan, Christine A., 'Women Attorneys and the Judiciary', *Denver Law Journal*, 1975.

Ginsburg, Ruth Bader, *Constitutional Aspects of Sex Based Discrimination*, St. Paul, West Publishing Co., 1974.

——, 'Women as Full Members of the Club: An Evolving American Ideal', *Human Rights* (ABA), 1976.

Glendon, Mary Ann, 'Marriage and the State: The Withering Away of Marriage', *Virginia Law Review*, 1976.

Graveson, R. H. and Crane, F. R., eds., *A Century of Family Law 1857–1957*, London, 1957. Foreword by Lord Evershed, Master of the Rolls

Grossblat, Martha and Sikes, Bette H., eds., *Women Lawyers: Supplementary Data to the 1971 Lawyer Statistical Report*, Chicago, American Bar Foundation, 1973.

Guggenheim, Malvina H. and Defeis, Elizabeth F., 'United States Participation in International Agreements Providing Rights for Women', *Loyola of Los Angeles*

Law Review, 1976.

Harding, Alan, *A Social History of English Law*, London, Penguin, 1966.

Harris, Nigel, *Belief in Society – The Problem of Ideology*, London, Penguin, 1971.

Harrison, Paul, 'Burn Your Jock Straps', *New Society*, 15 May 1975.

Hearst, Patty, *The Trial of* (complete transcript), San Francisco, The Great Fidelity Press, 1976.

Hewitt, Patricia, 'Women's Rights in Law and Practice', *New Community – Journal of the Community Relations Commission*, special edition, Vol. V, no. 1–2, Summer 1976.

Hiller, Dana V. and Sheets, Robin Ann, eds., *Women and Men: The Consequences of Power*, Cincinnati, 1977.

Holmes, Oliver Wendell, *The Common Law*, New York, 1881.

Horwitz, Morton J., *The Transformation of American Law, 1780–1860*, Cambridge, Harvard University Press, 1977.

House of Lords Select Committee on Anti-Discrimination Bill (H.L. 104), House of Lords 1972–73, Vol. VIII.

Jackson, David, *Law and Public Policy – The English Connection*, Inaugural Lecture, Southampton, 1974.

Johnston, John D. and Knapp, Charles L., 'Sex Discrimination by Law: A Study in Judicial Perspective', *New York University Law Review*, 1971.

Kamm, Josephine, *Rapiers and Battleaxes*, London, Allen and Unwin, 1966.

Kanowitz, Leo, *Women and the Law: The Unfinished Revolution*, Albuquerque, University of New Mexico Press, 1969.

Kay, Herma Hill, *Sex-Based Discrimination in Family Law*, St. Paul, West Publishing Co., 1974.

Kennedy, Helena, in Robert Hazel (ed.) *The Bar on Trial*, London, Quartet Books, 1978.

Knight, Holford, 'Women and the Legal Profession', *Contemporary Review*, May 1913.

Kraditor, Aileen S., *The Ideas of the Woman Suffrage Movement, 1890–1920*, Garden City, N.Y., Anchor Books, 1971.

Law Guardian Gazette, 26 February 1975.

Law Journal, Vol. 39, 1904.

Leach, Edmund, *Levi-Strauss*, London, Fontana Modern Masters, revd. ed., 1974.

Le Grand, Camille, 'Rape and Rape Laws: Sexism in Society and Law', *California Law Review*, 1973.

Lerner, Gerda, *The Female Experience: An American Documentary*, Indianapolis, Bobbs-Merrill Co., Inc., 1977.

——, *The Woman in American History*, Menlo Park, CA, Addison-Wesley Publishing Company, 1971.

Levenzey, Beth and Andersson, Joan, *Trials of a Woman Lawyer*, duplicated, Los Angeles, 1973.

Lockwood, David, *The Black-Coated Worker*, London, 1958.

Lytton, Lady Constance (alias Jane Warton), *Prisons and Prisoners*, London, 1914.

Mandela, Nelson, *No Easy Walk to Freedom*, ed. Ruth First, London, Heinemann, 1965.

Mannheim, Karl, *Ideology and Utopia*, London, 1936; 1946 edition, London.

Mansfield, Edward, *The Legal Rights, Liabilities and Duties of Women*, Salem, MA, Jewett and Co., 1845.

Martin, Del, *Battered Wives*, San Francisco, Glide Publications, 1976.

Mayhew, Judy, 'Women at Work' in Pat Carlen (ed.) *The Sociology of Law*, Sociological Review Monograph 23, University of Keele, Staffs, 1976, 134–42.

McGregor, O. R., 'The Social Position of Women in England, 1850–1914: A Bibliography', *British Journal of Sociology*, Vol. 6, 1955, p. 48.

Melder, Keith E. *Beginnings of Sisterhood: The American Woman's Rights Movement, 1800–1850*, New York, Schocken Books, 1977.

Meyer, Annie Nathan (ed.), *see* Ada Bittenbender.

Morgan, Robin, *Going Too Far: The Personal Chronicle of a Feminist*, New York, Random House, 1977.

Morris Committee Report on Jury Service, Cmnd. 2627, London, H.M.S.O., 1965.

Morris, Richard, *Studies in the History of American Law*, New York, Columbia University Press, 1930.

Nandy, Luise and Dipak, 'Towards True Equality for Women', *New Society*, 30 January 1975.

National Union of Women's Suffrage Societies, Papers in the Fawcett Library, London.

Nelson, William E., *Americanization of the Common Law: The Impact of Legal Change on Massachusetts Society, 1760–1830*, Cambridge, Harvard University Press, 1975.

Novarro, Virginia, *Right on Sister*, London, 1976; published by the author.

Pankhurst, E. Sylvia, *The Suffragette*, London, 1911.

Parkes, Bessie Rayner, *Essays on Women's Work*, London, 1865.

Parliamentary Debates, House of Commons, 25th March, 20th May, 1867.

Pascal, Harold J., *Battered Wives: The Secret Scandal*, Canfield, OH, Alfa Books, 1977.

Paterson, A. A., 'Judges: A Political Elite?' *British Journal of Law and Society*, Vol. 1, No. 2, 1974.

Prices and Incomes Board, Report on *Solicitors*, Report no. 134, Parliamentary Papers, 1969–70, Vol. XXV, Table 2.

Purcell, Susan Kaufman, 'Ideology and the Law: Sexism and the Supreme Court Decisions', in Jane Jaquette, ed., *Women in Politics*, New York, John Wiley & Sons, 1974.

Rabkin, Peggy A., 'The Silent Feminist Revolution: Women and the Law in New York State from Blackstone to the Beginnings of the American Women's Rights Movement', Ph.D. dissertation, University of New York, Buffalo, 1975.

Radzinowicz, Leon, 'Sir James Fitzjames Stephen', Selden Society Lecture, 30 July 1957.

Rendel, Margherita, 'Law as an Instrument of Oppression or Reform' in Pat Carlen (ed.) *The Sociology of Law*, Sociological Review Monograph 23, University of Keele, Staffs, 1976, pp. 143–71.

Renner, Karl, *The Institutions of Private Law and their Social Functions*, London, Routledge and Kegan Paul, 1976.

Rheinstein, Max, *see* Max Weber.

Ross, Susan C., *The Rights of Women: The Basic ACLU Guide to a Woman's Rights*, New York, Sunrise Books, 1973.

Rowbotham, Sheila, *Hidden from History: 300 Years of Women's Oppression and the Fight Against It*, London, Pluto Press, 2nd ed., 1974.

Russell, Diana E. H. and Van de Ven, Nicole, eds., *The Proceedings of the International Tribunal on Crimes Against Women*, Milbrae, CA, Les Femmes, 1976.

Ryan, Mary P., *Womanhood in America: From Colonial Times to the Present*, New York, New Viewpoints, 1975.

Sanders, Byrne Hope, *Emily Murphy – Crusader*, Toronto, Macmillan, 1945.

Sassower, Doris L., 'Women and the Judiciary: Undoing "The Law of the Creator"', *Journal of the American Judicature Society*, 1974.

——, 'Women, Power, and the Law', *American Bar Association Journal*, 1976.

Scarman, Sir Leslie, *Women and Equality before the Law*, Fawcett Lecture, Bedford

College, London, 27 October 1971.

Sex Bias in the United States Code: A Report of the U.S. Commission on Civil Rights, Washington, D.C., April, 1977.

Simons, H. J., *African Women – Their Legal Status in South Africa*, London, C. Hurst & Co., 1968.

Sinclair, Andrew, *The Better Half: The Emancipation of the American Woman*, New York, Harper and Row, 1965.

Singer, Linda, 'Women in the Correctional Process', *American Criminal Law Review*, 1972.

Soule, Bradley and Standley, Kay, 'Perceptions of Sex Discrimination in Law', *American Bar Association Journal*, 1973.

South African Law Journal, 1913, 1918.

The Spokeswoman, a monthly newsletter published in Chicago, Illinois.

Stanton, Elizabeth Cady, Anthony, Susan B., and Gage, Matilda Joslyn, eds., *History of Woman Suffrage*, New York, Source Book Press reprint, 1970.

Stephen, James Fitzjames, Q.C., *Liberty, Equality, Fraternity*, London, 1873.

Stetson, Dorothy McBride, 'English Family Law Reform and the Status of Women', unpublished manuscript.

Strachey, Ray, *Women's Suffrage and Women's Service*, London, 1927.

Switzer, Ellen, *The Law for a Woman: Real Cases and What Happened*, New York, Charles Scribners, 1975.

Thomas, Dorothy, ed., *Women Lawyers in the United States*, New York, The Scarecrow Press, Inc., 1957.

'. . . To Form a More Perfect Union . . .' *Justice for American Women: Report of the National Commission on the Observance of International Women's Year*, Washington, D.C., 1976.

Tribe, Laurence H., *American Constitutional Law*, Mineola, N.Y., Foundation Press, 1978.

Veblen, Thorston, *The Theory of the Leisure Class*, London, 1899.

Weber, Max, *On Law in Economy and Society*, ed. Max Rheinstein, Cambridge, Harvard University Press, 1954.

Wedderburn, K. W., *The Worker and the Law*, London, Penguin, 2nd ed., 1971.

Weitzman, Lenore J., 'Legal Regulation of Marriage: Tradition and Change', *California Law Review*, 1974.

White, James J., 'Women in the Law', *Michigan Law Review*, 1967.

Wilson, Joan Hoff, 'The Illusion of Change: Women and the American Revolution', in Alfred F. Young, ed., *The American Revolution: Explorations in the History of American Radicalism*, DeKalb, Illinois, Northern Illinois University Press, 1976.

——, 'The Legal Status of Women in the Late Nineteenth and Early Twentieth Centuries', *Human Rights (ABA)*, 1977.

'Women in Law Centres', unpublished discussion paper prepared by women from Camden and Islington law centres. London, 1975.

Women Law Reporter, a bimonthly legal service covering sex discrimination exclusively.

Women Lawyers Journal, a trimester publication of the National Association of Women Lawyers.

Women's Newsletter, a publication of the National Commission on Women's Oppression (NCWO) of the National Lawyers' Guild.

Women's Report, Vol. 1, No. 2, January 1973, London.

Women's Rights Law Reporter, a student-operated scholarly journal published quarterly by Rutgers Law School.

Wraith, R. E. and Hutchinson, P. G., *Administrative Tribunals*, London, George Allen and Unwin, 1973.

Notes and References

1 *Britain:* Are Women 'Persons'?

1. This now forgotten episode is fully documented in the many accounts of the nineteenth-century women's struggle, some of which are cited in the Bibliography.
2. Blease, law lecturer at Liverpool University and member of the radical section of the Liberal Party.
3. Ray Strachey, *Women's Suffrage and Women's Service* (London, 1927).
4. Personal communication, July 1975. This is one of a number of helpful formulations and suggestions made by Dr Stone, who has been rare among law teachers in the firmness with which she has campaigned for gender equality. She would have preferred a less radical critique of the legal profession than the one presented in the pages that follow.
5. This case was brought by Sophia Jex-Blake and six other women students, and accordingly was referred to as *Septem contra Edinem*, which in present-day parlance would translate as the Edinburgh Seven.
6. In his capacity as Chancellor he had in fact put his *imprimatur* on the regulations.
7. Lord Neaves' judgment was the most full-blooded of those representing the anti-feminist position. The passages most relevant to the later discussion are reproduced here in italics.
8. *Parliamentary Debates*, House of Commons (25 March 1867).
9. Sylvia Pankhurst used her father's papers as the basis for the discussion in her two books on the Manchester Voters' cases.
10. The term 'suffragette', which apparently has a rather derisory meaning in the United States, has a more favoured position in Britain. The militant wing of the women's suffrage movement led by the Pankhursts and organised in the Women's Social and Political Union called its newspaper *The Suffragette* and regarded the term as one of honour. Today all the campaigners for votes for women are popularly if not quite accurately known as the suffragettes.
11. Annual Report of the National Union of Women's Suffrage Societies (1880).
12. See Annual Reports of the National Union of Women's Suffrage Societies.
13. *The Times* (3 December 1903).
14. The remarks refer to Scottish judges as well.
15. *South African Law Journal* (1913), p. 462. But a later contributor argued that for women to practise law would be to revolt against Nature (*South African Law Journal* (1918), p. 290).
16. The case was brought by Henrietta Edwards, Emily Murphy and other Canadian feminists.
17. The passages quoted in support of this proposition and the following ones are:
    'Nihil autem neque publicae neque privatae rei, nisi armati, agunt' (Tacitus, *Germania*, C.13).
    'Inesse quin etiam sanctum et providum putant, nec aut consilia earum aspernantur aut responsa negligunt' (*Germania*, C.8).

'Feminae ab omnibus officilis civilibus vel publicis remotae sunt' (Ulpian, A.D. 211, Dig. 1.16.195).
Lord Sankey in fact took these references from an earlier case, but used them to support an opposite argument.

18. For a background to the case, see C. L. Clevedon, *The Woman Suffrage Movement in Canada* (Toronto, 1950).
19. J. Kamm, *Rapiers and Battleaxes* (London: Allen and Unwin, 1966).
20. Calculations by Harold Laski, quoted in B. Abel-Smith and R. Stevens, *Lawyers and the Courts* (London: Heinemann, 1967).
21. Cf. K. W. Wedderburn *The Worker and the Law* (London: Penguin, 2nd ed. 1971); Abel-Smith and Stevens, as in previous note.
22. Quoted in A. Harding, *A Social History of English Law* (London: Penguin, 1966).
23. *The Queen v. Jackson* (1891) 1 Q.B. 671 (the Clitheroe case); cf. *In re Cochrane* 8 Dowl. 630 (1840).
24. Generally, see R. Cross, *Precedent in English Law* (Oxford: Clarendon Press, 2nd ed. 1969).
25. Max Weber, *On Law in Economy and Society* (Harvard University Press, 1954).
26. Lord Alverstone in *Leigh v. Gladstone* (1909) 26 T.L.R. 139.
27. Pankhurst, *Portrait.*
28. Mandela, application that the judicial officer recuse himself on the grounds of bias.
29. But there were criticisms of his vacillation.
30. Karl Mannheim, *Ideology and Utopia* (London, 1936 and 1946).
31. Cf. Thurman Arnold, *The Symbols of Government* (New York, 1962).
32. Karslake, House of Commons *Parliamentary Debates* on Second Reform Bill (1867).
33. *R v. Tyrell* (1894) 1 Q.B. 710.
34. Probably written by Harriet Martineau: see A. Deacon and M. Hill *The Problem of Surplus Women* (London: S.C.M.P., 1972).
35. *Parliamentary Debates* Second Reform Bill (1867).
36. B. Ehrenreich and D. English, *Witches, Midwives and Nurses* (Detroit, 1973).
37. Deacon and Hill.
38. Quoted in Ehrenreich and English, *op. cit.*
39. B. R. Parkes, *Essays on Women's Work* (London, 1865).
40. S. Rowbotham, *Hidden from History* (London: Pluto Press, 2nd ed. 1974).
41. Deacon and Hill.
42. *Howard v. Earl of Digby* (1834) 2 X1 and Fin 634 H.L.
43. *Parliamentary Debates* on Second Reform Bill (1867).
44. *Finer Report on One Parent Families* (London: HMSO, 1974), Section One, probably drafted by O. R. McGregor.
45. R. Fulford, *Votes for Women* (London, 1957).

2   *United States:* Are Women Citizens?

1. Elizabeth Cady Stanton, Susan B. Anthony, and Matilda Joslyn Gage, eds., *History of Woman Suffrage* (New York: Source Book Press, 1970: reprint of original 1881 edition), 2:627.
2. Unless otherwise noted all references and quotations for this section can be found

in Joan Hoff Wilson, 'The Illusion of Change: Women and the Revolution', in Alfred F. Young, ed., *The American Revolution: Explorations in the History of American Radicalism* (DeKalb, Illinois: Northern Illinois University Press, 1976), pp. 375, 394–99, 422–23, and idem, 'Historical Overview: 1776–1870', first segment of *Women and the Law: A Video Course in Color* developed by Elizabeth F. Defeis, Seton Hall University School of Law, Newark, N.J. 07102.

3. Equity was a separate form of jurisprudence designed to achieve justice when common law legal procedures proved inadequate because of their strict adherence to rigid writs and forms of action. Only the wealthy in England and colonial America could afford the luxury of utilising equity courts to establish private trusts. Although equity survived the American Revolution it remained largely unavailable to average American women.

4. Richard B. Morris, *Studies in the History of American Law* (New York: Columbia University Press, 1930), pp. 126–200; Alexander Keyssar, 'Widowhood in Eighteenth-Century Massachusetts: A Problem in the History of the Family', *Perspectives in American History* 8 (1974): 101, 118; George Lee Haskins, *Law and Authority in Early Massachusetts: A Study in Tradition and Design* (New York: Macmillan, 1960), pp. 180–82; George Athan Billias, ed., *Selected Essays: Law and Authority in Colonial America* (Barre, Massachusetts: Barre Publishing Co., 1965), pp. 23–26; Allan Kulikoff, 'The Progress of Inequality in Revolutionary Boston', *William and Mary Quarterly* 28 (July 1971): 388.

5. Statistics computed by author from data found in South Carolina State Archives. Dower decisions cited in Morton J. Horwitz, *The Transformation of American Law, 1780–1860* (Cambridge: Harvard University Press, 1977), pp. 56–58, and William E. Nelson, *Americanization of the Common Law: The Impact of Legal Change on Massachusetts Society, 1760–1830* (Cambridge: Harvard University Press, 1975), pp. 9, 48, 228 n175, 249 n34, 253 n100.

6. Elizabeth F. Defeis and Joan Hoff Wilson, *Experiment in Equality: The Woman's Vote*, a video presentation in color, Seton Hall University School of Law, Newark, N.J. 07102.

7. Horwitz, *Transformation of American Law*, at 4; Peggy A. Rabkin, 'The Silent Feminist Revolution: Women and the Law in New York State From Blackstone to the Beginnings of the American Women's Rights Movement' (Ph.D. dissertation, University of New York, Buffalo, 1975), p. 147.

8. Eric Foner, 'Get a Lawyer!' *New York Review of Books*, April 14, 1977, p. 38.

9. Joseph Story, *Commentaries on Equity Jurisprudence as Administered in England and America* (Boston: Charles C. Little and Brown, 1839), 2: 654–55.

10. Quotations from Barbara Allen Babcock, Anne E. Freedman, Eleanor Holmes Norton, and Susan C. Ross, *Sex Discrimination and the Law: Causes and Remedies* (Boston: Little, Brown and Company, 1975), pp. 593, 594. Also see Rabkin, 'Silent Feminist Revolution', pp. 176–86; Mary Jane Hamilton, 'A History of Married Women's Rights', in Dana V. Hiller and Robin Ann Sheets, eds., *Women and Men: The Consequences of Power* (selected papers from the bicentennial conference, Pioneers for Century III) (Cincinnati: Office of Women's Studies and University of Cincinnati Press, 1977), pp. 168–83, and Keith E. Melder, *Beginnings of Sisterhood: The American Woman's Rights Movement, 1800–1850* (New York: Schocken Books, 1977), pp. 4–6, 143–4.

11. Blackstone had said: 'By marriage, the husband and wife are one person in law: that is, the very being or legal existence of woman is suspended during marriage. . . .'

12. The first sections of the Fourteenth and Fifteenth Amendments read respectively: Fourteenth: 'All persons born or naturalised in the United States, and subject to

the jurisdiction thereof, are citizens of the United States and of the State wherein they reside. No State shall make or enforce any law which shall abridge the privileges or immunities of citizens of the United States; nor shall any State deprive any person of life, liberty, or property, without due process of law; nor deny to any person within its jurisdiction the equal protection of the laws.'

Fifteenth: 'The right of citizens of the United States to vote shall not be denied or abridged by the United States or by any State on account of race, color or previous condition of servitude.'

13. Gerda Lerner, *The Woman in American History* (Menlo Park, California: Addison-Wesley, 1971), pp. 95–105; Stanton, Anthony and Gage, *History of Woman Suffrage*, 1: *passim*.

14. Quoted in Andrew Sinclair, *The Better Half: The Emancipation of the American Woman* (New York: Harper & Row, 1965), p. 185.

15. *Id.*

16. The Fifth Amendment provides that no person shall be held for a 'capital or other infamous crime without indictment, be twice put in jeopardy of life or limb', for the same offense, be compelled to testify against himself, or 'be deprived of life, liberty, or property without due process of law'. This amendment is applicable only to the actions of the federal government.

17. Unless otherwise noted all references and quotations for this section can be found in Stanton, Anthony and Gage, *History of Woman Suffrage*, 2: 627–715.

18. This common law position was not officially abandoned until the decision in *Eisenstadt v. Baird*, 405 U.S. 438 (1972) which stated that 'the marital couple is not an independent entity . . . but an association of two individuals'. As late as 1966 Justice Black insisted in a dissenting opinion that 'husband and wife are one . . . and that one . . . is the husband'. See *U.S. v. Yazell*, 382 U.S. 341 (1966). After surveying marriage laws in 50 states, Shana Alexander concluded in 1975 that 'when two people marry they become in the eyes of the law one person, and that one person is the husband! . . . When a woman marries she legally to some degree ceases to exist. Only the loss of her husband through death or divorce can bring about the full restoration of her legal self'. (Shana Alexander, *State-by-State Guide to Women's Legal Rights*, Los Angeles: Wollstonecraft, 1975, p. 10).

19. Selden to Anthony, November 27, 1872. Complete text of this letter can be found in *History of Woman Suffrage*, 2: 935.

20. *Id.* at 949.

21. *Id.* at 934–35.

22. *Konigsberg v. State Bar*, 353 U.S. 252 (1957) and *Schware v. Board of Examiners*, 353 U.S. 232 (1957).

23. Quoted in Dorothy Thomas, ed., *Women Lawyers in the United States* (New York: Scarecrow Press, 1957), p. vii.

24. *Id.*

25. Quoted in Janette Barnes, *Women and Entrance to the Legal Profession*, 23 J of Legal Ed. 283 (1970).

26. *State v. Goodell*, 39 Wisc. 232 (1875).

27. *In re Goodell*, 48 Wisc. 693 (1879).

28. Babcock *et al.*, *Sex Discrimination and the Law*, p. 8.

29. *Id.* quoting Fairman, *History of the Supreme Court of the United States* (1971).

30. Stanton, Anthony and Gage, *History of Woman Suffrage*, 2: 946.

31. 28 American L. Rev. 278–83 (1894).

32. W. William Hodes, *Women and the Constitution: Some Legal History and a New Approach to the Nineteenth Amendment*, 25 Rutgers L. Rev. 35, 43–46 (1970).

33. Stanton, Anthony and Gage, *History of Woman Suffrage*, 2: 952.

34. Quoted in Madeline Stern, *We the Women: Career Firsts of Nineteenth-Century*

America (New York: Schulte, 1963), p. 211.

35. *Reed v. Reed*, 404 u.s. 71 (1971).

36. Quoted in Gerda Lerner, *The Female Experience: An American Documentary* (Indianapolis: Bobbs-Merrill, 1977), pp. 418–19.

37. Babcock *et al.*, *Sex Discrimination and the Law*, p. 19.

38. Eleanor Flexner, *Century of Struggle: The Woman's Rights Movement in the United States* (Cambridge: Harvard University Press, 1959), p. 145.

39. Elizabeth Cady Stanton, *Eighty Years and More: Reminiscences 1815—1897* (New York: Schocken Books, 1971; reprint of original 1898 edition), p. 150. Unless otherwise footnoted all references and quotations for this and the following section can be found in Joan Hoff Wilson, *The Legal Status of Women in the Late Nineteenth and Early Twentieth Centuries*, 6 Human Rights (ABA) 125 (1977).

40. Equal pay for equal work was first proposed at the National Labor Union Convention of 1868. It did not become a federal issue until World War I and did not become law until the 1963 Equal Pay Act – ninety-five years after it was first conceptualised and seventy years after it was taken up by the first women's rights movement.

41. Blanche Crozier, *Constitutionality of Discrimination Based on Sex*, 15 Boston L. Rev. 724 (1935) at 748.

42. Laurence H. Tribe, *American Constitutional Law* (Mineola, New York: Foundation Press, 1978), Chapter 8.

43. Burnita Shelton Matthews, *Women Should Have Equal Rights with Men: A Reply*, 12 American Bar Assoc. J. 117–20 (1926).

44. Quotation from Crozier, *Constitutionality of Discrimination Based on Sex*.

45. *Id.*

46. For the complex reasons distinguishing fundamental rights from other kinds of suspect classifications see: John Hart Ely, *The Wages of Crying Wolf: A Comment on Roe v. Wade*, 82 Yale L. J. 920 (1973) at 932 and Ruth Bader Ginsberg, *Women as Full Members of the Club: An Evolving American Ideal*, 6 Human Rights (ABA) 1 (1976).

47. *Goesart v. Cleary*, 335 u.s. 464 (1948).

48. *Daindridge v. Williams*, 397 u.s. 471 (1970).

49. John D. Johnston, Jr., and Charles L. Knapp, *Sex Discrimination by Law: A Study in Judicial Perspective*, 46 N.Y.U.L. Rev. 687–89 (1971).

50. *Strauder v. West Virginia*, 100 u.s. 303 (1879).

51. Johnston and Knapp, at 709–10.

52. *Id.* at 711.

53. *Id.* at 719.

54. *Id.* at 737.

55. Linda Singer, *Women in the Correctional Process*, 2 Am. Crim. L. Rev. 295 (1972).

56. Stuart Nagel and Lenoire Weitzman, *Women as Litigants*, Hastings L. J., 23 171–98 (1971).

57. For latest data relating to California, which has the best crime reporting system in the United States, see Elizabeth F. Moulds, *The Chivalry Factor and Disparities of Treatment in the Criminal Justice System*, paper delivered in April, 1976, at the Annual Meeting of the Western Political Science Association. Also see Eve Cary and Kathleen Willert Peratis, *Woman and the Law* (Skokie, Illinois: National Textbook 6, 1977), pp. 134–43.

58. Babcock, *et al.*, *Sex Discrimination and the Law*, pp. 939–41.

59. Diane Johnson, 'The People v. Patty Hearst', *New York Review of Books*, April 29, 1976, p. 17.

60. *Id.* at 15.

61. Unless otherwise noted all quotations and references for this section are from *The Trial of Patty Hearst* [complete transcript] (San Francisco: The Great Fidelity Press, 1976).

62. Kathleen Barry, "'Did I ever have a chance?" Patriarchal Judgement of Patricia Hearst', *Chrysalis*, no. 1 (1977): 10–11.

63. *San Francisco Chronicle*, January 8, 1977, p. 2.

64. *Boston Evening Globe*, April 14, 1977, p. 19.

65. For such theories see Philip G. Zimbardo *et al.*, *Influencing Attitudes and Changing Behavior*, 2nd ed. (Reading, Massachusetts: Addison-Wesley, 1977), pp. 4–17.

66. The trade in what I am calling sexual slavery is now euphemistically referred to as illicit traffic in women and children. It is an international business of such gigantic, but well-protected, proportions that it has proven impenetrable despite multilateral UN treaties calling for its suppression. One of the reasons for this is that among the forty-two countries (not including the U.S.) which have ratified the 1951 Convention for the Suppression of the Traffic in Persons and of the Exploitation of the Prostitution of Others as of June 30, 1975 (Malvina H. Guggenheim and Elizabeth F. Defeis, *United States Participation in International Agreements Providing Rights for Women*, 10 Loyola of Los Angeles L. Rev. 1 (1976), at 18–19), were the very ones in which this illicit traffic in women and children is most rampant. Another reason for its thriving existence is that it has the covert support of the multilateral corporations operating in these same countries and of the international lawyers who represent them. No serious UN or scholarly investigation has ever been conducted of sexual slavery and most feminist accounts to date limit themselves to documenting sensational testimony from those few exceptional women who have managed to escape. This issue like international crimes against women is one that patriarchal societies and institutions simply will not expose, let alone eradicate (Diana E. H. Russell, ed., *Proceedings of the International Tribunal on Crimes against Women*, Milbrae, California: Les Femmes, 1976). While feminists of the 1920s, 30s and 40s were actively concerned with sexual slavery, members of the second women's movement have only recently begun to organise around it. Unfortunately, even these contemporary feminists are without much historical consciousness about past attempts to deal with it and usually find themselves with limited economic and legal skills to project viable new solutions.

67. *New York Times*, May 10, 1977, p. 18; *Los Angeles Times*, 3 November 1977, pp. 1, 32; 4 February 1978, p. 23.

68. Robin Morgan, *Going Too Far: The Personal Chronicle of a Feminist* (New York: Random House, 1977), pp. 17, 116, 124, 128, 130, 222–226.

69. Alexander, *State Guide to Women's Legal Rights*, p. 117; Jim Wood, *The Rape of Inez Garcia* (New York: Putnam, 1976). For the legal complexities of rape see: Camille Le Grand, *Rape and Rape Laws: Sexism in Society and Law*, 61 Calif. Law R. 923 (1973), and *Rape and Its Victims: A Report for Citizens, Health Facilities, and Criminal Justice Agencies* published by the Law Enforcement Assistance Administration (LEAA), Washington, D.C.; Cary and Peratis, *Woman and the Law*, pp. 122–34; and review article on recent rape cases in 46 *Law-Week* 3061.

70. *Spokeswoman*, May 15, 1977, p. 6. Recently feminist groups have taken to picketting or asking for the recall of judges who make sexist remarks in the course of rape trials. For example, one judge in California said in overturning a guilty verdict in the rape of a woman hitchhiker: 'It may not speak well of the prevailing standard of morality in society, but women hitchhikers should anticipate sexual advances from men who pick them up.' In a Wisconsin case a judge questioned

whether in a sexually permissive community we should 'punish a 15- or 16-year boy who reacts to it normally?' See *New York Times*, July 31, 1977, p. 24.

71. Del Martin, *Battered Wives* (San Francisco: Glide, 1976), Harold J. Pascal, *Battered Wives: The Secret Scandal* (Canfield, Ohio: Alba Book, 1977) and Lisa Leghorn, 'Social Responses to Battered Women', speech delivered at Wisconsin Conference on Battered Women, October 2, 1976.

72. *New York Times*, June 12, 1977; July 21, 1977, p. 19.

73. The distinction between legalisation and decriminalisation of prostitution is crucial to feminists because the former would create a state-controlled pool of 'clean' women subject to even greater male exploitation than now exists. Decriminalisation would eliminate all male control, whether in the form of state boards of health, the police, or pimps.

74. Marilyn C. Zilli, *Feminism and the Legalization of Prostitution: How Far Down the River?* 2 Iustitia [Indiana Univ. Law School] 39 (1974). Charles Rosenbleet and Barbara J. Pariente, *The Prostitution of the Criminal Law*, 11 Am. Crim. L. Rev. 373 (1973) and Cary and Peratis, *Woman and the Law*, pp. 107–22.

3   *Britain:* From Head Servant to Junior Partner

1. *The Queen v. Jackson* (1891), 1 Q.B. 671.

2. H. J. Simons, *African Women – Their Legal Status in South Africa* (London: Hurst, 1968).

3. Unpublished lectures at Bedford College, University of London, Summer 1973.

4. S. M. Cretney, *Principles of Family Law*, 2nd edition (London: Sweet and Maxwell, 1976), p. 256.

5. Karl Renner, *The Institutions of Private Law and their Social Functions* (London: Routledge and Kegan Paul, 1976), p. 41.

6. Sue in Thomas Hardy's *Jude the Obscure* (Macmillan).

7. Simons, *African Women, op. cit.*

8. J. F. Stephen, *Liberty, Equality, Fraternity* (London, 1873).

9. Lord Justice Atkinson in *Roberts v. Hopwood* (1925) A.C. 591.

10. Introduction to R. H. Graveson and F. R. Crane (eds.), *A Century of Family Law 1857–1957* (London, 1957).

11. See Scarman, *Women and Equality before the Law*, Fawcett Lecture (27 October 1971).

12. The Matrimonial Homes Act, 1967, gives limited protection from eviction to spouses. More recently there have been a number of provisions dealing with domestic violence, the main effect of which has been to give wives the possibility of getting speedy injunctions against violent husbands (Domestic Violence and Matrimonial Proceedings Act, 1976). See Anna Coote and Tess Gill, *Battered Women and the New Law* (London: National Council for Civil Liberties and Interaction, 1977).

13. Divorce Reform Act, 1969, incorporated into the Matrimonial Causes Act, 1973.

14. Cretney, *op. cit.* p. 258.

15. The Matrimonial Proceedings and Property Act, 1970, and the Matrimonial Causes Act, 1973.

16. *Wachtel v. Wachtel* (1973).

17. Per Lord Denning, Master of the Rolls, and one of the main judicial proponents of strengthening the wife's claim on family assets.

18. Inheritance (Provision for Family and Dependants) Act, 1975.

19. Abortion Act, 1967.
20. Sexual Law Reform Act, 1967.
21. Employment Protection Act, 1975.
22. Cf. Cretney, *op. cit.* p. 258.

4   *United States:* Control by Husbands, Control by State

1. Theodore Stanton and Harriot Stanton Blatch, eds., *Elizabeth Cady Stanton As Revealed In Her Letters, Diary and Reminiscences* (New York: Harper and Brothers, 1922), 2: 49.
2. Timothy Walker, *Introduction to American Law* (Boston: Charles C. Little and James Brown, 1837), p. 260.
3. Warren, *Husband's Rights to Wife's Services*, 38 Harv. L. Rev. 421, 423 (1925).
4. Quoted in Leo Kanowitz, *Women and the Law: The Unfinished Revolution* (Albuquerque: University of New Mexico Press, 1969), p. 263 n48.
5. Babcock, *et al., Sex Discrimination and the Law*, pp. 151–52.
6. Quoted in *The Spokeswoman*, January 15, 1977, p. 11.
7. Lenore J. Weitzman, *Legal Regulation of Marriage: Tradition and Change*, 62 Calif. L. Rev. 1249–50 (1974).
8. *Id.* at 1250–58, 1278–88.
9. *Id.* at 1258–66 (quote at 1260).
10. *Id.* at 1173–97 for full implications of the husband as head of the family.
11. Currently 48 percent of all adult women (over sixteen) or 38.6 million hold jobs or are seeking employment. Most women still find work in traditional female occupations which offer few opportunities for advancement. Working mothers constitute almost 40 percent of all female laborers and one-third of these have children under six years old. Being married and having children no longer means a woman will not also work outside her home. Unless a woman marries a man already earning over $25,000 she has less than a 50–50 chance of not working because currently almost 60 percent of average middle income American families (those earning between $10,000 and $15,000) maintain that level of economic existence because *both* husband and wife work. Yet full-time working women routinely earn 58 cents for every dollar earned by full-time working men due to unequal pay scales based on gender differentiation. The gap between the earnings of women and men has nearly doubled since 1955 and is continuing to increase. The 1978 median income for women was only $7,531 compared with $12,770 for men.
12. Weitzman, *Legal Regulation of Marriage* at 1180–97; Guggenheim and Defeis, *United States Participation in International Agreements* at 59–65.
13. Herma Hill Kay, *Sex-Based Discrimination in Family Law* (St. Paul: West Publishing Co., 1974), *passim*; Cary and Peratis, *Woman and the Law*, pp. 145–77; and Riane Tennenhaus Eisler, *Dissolution: No-Fault Divorce, Marriage, and the Future of Women* (New York: McGraw-Hill, 1977), pp. 10–13, and *passim*.
14. Kay, *Sex-Based Discrimination in Family Law*, pp. 165–69; Babcock, *et al., Sex Discrimination and the Law*, pp. 609–19; and Eisler, *Dissolution*, pp. 20–40.
15. Quoted in *The Spokeswoman*, January 15, 1977, p. 1.
16. *Boston Evening Globe*, May 3, 1977, p. 9.
17. *Women's Newsletter* [a publication of the National Commission on Women's Oppression (NCWO) of the National Lawyers' Guild] (Winter 1977): 11.

18. Quoted in *The Spokeswoman*, April 15, 1977, p. 1.

19. *Id.*

20. *Nashville Gas Company v. Satty* and *Richmond Unified School District v. Berg.*

21. Since laws discriminating against homosexuals affect gay males as well as lesbians, they are not strictly speaking sexist and will not be discussed in detail. Although no case involving lesbian rights has ever reached the Supreme Court, lesbian mothers fighting for custody of their children is on the increase at the state level. See: Carrington E. Boggan *et al.*, *The Rights of Gay People: A Basic ACLU Guide to a Gay Person's Rights* (New York: Avon, 1975); Randy Von Beitel, *The Criminalization of Private Homosexual Acts: A Jurisprudential Case Study of a Decision by the Texas Bar Penal Code Revision Committee*, 6 Human Rights (ABA) 23 (1976); and Kay Whitlock and Wendy Kellogg, 'With Liberty and Justice for Some: Lesbian Rights Update', *Do It Now*, November, 1977, p. 3. To date the Supreme Court has usually chosen not to hear any cases involving homosexuals, thus allowing state regulations to prevail. On October 3, 1977, for example, the Justices refused to review the case of James Gaylord who had been dismissed from his high school teaching job solely on the grounds that a Washington State court had ruled that homosexuals were 'immoral'.

22. Unless otherwise cited all quotations and references for the remainder of this section are from Mary Ann Glendon, *Marriage and the State: The Withering Away of Marriage*, 62 Virginia L. Rev. 663 (1976).

23. M. Sussman, 'The Four F's of Variant Family Forms and Marriage Styles', *The Family Coordinator*, 24 (1975): 563, 575–76.

24. *New York Times*, July 7, 1975, p. 36; January 8, 1976, p. 58.

25. Daniel Bell, 'The Revolution of Rising Entitlements', *Fortune Magazine*, April, 1975, pp. 98–100.

26. See *King v. Smith*, 392 U.S. 309 (1968), *Lewis v. Martin*, 397 U.S. 552 (1970), and *Cahill v. New Jersey Welfare Rights Organization*, 411 U.S. 619 (1973).

27. Colin C. Blaydon and Carol B. Stack, 'Income Support Policies and the Family', *Daedalus: The Family*, 106 (Spring 1977): 148.

28. Stanton to Anthony, March 1, 1853, in Blatch, *Stanton as Revealed*, 2: 48. She added in this letter that she did 'not know whether the world is quite willing or ready to discuss the question of marriage'.

29. GFWC (General Federation of Women's Clubs) September 1976, pp. 20–21; *Spokeswoman*, April 15, 1977, p. 8; and Cynthia Holcomb Hall, *The Working Woman and the Federal Income Tax*, 61 APA Journal 716 (1975).

30. GFWC, September 1976, pp. 20–21; *Spokeswoman*, January 15, 1977, p. 4; Eleanor Cutri Smeal, 'Testimony on Equity in Social Security Impact on Women', House of Representatives Subcommittee on Social Security of the Ways and Means Committee, July 21, 1977.

31. As of 1976 22 states had passed affirmative action legislation to extend credit to married women. See Guggenheim and Defeis, *U.S. Participation in International Agreements* at 62 n387, and *Spokeswoman*, April 15, 1977, p. 4.

32. Gerda Lerner, 'Women's Rights and American Feminism', *American Scholar* 40 (Spring 1971): 237.

33. See *Griswold v. Connecticut*, 381 U.S. 479 (1965), and *Eisenstadt v. Baird*, 405 U.S. 438 (1972).

34. *Spokeswoman*, February 15, 1977, p. 4. Some estimates range as high as 400,000 to 900,000. See 'Congress Votes Against Women's Rights', *Dollars & Sense*, no. 23 (January 1977): 4.

35. Quoted in *The Spokeswoman*, April 15, 1977, p. 3; *Ms*, February, 1978, pp. 46–9, 97–8.

36. Title XIX established a Medical Assistance Program (Medicaid) under which

participating states could provide federally funded medical assistance to needy persons.

37. The compromise language of the Hyde Amendment would permit a poor woman to have a Medicaid abortion only if her life were threatened by the pregnancy *or* if she had been a rape or incest victim and had reported the incident to proper federal authorities *within* 60 days. See *Los Angeles Times*, December 8, 1977, pp. 1, 18; January 27, 1978, p. 4.

38. *The Spokeswoman*, November 15, 1976, pp. 3–4; December 15, 1976, p. 3; 'Congress Restricts Medicaid Payment for Abortion', *Clearinghouse Review*, 10 (December 1976): 700–3; Carter quoted in *New York Times*, July 13, 1977, pp. 1, 10.

39. *Boston Globe*, July 13, 1977, p. 2; General Electric quoted in NCWO *Women's Newsletter* (Winter 1977): 2.

40. Quotation from *New York Times*, November 27, 1977, p. 1. For the latest estimates of the financial impact of the Hyde Amendment see *Spokeswoman*, October 15, 1977, pp. 3–4; Susan Tenenbaum, 'Will America Bribe Poor to Breed for Adoptions?' *Los Angeles Times*, September 17, 1977, Part II, p. 7.

41. Laurence H. Tribe, *Structural Due Process*, 10 Harv. Civil Rts.-Civil Lib. L. Rev. 297 (1975) and Ely, *The Wages of Crying Wolf, passim*.

42. Tribe, Structural Due Process at 296–7; *idem, American Constitutional Law*, Chapter 17.

43. Tribe, *Structural Due Process* at 301, 319, 321.

44. *Time*, April 4, 1977, p. 46.

45. *Phillips v. Martin Marietta Corporation*, 400 US 542 (1971). Oral Arguments.

5 *Britain:* Barristers and Gentlemen

1. House of Lords Select Committee Report on Anti-Discrimination Bill (H.L. 104), House of Lords 1972–3, vol. VIII.

2. Helena Kennedy, in Robert Hazel (ed.) *The Bar on Trial* (London: Quartet Books, 1978) p. 148.

3. Abel-Smith and Stevens, *Lawyers and the Courts*, p. 193, give a brief history of attempts by women to enter the profession.

4. Lockwood's study (*The Black-Coated Worker*, London, 1958) was unusual for its period in that it focused on gender relationships at work.

5. *Law Journal*, vol. 39 (1904).

6. Cf. Holford Knight: *The Times*, 4 July 1913.

7. Figures from Vera Brittain *Women's Work in Modern England* (London, 1928); Ruth Miller in *The Times*, 1 January 1973; *Legal Action Group Bulletin*, (December 1975); Kennedy, *op. cit.* p. 149.

8. Kennedy, *op. cit.* p. 153.

9. *ibid.*

10. Figures from Brittain, *op. cit.*; *Legal Action Group Bulletin* (December 1975).

11. Table taken from Kennedy *op. cit.* p. 153.

12. Kennedy, *op. cit.* p. 149.

13. John Baldwin, 'The Social Composition of the Magistracy', *British Journal of Criminology*, vol. 16, no. 2 (1976) pp. 171–4.

14. *Morris Committee Report on Jury Service*, Cmnd. 2627 (HMSO: 1965).

15. R. E. Wraith and P. G. Hutchinson, *Administrative Tribunals* (London: Allen and Unwin, 1973).

16. Jean Coussins, *Equality Report* (London: National Council for Civil Liberties, 1977).
17. 'Barristers Diary' by Furnival, *Law Guardian Gazette* (26 Feb. 1975).
18. Diana Cheeld, 'The Rise of an Angry Young Woman', *Law Guardian Gazette* (28 July 1976) p. 635.
19. Pamela Brookes, *Woman at Westminster* (British American books).
20. Cf. Kamm, *Rapiers and Battleaxes*, pp. 199–203.
21. See, too, evidence by Bow Group (a pressure group inside the Conservative Party) to Royal Commission on Legal Services, reported in *The Times* (13 June 1977) under heading: 'Outrageous' treatment of women barristers: Kennedy *op. cit.* p. 151.
22. Evidence by Bar Council to the Monopolies Commission, quoted by Kennedy, *op. cit.* p. 158.
23. Kennedy, *ibid.* 158.
24. 'Women in Law Centres', unpublished discussion paper (London, 1975).
25. *Positive Discrimination*, Fabian Society pamphlet.
26. Novarro argues for the extension of American experience in this regard to Britain (*Right On Sister*, 1976).

6 *United States:* Portia's Plight

1. *Time*, May 26, 1975, p. 41.
2. Jurate Jason, Lizabeth Moody, and James Schuerger, *The Woman Law Student: The View from the Front of the Classroom*, 24 Cleveland State L. Rev. 223 (1975); Doris L. Sassower, *Women, Power, and the Law*, 62 Amer. Bar Assoc. J. 615 (1976).
3. James F. Gilsinan, Lynn Obernyer, and Christine A. Gilsinan, *Women Attorneys and the Judiciary*, 52 Denver L. J. 887 (1975).
4. Sassower, *Women, Power, and the Law*, at 615.
5. Cynthia Fuchs Epstein, *Woman's Place: Options and Limits in Professional Careers* (Berkeley: University of California Press, 1970), p. 12; Barnes, *Women and the Legal Profession*, at 28.
6. *Id.* at 153.
7. Eva Figes, *Patriarchal Attitudes* (New York: Stein and Day, 1970), pp. 11, 57, 103–4, 106, 116, 122, 131, 149, 184; Florida Scott-Maxwell, *Women and Sometimes Men* (New York: Harper & Row, 1971; reprint of original 1957 edition), pp. 38–39, 44–46, 2 3–6; Germaine Greer, *The Female Eunuch* (New York: McGraw-Hill, 1971), pp. 6, 59, 101–2, 146, 216–17, 245–69, 338 n8.
8. Herbert Marcuse, *One-Dimensional Man*, pp. 123–43, 247–57; Greer, *Female Eunuch*, pp. 101–2, 106–8, 298.
9. Richard Goodwin, 'The Social Theory of Herbert Marcuse', *Atlantic*, June, 1971, pp. 81–82.
10. Barnes, *Women and the Legal Profession*, at 276; Gordon and Popkin, 'Women's Liberation: "Let Us Now Emulate Each Other"', in Boskin and Rosenstone, eds., *Seasons of Rebellion* (1972), p. 286.
11. James J. White, *Women in the Law*, 65 Mich. L. Rev. 1062 (1967); Barnes, *Women and the Legal Profession*, at 277.
12. Epstein, *Woman's Place*, pp. 160–62; Barnes, *Women and the Legal Profession*, at 292.

13. Shirley Raissi Bysiewicz, *1972 AALS Questionnaire on Women in Legal Education*, 25 J. of Legal Ed. 506–8 (1973); White, *Women in the Law*, at 1051, 1057, 1085–86; Joan E. Baker, *Employment Discrimination Against Women Lawyers*, Amer. Bar Assoc. J. 1029–32.

14. *American Bar News* cited in address by Dorothy W. Nelson, 26 Okla. L. Rev. 375 (1973); *New York Times*, March 25, 1975, p. 28.

15. Gilsinan and Obernyer, *Women Attorneys*, at 888–89; Sassower, *Women and the Judiciary: Undoing 'The Law of the Creator'*, 57 J. Amer. Jud. Society 282 (1974).

16. Karen DeCrow, *Sexist Justice* (New York: Vintage, 1975; reprint of original 1974 edition), pp. 37–38; Bradley Soule and Kay Standley, *Perceptions of Sex Discrimination in Law*, 59 Amer. Bar Assoc. J. 1144–1147 (1973).

17. Beth Levenzey and Joan Andersson, 'Trials of a Woman Lawyer', dittoed, 1973. For similar statements see D. X. Fenton, *Ms. Attorney* (Philadelphia: Westminster Press, 1974).

18. Testimony at Boston Women's Law Day Conference, March 26, 1977.

19. Gilsinan and Obernyer, *Women Attorneys*, a 881–909. For similar statements see Sophie Douglass Pfeiffer, *Women Lawyers in Rhode Island*, 61 Amer. Bar Assoc. J. 742–43 (1975).

20. Generally speaking the number of female and minority policy makers in government remains low. Of the more than 1,200 federal advisory committees in existence at the end of 1975, 35 percent had no women members and 50 percent had no minority representation. More than 22,000 people serve on such committees and only 11 percent are women and 4 percent black. The Carter administration has been criticised by the National Women's Political Caucus (NWPC) for the 'disappointingly small' number of women appointed thus far to top policy making positions: only two out of 13 high-level appointments in the Justice Department; 10 in Labor; 14 in Defense; none in the State or Interior Departments; one in Agriculture. However, over one-half the policy making positions in Commerce are now held by women; one-third in HEW and HUD. On March 10, 1977, President Carter chided the Ad Hoc Coalition for Women for not being grateful enough for the appointments they had received. (*Spokeswoman*, April 15, 1977, p. 7; May 15, 1977, pp. 8–9.)

21. *New York Times*, May 1, 1977, pp. F1, F4.

22. Jerold S. Auerbach, *Unequal Justice: Lawyers and Social Change in Modern America* (New York: Oxford University Press, 1976), p. 308. Women are also playing an increasingly important role in the government-financed program of legal services for the poor. This nonprofit Legal Services Corporation now has a budget in excess of $200 million and employs 3,200 lawyers in about 700 offices across the nation. In agreeing to continue funding this essential corporation Congress has placed some severe restrictions on its operations, namely, that legal advice and representation *cannot* be provided in cases involving abortion, school desegregation, the draft, military desertion, or homosexual rights. See *New York Times*, July 31, 1977, p. E4.

23. *Newsweek*, January 10, 1977, pp. 43–47. For other articles about current problems within the legal profession see *Boston Evening Globe*, January 4, 1977, p. 23; *New York Times*, April 1, 1977, p. B1; April 9, 1977, p. 19; April 24, 1977, pp. 1, 50; Russell Baker, 'Terminal Jurisprudence', *New York Times Magazine* March 20, 1977, p. 12.

24. Quoted in *New York Times*, May 28, 1977, p. 1.

7 *Britain:* Citizens, Workers and Parents

1. *Roberts v. Hopwood* (1925) A.C. 578.
2. *Price v. Rhondda UDC* (1923) 2 Ch. 372; *Short v. Poole Corporation* (1926) Ch. 66. See discussion in Margareta Rendel, 'Law as an Instrument of Oppression or Reform' in Pat Carlen (ed.) *The Sociology of Law*, Sociological Review Monograph no. 23, University of Keele (1976) pp. 143–71.
3. *Nagle v. Fielden* (1966) 2 Q.B. 633.
4. Notably the Race Relations Acts of 1965 and 1968, now consolidated and amended in the Race Relations Act, 1976.
5. Patricia Hewitt, 'Women's Rights in Law and Practice', *New Community* Vol. V, no. 1–2, Summer 1976.
6. See Patricia Ashdown-Sharp, 'Women's Rights: the Missed Opportunity', *Sunday Times* (20 Feb. 1977); Coussins, *Equality Report.*
7. Coussins, p. 9.
8. According to press reports, the Court of Appeal upheld a rule permitting women to leave a factory five minutes before men, the Master of the Rolls declaring that the new legislation did not outlaw chivalry (July 1977).
9. Virginia Novarro, *Right on Sister* (1976); Rendel, *op. cit.*
10. Tessa Blackstone, 'The Limits of Legislating for Equality for Women', *New Community* Vol. V, no. 1–2, Summer 1976.
11. Judith Mayhew, 'Women at Work' in Pat Carlen (ed.) *The Sociology of Law*, *op. cit.*, pp. 134–42.
12. Ashdown-Sharp, *op. cit.*; Coussins *op. cit.*
13. TUC survey quoted in Coussins, p. 78.
14. Blackstone, *op. cit.* p. 27.
15. Coussins, p. 103.
16. *ibid.*, p. 83; see, too, National Council for Civil Liberties, *Women Factory Workers.*
17. *ibid.*
18. See Mayhew, *op. cit.*; cf. Luise and Dipak Nandy, 'Towards True Equality for Women', *New Society* (30 Jan. 1975). p. 37.

8 *United States:* Recent Congressional Acts and Supreme Court Decisions

1. Quoted in Guggenheim and Defeis, *U.S. Participation in International Agreements*, at 51 n314.
2. Miller, *Sex Discrimination and Title VII of the Civil Rights Act of 1964*, 51 Minn. L. Rev. 877, 883 n34 (1967); *Congressional Record*, House, February 8, 1964.
3. Jo Freeman 'Women and Public Policy', paper delivered at 1975 conference *Pioneers for Century III: Women and Power*, Cincinnati, Ohio.
4. The BFOQ has proven particularly cumbersome even though EEOC guidelines technically limit it to physical attributes crucial to job performance and sexual attributes necessary for authenticity such as in modeling or acting careers. In practice a heavy burden of persuasion is placed on the individual litigant to overturn a BFOQ exception claimed by an employer. Litigation under Title VII first focused primarily on the BFOQ, then moved to protective legislation at the state level, and most recently has concentrated on pregnancy related employment practices. (Guggenheim and Defeis, *U.S. in International Agreements*, at 51–52,

and Lynn Andretta Fishel and Clarine Nardi Riddle, *The Equal Rights Amendment as an Instrument for Social Change*, 2 Iustitia [Indiana Univ. Law School] 17–18, 1974.) The BFOQ provision allows 'an employer to hire and employ employees . . . on the basis of his [sic] religion, sex, or national origin in those certain instances where religion, sex or national origin is a bona fide occupational qualification reasonably necessary to the normal operation of that particular business or enterprise. . . .' See the *Phillips* decision below for an example of how the continued existence of the BFOQ is an obstacle to obtaining complete sexual equality.

5. *Spokeswoman*, November 15, 1976, pp. 2–3; March 15, 1977, p. 3. Edelsberg quoted in *Labor Relations Reporter* 61 (August 25, 1966): 253–55.
6. Other nationally organised activist groups include: Women's Equity Action League (WEAL), Federally Employed Women (FEW), Human Rights for Women, Inc. (HRW) – all formed in 1968; Professional Women's Caucus (PWC) organised in 1969; the National Women's Political Caucus (NWPC) formalised in 1971, and the National Black Feminist Organisation of 1973. No less important but usually of a more temporary and regional nature were the numerous radical feminist groups such as Radical Women (1967), the Jeannette Rankin Brigade (1967), the Berkeley Women's Sociology Caucus (1967), Sudsofloppen (1968), WITCH (1968), Redstockings (1969), The Feminists (1969), New York Radical Feminists (1969). There have also been numerous consciousness raising groups all over the country and many feminist journals and newspapers.
7. *New York Times*, March 22, 1977, p. 28; July 8, 1977, p. 8; *Spokeswoman*, April 15, 1977, pp. 3–4.
8. For a review of recent state cases see Ginsborg, *Women as Full Members*, pp. 10–14.
9. Quoted in *San Francisco Chronicle*, December 21, 1976, p. 1; *Boston Evening Globe*, January 3, 1977, p. 15. Also see Guggenheim and Defeis, *U.S. in International Agreements*, at 61, and *Spokeswoman*, March 15, 1977, p. 6.
10. Susan Kaufman Purcell, '*Ideology and the Law*: Sexism and Supreme Court Decisions', in Jane Jaquette, ed., *Women in Politics* (New York: John Wiley, 1974), pp. 142, 149; and Babcock *et al.*, *Sex Discrimination and the Law*, pp. 330–31.
11. *New York Times*, June 1, 1977, pp. 1, 32; June 2, 1977, pp. 1, 40.
12. Guggenheim and Defeis, *U.S. in International Agreements*, at 49–50.
13. John H. Bunzel, '*Bakke v. University of California*', *Commentary*, March, 1977, p. 60; *San Francisco Chronicle*, November 12, 1976, p. 20; November 16, 1976, p. 1; November 17, 1976, p. 16; and *New York Times*, July 24, 1977, p. 27; 63 A.B.A. Journal 1551 (1977).
14. Quoted in *San Francisco Chronicle*, November 16, 1976, p. 1.
15. *New York Times*, March 18, 1977, p. 1; April 1, 1977, p. 1; July 3, 1977, p. 28. *Spokeswoman*, November 15, 1976, p. 6.
16. Title IX of the Education Amendments 20 U.S.C. §1681, *et seq.* (1975 supp.). HEW has compliance responsibility for the act and issued the *Final Regulation Implementing Title IX of the Education Amendments of 1972* in June, 1975. The long delay was primarily due to disputes over guidelines about athletic programs. Regulations for such programs can be found in 45 C.F.R. §86.41 (1975), 'Athletics'.
17. Pamela L. Jacklin, 'Sexual Equality in High School Athletics: The Approach of Darrin v. Gould', forthcoming in Gonzaga Law Review (1977).
18. Copus quoted in *New York Times*, June 2, 1977, p. 40; EEOC quoted in *New York Times*, July 13, 1977, p. 13.
19. Morgan, *Going Too Far*, pp. 90, 92.

20. Freeman, 'Women and Public Policy'.
21. *New York Times*, April 1, 1977, p. 16; *Boston Globe*, March 26, 1977, p. 18.
22. Fishel and Riddle, *ERA*, at 17. Also see Barbara Brown *et al.*, *The Equal Rights Amendment: A Constitutional Basis for Equal Rights for Women*, 80 Yale L. Rev. 871 (1971).
23. Women's Law Project, Philadelphia, 'Report on State Court Interpretations of State ERAs', for National Committee on the Observance of International Women's Year, dittoed, February, 1977.
24. *Id.* Also see *Note, Sex Discrimination in the Criminal Law: The Effect of the Equal Rights Amendment*, 11 Amer. Criminal L. Rev. 469 (1973).
25. Brown *et al.*, *ERA*, at 873. Also see *Note, Sex Discrimination and Equal Protection: Do We Need a Constitutional Amendment?* 84 Harvard L. Rev. 1499 (1971). Kenneth L. Krast, *'A Discrimination so Trivial': A Note on Law and the Symbolism of Women's Dependency*, 49 Los Angeles Bar Bulletin 499 (October 1974); Joan M. Krauskopf, *The Equal Rights Amendment: Its Political and Practical Contexts*, 50 California State Bar Journal 79 (March/April 1975); and Eisler, *Dissolution*, pp. 198–220.
26. Raoul Berger, *Government by Judiciary: The Transformation of the Fourteenth Amendment* (Cambridge: Harvard University Press, 1977), *passim*; Hodes, *Women and the Constitution* at 50.
27. *Newsweek*, June 13, 1966, p. 71.

Index